Ladies of Lost Causes

Rehabilitation, Women Offenders
and the Voluntary Sector

Ladies of Lost Causes

Rehabilitation, Women Offenders and the Voluntary Sector

Judith Rumgay

PUBLISHED BY
WILLAN PUBLISHING
CULMCOTT HOUSE
MILL STREET, UFFCULME
CULLOMPTON, DEVON
EX15 3AT, UK
TEL: +44(0)1884 840337
FAX: +44(0)1884 840251
E-MAIL: INFO@WILLANPUBLISHING.CO.UK
WEBSITE: WWW.WILLANPUBLISHING.CO.UK

PUBLISHED SIMULTANEOUSLY IN THE USA AND CANADA BY
DE SITTER PUBLICATIONS
1288 RITSON RD NORTH, SUITE 417
OSHAWA, ON, LIG 8B2, CANADA
TEL: +1(905)430-5696
E-MAIL: ISHWARAN@DESITTERPUBLICATIONS.COM
WEBSITE: WWW.DESITTERPUBLICATIONS.COM

FIRST PUBLISHED 2007
PAPERBACK
ISBN-13: 978-1-84392-298-8 (OUTSIDE NORTH AMERICA)
ISBN 10-ISBN 1-897160-16-X (WITHIN NORTH AMERICA)

BRITISH LIBRARY CATALOGUING-IN-PUBLICATION DATA
A CATALOGUE RECORD FOR THIS BOOK IS AVAILABLE FROM THE BRITISH
LIBRARY

PRINTED AND BOUND BY TJI DIGITAL, PADSTOW, CORNWALL

To the inspiration of Kuan Yin:

Great Lady of Compassion

Table of Contents

List of Figures and Tables

Acknowledgements

This book would not have been possible without the help of many people.

First, a deep debt of gratitude is owed to Angela Camber, the current chair of the Griffins Society, who saw the organisation's research potential and invited me to evaluate its contribution to rehabilitation of female offenders. Her unflagging support and enthusiasm for the project sustained me through many periods of doubt and anxiety. Without her initiative and encouragement this story would not have been told.

Thanks are due to the current and former Council members, project staff, probation officers, housing association officers, social workers and other professionals who participated in the research through personal interviews, contribution of archival materials, facilitation of and participation in observation at the projects and introductions to further relevant contacts. The organisation that currently manages the surviving hostels of the Griffins Society provided considerable assistance to and support for the research, at cost to the convenience of its own personnel. Thanks are also given in deep appreciation of the contributions of hostel residents to the project. I hope that the passionate accounts of all these individuals of the impact of the Griffins Society on their professional and/or personal lives are adequately expressed in the pages to follow.

The Inner London Probation Service (as it then was called) provided generous support in tracing archival material for the file survey and in attempts to facilitate contact with former residents.

A number of academics, professionals and Council members have dedicated time to reading drafts of part or all of the manuscript. I am grateful to Rachel Benson, Angela Camber, Derek Cornish, Carol Hedderman, Jane Leaver, Shadd Maruna, Adrian Moran, Susannah Morris, Sally Sainsbury, Michael Shiner and Mary Walton for their insightful comments and hope that they feel that they have received my proper attention in the final version. My thanks also go to Tim Newburn for strategic guidance in the production of the finished manuscript. As always, Helen, Mary and

Stuart, at the Radzinowicz Library at the Institute of Criminology, Cambridge, facilitated my access to literature with patience and fortitude.

The research would not have been feasible without the commitment of Kate Steward, who devoted more time, energy, persistence, resourcefulness and imagination to the project than I should reasonably have expected from a research assistant.

Finally, during the life of this enterprise, I have benefited from the personal support of people who were probably unaware of their contribution to its completion. My thanks to Alan, Ann, Debbie, Guhyaprabha, Kamalashila and Steen.

Foreword

This is a remarkable book, both because of the story it tells and the way in which Judith Rumgay discovered and presents it. She has unearthed a treasure trove of archive material on a remarkable project, the Griffins' Society. She also interviewed members of Griffins' Council, staff, residents and professionals from other organisations in the field. She is thus able to give us a very full picture, as well as a clear and thoughtful evaluation, of what she aptly calls 'an extraordinary organisation'.

The Griffins Society acquired its name from the heraldic beasts who used to adorn the entrance to Holloway Prison in London, Britain's main and best known gaol for women offenders. Its aims were to provide hostels and aftercare for women leaving Holloway. What made the Society distinctive was not only that the volunteers—the members of the Council—were upper middle-class 'ladies', but that they participated fully in the rehabilitation work to which the Society was dedicated. They intervened directly in the women's lives, though the Society also employed professional, paid staff and other agencies with a modern approach were involved too. Even in 1965, when the Society was founded, this was most unusual; as many writers on women's role in the development of welfare have noted, professionalisation and bureaucratisation had been major trends since at least the 1920s.

Yet, as Judith Rumgay records, it seemed as though 'this particular group of volunteers had leaped fully formed from the pages of a text on nineteenth century female philanthropy and simply taken up in the mid-twentieth century where they had left off in the previous one *without noticing the lapse of time*'. *Ladies of Lost Causes* charts how this happened: why, in their first three decades they were very successful—in 1994 they ran five hostels for sixty five women; and why, eventually, their project ceased to be viable. Their access to what Judith Rumgay calls 'the hidden iceberg of power' was crucial, she suggests. As a study of high status women who set out to help other women who are 'doomed to deviance', this book offers notable insights into work on women's voluntary activities and organisations. It enables comparisons to be made with other studies of

xi

first wave feminist 'do gooding', both in the USA and the UK, although, as Judith Rumgay stresses, the Griffins Society was not, in any recognisable sense, a feminist body.

The book offers, too, new perspectives on organisations run by women, women's role in voluntary work and on concepts such as maternalism. It is the period when all this took place, the late twentieth century, which is so striking and Judith Rumgay shrewdly evaluates how the Griffins ran out of steam, entered a cycle of decline and finally gave up providing their services. As a case study of a welfare body's natural history, in an era of rapid change in the 'mixed economy of welfare' *Ladies of Lost Causes* is most revealing.

It gives the reader, too, rich material on the residents who used Griffins services, drawn both from files which Judith Rumgay examined and the interviews she undertook with those who could be traced. These were among the most troubled and troublesome women to be found in the penal system—with very long prison records, chaotic lifestyles, patterns of offending and of self harm. Judith Rumgay gives telling accounts of their suicide attempts, broken lives and histories of abuse, but also of positive outcomes, often achieved through devotion and unorthodox methods. She notes that some professional staff and other observers praised, sometimes reluctantly, the Griffins ladies and their successes.

Judith Rumgay brings her understanding of female offenders, based on her experience as a probation officer, as well as her expertise as a researcher, to her analysis of the Griffins Society. She points out that, while the ladies were passionately dedicated to their residents and the staff heroic and stoical, it was not a feminist enterprise in the modern mode. She raises a number of fascinating questions for scholars, students and professionals: could such an organisation be set up today? What have we lost if there is no scope for such an amateur approach? What can we learn to do from these ladies who acted so boldly 'in the style of women…getting their way'? It is a privilege to write a foreword for a book which speaks to so many of the concerns that I and others share about work for, by and about women.

Frances Heidensohn
London School of Economics

Chapter One

Introduction

I just want to say that, whilst going through the Griffins Society, I didn't think it would help me, but it has. I've really achieved a lot since going through and leaving. I'd just like to thank any of the people that are still (there), like who you ever come across within the Griffins Society, I'd just like to thank them. And that's it. (Former resident)

What would persuade a small group of wealthy, upper middle-class women voluntarily to set up an after-care hostel for discharged female prisoners? And what, given the trials and tribulations of their experience of accommodating those unruly women, would motivate them to spend the following thirty years pioneering another four hostels for the most challenging female offenders? Could such an unlikely enterprise, bringing together opposing extremes of class, privilege and stability, possibly benefit the rehabilitation of serious, recidivist and disturbed offenders? If so, how can we explain the positive outcomes of a venture embarked upon by unpaid 'amateurs', when, almost ten years after their withdrawal from hostel provision, academic and professional disputes about the necessary components of effective offender rehabilitation rage ever more fiercely?

This book attempts to answer these questions. It comprises a retrospective evaluation of the contribution to female offender rehabilitation of the Griffins Society, a voluntary organisation established in the wake of and, partly, in protest against the professionalisation of prison welfare and after-care during the mid-1960s. Over three decades, the Griffins Society developed a range of hostel provision that broke new ground in accommodating women offenders who were very often excluded from alternative

services. The Griffins Society was most notably characterised by its idiosyncratic governing Council, constituted by wealthy, upper middle-class
women, whose philanthropic activity commonly earned them the soubriquet 'Lady Bountiful'. This epithet, with its derogatory associations of
superficiality, patronisation and class-consciousness, encapsulates for most
of us the only available account of the motivations of such volunteers in the
contemporary landscape of penal and social welfare, since they are not
commonly personally encountered, either by the recipients of state or philanthropic aid or by the professionals who generally dispense it.

The invitation to study the Griffins Society's contribution to the
rehabilitation of women offenders presented a unique opportunity to
confront this social stereotype. The initially modest request to evaluate its
hostel provision in order to assess whether it had 'all been worthwhile',
overlooked the fact that the practical enterprise of accommodating difficult,
damaged, and disadvantaged women could not be adequately understood
independently of the context of the philanthropic outlook of its Council
members and its increasingly anachronistic organisational style.
Consequently, this research takes a very different approach from the
conventional method of studying the impact of a discrete and specific
programme of rehabilitative treatment, largely in isolation from its broader
social, organisational and environmental context. Instead, this project is a
holistic evaluation of an organisation's unique contribution to the provision
and practice of rehabilitation of women offenders. Framed in this way, the
study reveals a powerful initiative on the part of women in the voluntary
sector to influence the penal system's traditional disregard of female
offenders. Moreover, this endeavour pre-dates most contemporary efforts to
raise awareness of the plight of females in the predominantly masculine
world of deviance and punishment: feminism was only just beginning to
inspire academic criminological interest in gender disparities in crime and
its treatment (Heidensohn 1968); and it would be thirty years before
'gender-specific programming' became a catch-phrase for professional
rehabilitative practice with women (Bloom and Covington 1998).

The Council, however, was only one of three groups of women
whose distinctive characteristics turned the Griffins Society into an extraordinary organisation. A second group was comprised of strong-minded
project staff whose enthusiasm, initiative and determination enabled the

2

Council to turn ambition into reality. Lastly, the residents were women who were candid and colourful during participant observation. Their personal stories speak poignantly from the pages of normally dry archival records. They were vividly remembered, sometimes years later, with emotions ranging from sorrow, through humour to admiration by professionals whose powers of recall might reasonably be expected to have become blunted through daily saturation with individual need. It is a matter of regret that, despite numerous efforts, it was not possible to trace more of them for interview.

This study draws on rich archival, interview and observational sources to explore the Griffins Society's significance and achievements. The data, collected over an extended period of two years, succeeded in accumulating a wealth of information yielding diverse perspectives from which to view the organisation's character and achievements: 87 interviews with Griffins Society Council members, project staff, allied professionals and residents; a survey of 79 case files of former residents of the hostels; 67 observation days at the three projects that survived the organisation's withdrawal from service provision; and collation of its archives.

The extensive time period required for data collection derived from a number of causes, of which three deserve particular mention. First, while the principle of entry to the hostels as participant observers and for file surveying was initially readily accepted, in practice it was difficult to achieve. Concerns raised by staff about confidentiality had to be negotiated not only in terms of general principles at the outset, but again separately at the point of entering each project. While this issue is an entirely appropriate concern, its constant re-emergence seemed to reflect staff ambivalence about the research: on the one hand they wanted recognition for pioneering projects; on the other, they feared negative exposure from evaluation. Notably, however, once access was achieved, staff rapidly became helpful, open and generous in their assistance, displaying not only their pride in their projects but also a capacity for abrasive self-critique that greatly enriched the qualitative findings. Thus, despite delays prior to entry, time spent in intensive involvement in the life of each project in turn was richly rewarded. Second, much effort was applied to tracing former Council members, staff and allied professionals who played key roles in the organisation's development for interview. Interviewing thus extended over a substantial period, yielding multi-faceted perspectives on the Society's history, its rehabilitative practice and its impact on provision for female offenders. Unfortunately, equal effort applied to tracing former residents was less successful. The difficulties of establishing personal contact with active offenders and retired offenders are well documented (see, for example, Farrall 2002; Wright and Decker 1994, 1997) and that exercise alone could have comprised a research study in itself: ultimately, a choice was forced between the further expenditure of time and resources with potentially little result and the deeper exploitation of more readily available material. Third, although the Griffins Society retained many of the relevant records, archival data was gathered in a partly piecemeal fashion, as contacts established with former Council members, staff and other professionals led to the contribution of additional materials. The consequent task of trawling these records and analysing them for their insights into the organisation's history and character was formidable.

Some terminology should be clarified. The management of the Griffins Society included a system of sub-committees that evolved as the organisation's hostels increased and was subject to various adaptations to meet new contingencies. These fluctuating arrangements were not, however, of great significance in understanding the broader organisational ethos, since the small central core of volunteers remained relatively stable, with a number of individuals participating in several different sub-committees. However, committees also included a range of professional representatives, for example, from project staff, the probation service, police and housing associations. Although interview excerpts will show that the words 'committee' and 'committee member' were used quite loosely to allude to these various arrangements and participants, it is necessary for the purposes of the research to distinguish between the volunteer women whose philanthropic enterprise lay at the heart of the Griffins Society and those other contributors to its management. For the sake of clarity, the terms 'Council' and 'Council member' are reserved for the former group. Moreover, it was customary to refer both to the organisation generally and to Council members collectively as 'the Griffins'. The research follows this custom with regard to Council members, both for convenience and because the soubriquet is rightly suggestive of the extent to which these individuals were identified with the core ethos of the Society.

Care has been taken to preserve confidentiality. Council members are identified throughout the text only in terms of that particular status. With only two exceptions, project staff and other professionals are identified in terms of their primary role in relation to the organisation. The identity of Joanna Kelley, who, as governor of Holloway prison, played midwife to the Society's birth, could not have been concealed from anyone with some knowledge of that penal institution's history: moreover, this book is in part a tribute to her humanitarian vision. Sir Edmond Stockdale, as Lord Mayor of the City of London, was a crucial benefactor to the Society in its early years. While these individuals are now deceased, their acknowledgment in this book appropriately testifies to their philanthropic energy and lasting influence on the Society's fortunes. The identities of hostel residents were disguised during data collection through the assignment of pseudonyms, which are reproduced here in the text. Undertakings were also given at the outset of the research to protect the identities and locations of the hostels themselves, since three surviving projects continue, under the management of another voluntary organisation, to accommodate vulnerable women. The Society's first, flagship hostel has been called here by the name given to it in recognition of the afore-mentioned benefactor, Sir Edmond Stockdale. Since that hostel has closed and the building is no longer known by that name, it has been reproduced, since it helps to convey the Griffins' preference for 'personalisation' of their projects. Pseudonyms reflecting their status have been adopted for each of the other hostels.

In the following chapters, all verbatim interview excerpts are identified in terms of the status of the respondent in relation to the Griffins Society, for example by the inclusion of 'Council member' or 'hostel manager' in parentheses after the quotation. Data from other sources are identified by reference to the methodology used in their collection. In particular, these include: 'observation notes' in parentheses after verbatim excerpts from contemporaneous records; 'case notes' denoting an extract from the file survey; and citations of specific archival documents included in the bibliography.

Chapter 2 charts the history of the Griffins Society, from its origins in the dismantling of voluntary provision of after-care services to its ultimate surrender to the pressures of professionalisation in the voluntary sector itself. It includes an analysis of the organisation's distinctive qualities of maternalism, boldness, and a 'hands on' management style, that accounted in large part for its influence and energy as an innovator in female offender rehabilitation. Chapter 3 profiles the Griffins Society's Council members, studying their social and personal characteristics to reveal how a small group of volunteer women from an elite sector of society became powerful contributors to the development of residential rehabilitation of female offenders. Chapter 4 studies the contribution of project staff to the pioneering practice within the hostels. It includes exploration of the mutually dependent relationship between staff and Council and the impact of breaches of that trust. Chapter 5 considers the social histories and personal characteristics of residents of Griffins Society projects, illuminating the ways in which offending was embedded in the turbulence of the women's lives and revealing the inability or unwillingness of formal agencies of support to engage effectively with them. Chapter 6 explores the daily practice of rehabilitation within the projects, showing that the complex moral dilemmas facing female offenders obscure simple choices between right and wrong responses to their problems. It illustrates the volatility of the hostel environment, the impact of women's deviant lifestyles on hostel safety and management and staff members' narratives of dangerous incidents and their impact, including traumatisation and the 'normalisation of trauma' in the hostel environment. Chapter 7 compares professional accounts of successful and failed placements at the hostels, developing a theoretical account of successful outcomes as the product of 'normal-smithing' (Lofland 1969), which facilitates processes of natural desistance from crime. It illustrates the processes through which successful women established alternative, prosocial personal identities, became masters of their destinies and optimistic for their futures. Finally, Chapter 8 considers the importance of the Griffins Society's philanthropic mission in the contemporary penal landscape.

It was not the intention behind this evaluative study to produce an enthusiastic endorsement of the Griffins Society's enterprise. Indeed, I wondered uneasily at the outset whether such an egregious bunch of non-professional 'ladies of leisure' could have masterminded pioneering projects in offender rehabilitation with any real success. The study forces a reappraisal of the grounds on which such instinctive scepticism is based. This account is testimony to the powerful challenge to such reflex, prejudiced presumptions posed by the strength of evidence asserting the organisation's accomplishments. More broadly, and again unexpectedly, it offers persuasive evidence of the importance of philanthropic endeavour in the voluntary sector in pursuit of humanitarian values in contemporary penal treatments.

Chapter Two

A Philanthropic Phoenix

The Griffins was old-fashioned and quirky and it was absolutely in touch with the women it was seeking to help. They were part of our lives. (Council member)

This chapter charts the origins of the Griffins Society, its pioneering activities as a provider of hostels for women in the criminal justice system and its withdrawal from that role. In so doing, themes to be explored and developed during the remainder of the book are identified.

THIS WAS A NECESSITY

The first—and apparently last—newsletter of the Griffins Society unconsciously reveals a great deal about the organisation. It begins, without preamble:

> On October 27th 1964 John Cavanagh showed his collection of dresses to an audience of about 150, and a total of £2,600 was collected for the Holloway Discharged Prisoners' Aid Society. The Lady D- was the Chairman of the Appeal Committee, and Dame B-, now Baroness B- of Y-, was one of the members. (Griffins Society undateda:1)

The involvement of titled ladies in the benevolent work of the Griffins Society remained key to its character throughout the 30 years of its existence as a provider of accommodation for women offenders. The wealthy, upper middle-class women at the core of the Council gave the organisation its distinctive stamp of philanthropic endeavour derived from the sense of *noblesse oblige* accompanying social privilege (Daniels 1988; Freedman 1996; Jones 1966; Odendahl 1990; Ostrower 1995). Moreover, these women appeared oblivious to the incongruity—remarked by others many times over the following years—of this grand 'Charity Ball' approach to fundraising and advertising for a cause which is not generally noted for its popular appeal. The unapologetic alignment of two worlds, comprising wealth, establishment, and prestige on the one hand and poverty, deviance, and stigma on the other, became the hallmark of the Griffins Society's organisational tradition.

The newsletter goes on to explain the founding of the organisation in 1965 from the funds of the Holloway Discharged Prisoner's Aid Society (DPAS), upon the transfer of prison welfare and after-care services from the voluntary sector to the probation service. The 1960s was a crucial decade in the professionalisation of penal welfare, following a succession of calls during the 1950s (Home Office 1953, 1958). Professionalisation, in effect, meant expansion of state involvement, there being no agency to rival the probation service in terms of comprehensive social work training and geographical coverage. Thus, during this period, probation officers were endowed with professional status as advisors to the courts (Home Office 1961) and experts in social work methods of offender rehabilitation (Home Office 1962). Professional recognition of the probation service reflected the contemporary faith in the rehabilitative ideal (Bottoms and McWilliams 1986). The report of the Advisory Council on the Treatment of Offenders (ACTO 1963), exemplifies the spirit of optimism which characterised the period, in its endorsement of 'the employment of professional social workers on after-care work both in penal institutions and in the community' (p. 21).

The dissolution of local Discharged Prisoners' Aid Societies thus marked the closure of an era during which society's compassion for its offending members was symbolized by the efforts of local philanthropic voluntary bodies. The decision at Holloway to preserve an independent voluntary organisation dedicated to resettlement of women prisoners was facilitated by its recent fundraising venture; the proceeds from the dress show, as one early Council member observed, 'provided a kernel for them to do something.' Crucially, however, it was born from the initiative of the prison governor at that time. Joanna Kelley brought to her governorship of

Holloway Prison a combination of humanitarian instincts, therapeutic ideals and determination which, literally, transformed the institution: under her leadership, the prison redevelopment project replaced the squalid Victorian structure with a modern complex intended to promote the use of psychological therapies as the primary tools of a rehabilitative regime (Rock 1996). In addition to her pursuit of reform, moreover, Kelley was unimpressed by the proposals to transfer prison welfare to the probation service. She did not dispute the inadequacy of the DPAS, which 'had rather run to seed, like so many good things started in the nineteenth century. There were about five or six hundred women in Holloway at that time and we had one middle-aged...[DPAS] full-time worker. She could not, even if she had been brilliant, have covered all their needs.' Her complaint lay in the implied denigration of prison staff, which flew in the face of her own reform efforts.

> I must say I did not really approve...We were trying at Holloway to undertake a very difficult piece of work, which was to persuade the prison officers that they were social workers, not simply turnkeys...We were getting some success...Quite a few of the officers were turning to this, [finding it] much more satisfying...They were much more useful, because they saw much more of the prisoners than anyone else...Then we were told the probation service was taking over. We were no longer to do any of the welfare. It was their job. The first probation officers we had were very determined that should be...So they really got the officers' backs up! They got my back up too...Then the officers began to say, 'If that is all we are, that is all that we will be.' I think that many of the problems in the prison service really stem from that time.

Thus, Kelley recounted: 'When the re-organisation began, they decided, very much encouraged by me, that we would not go in with the rest. We would stay in our own Holloway Prisoners Aid Society and do what *we* wanted with it.' The Holloway DPAS appears to have fallen in with Kelley's plans willingly: 'it was quite easy to persuade them.' Kelley attributed the susceptibility of DPAS members to her influence to their multi-faceted involvement in penal affairs at the local level: many were

11

magistrates and members of Holloway's Board of Visitors. An early Council member, herself a Justice of the Peace and representative of the Board of Visitors, also recalled the participation of prison visitors: 'A prison visitor stems from the old-fashioned day when ladies and men of leisure wanted to help people and went to see them in prison to talk to them, help them, have a personal friendly relationship.' Here, then, Kelley was able to rally to her cause a collection of people who shared a common interest, participation and influence in penal issues generally and prison welfare at Holloway in particular. Having persuaded her audience to take up her ideas, Kelley provided a practical stimulus before withdrawing from the project: 'I was running the prison. I could not do much more. I held an auction at Holloway; people brought very nice things in. We had a champagne supper with very expensive tickets to get the thing started.'

The organisation which sprang from the demise of the DPAS called itself The Griffins Society. The newsletter explains that it was 'thought best to select a name with no obvious link with ex-prisoners' (undateda:1). The choice was not, however, random, but inspired by the stone griffins which adorned the gate of the Victorian prison building, representing its original status as a gaol of the City of London. Kelley recalled: 'There were two enormous creatures over the door. One was holding a set of keys. The other was holding a pair of gyves—leg irons.' These mythical creatures, with lions' bodies and eagles' beaks and wings, are traditionally depicted holding the heraldic crest of the City of London. Although the old prison has been demolished, images of griffins continue to guard the entrances to the City.

The Society's close originating association with Holloway held several implications for its future development. Firstly, as will be seen, it facilitated a remarkably cooperative enterprise in developing community-based opportunities for women prisoners. Secondly, Joanna Kelley's later appointment as Assistant Director of Women's Prisons at the Home Office enabled her to promote the Society's work at the level of central government. Thirdly, the link to the City of London brought the support of the then Lord Mayor, who coincidentally was greatly concerned by the problems of Holloway's prisoners.

Sir Edmund Stockdale was chairman of the prison visitors at Holloway. I'm sure this is right, that he used to give ten shillings...to the women who were going [out] and say 'Don't you come back again.' There they were, all homeless, absolutely. It used to really worry him stiff. That's why...he made [the Griffins] his charity. That's why he started it, decided this was a necessity, that these homeless women should [have somewhere to go]. (Council member)

Whether or not this particular story is apocryphal, there is no doubt that Sir Edmund Stockdale strongly encouraged the Griffins Society's work, not least by ensuring considerable financial support over several years, from both public funds and his private means. It became the tradition for the incumbent Lord Mayor of the City of London to hold the presidency of the Griffins Society, following this philanthropic individual's acceptance of the first tenure of the appointment, offered in recognition of his assistance. This tradition continued until the Society withdrew from direct service provision.

A 'CAN DO' ORGANISATION

The project which Kelley proposed as a worthy successor to the DPAS offered a modest, practical solution to the humiliation awaiting the discharged prisoner.

Before the '39 war, Holloway used to have a big room in a nearby house where they kept prisoners' property...[In those days] they had the women in uniform. All their clothes were bundled into sacks. Each sack had the woman's name on it. They were stored like sacks of potatoes until she went out. Then, if they had nowhere to press and iron them, they had to go out in unpressed clothes, from the bottom of a pile from years ago. It was really terrible. We did manage to press people's clothes in the reception area before they went out, but only if we had time from other things...So it was very unsatisfactory. This hall was bombed in the war, razed to the ground. I said they needed [a place] where the woman herself, perhaps the day before her release, could have her clothes, shake them out, iron them...

Warming to her theme of putting premises near the prison to practical use, Kelley elaborated: 'It could be used for family visits. If it was near the prison she could be taken out and her family could visit her there...You might use it for bed and breakfast for families who had come a long way...That was the kind of thing I had in mind as necessary.'

The fundraising efforts permitted the purchase of a terraced house in Camden, not far from the prison. Supported by grants from London Parochial Charities, the first project of the Griffins Society opened its doors on May 6, 1966. Its services reveal an imaginative development of Kelley's early plan: accommodation for six women; twice weekly group therapy offered by the consultant psychiatrist attached to Holloway; legal surgeries offered voluntarily by two solicitors; an evening coffee bar 'where women can bring their friends, associates, husbands or boy-friends for a snack meal and coffee' (Griffins Society undatedb:3). The project thus combined, as Kelley had suggested, community support services for discharged prisoners with an active relationship with the prison. It would continue to develop this dual approach for some years.

The consultant psychiatrist, quoted in an early brochure produced by the Society, expressed great confidence in the project's predicted achievements:

> I am more convinced than ever before that the therapeutic atmosphere which we are building up at the Griffins is the right one and will have far reaching effects in helping keep women out of prison and as an important piece of sociological work. (Griffins Society, undatedb:4)

Although few records survive from the Griffins Society's first 10 years of operation, it seems clear that the psychiatrist was not alone in this cheerful certainty. Already, at the time of publication of that brochure, the Griffins were taking an interest in the property next door to their project, with a view to extending their residential provision. A circular letter appealing for funds some time later declared:

It soon became evident that more accommodation was needed so further funds were raised to enable the Society to purchase another house. Fortunately the adjoining terraced house became vacant in March 1968 and, largely owing to the generosity of Sir Edmund Stockdale, the Society were *(sic)* in a position to purchase. (Griffins Society undatedc:1)

This letter also reports an ingenious extension of the cooperative relationship with Holloway: 'The cost of decoration in this house has been considerably reduced by a party of up to 5 women from Holloway who have come out daily with an Officer during the last few weeks to help paint the walls and ceilings and work on the garden' (Griffins Society undatedc:1).

These records reveal a striking pace of development, testifying both to the vigour of the Griffins and to the continuing generosity of Sir Edmund Stockdale and the London Parochial Charities. Moreover, the Society rapidly attained public recognition and political support for its enterprise, due partly to the social elite from which it drew its members and partly to the continuing efforts of Joanna Kelley who, as vice-president of the Society, promoted its work within the Home Office. In 1969, the front page of 'The North London Press' carried a photograph captioned 'Home Secretary Mr James Callaghan, and house supervisor Miss W-, cut the celebration cake at the opening of Stockdale House, a home for the rehabilitation of women ex-prisoners' (p.1). The story was also carried by a local newspaper, 'The Ham and High', which reported Mr Callaghan as saying, with a somewhat odd choice of metaphor: 'I regard this kind of venture as being one of the most important things the Home Office ought to be stepfather too *(sic)*.' He went on to admire 'voluntary service freely given by people who look beyond their own needs to those of society as a whole. The tradition of service and idealism is part of the British genius' (Camden Borough News 1969:9). The naming of the house after their benefactor began the Griffins' tradition of calling a project after an individual whose influence had been key to its development.

Fortunately, the Annual Report of 1975, which was the first to be produced as a glossy, therefore apparently durable, booklet, bearing the dramatic figure of a rampant griffin, took the opportunity to summarise activities over the decade. Reflecting the enthusiastic energy which had been expended on the organisations' development, the report begins breathlessly: 'Ten years old! A milestone in any life and a considerable one in the life of a voluntary society seeking to serve the needs of women offenders' (Griffins Society 1975:4).

Despite the departure of Holloway's consultant psychiatrist, which brought to an end the group therapy sessions, the account reveals more continuity than dislocation in the relationship with the prison. It records the provision of visiting facilities for women prisoners and their children, occasional (space permitting) accommodation of relatives visiting Holloway from afield, and the involvement of a retired prison officer, Miss O-, who became, as will be seen, a legend in the lifetime of the Griffins Society.

Notwithstanding its opening excitement, this report later reveals an extraordinary development with remarkable calm: 'At the request of the Home Office in 1973 we started an experiment by taking women on bail who might otherwise be remanded in custody, thus widening the scope of our work. For the first two years we provided two bail beds and for the last year we have provided five, but this has meant reducing the number of beds available for after care *(sic)* residents' (Griffins Society 1975:5). In the style of women accustomed to getting their way, the Griffins at this point asked the Home Office to increase its grant for the bail beds. The Home Office, however, in a curiously inverted bargain, not only agreed to their request, but capped it by inviting them to establish an approved bail hostel for women: 'This your committee agreed to do and at the same time we agreed to increase our bail provision to five beds, for the time being until a suitable building could be found...' (Griffins Society 1975:6).

Thus we discover that, in the space of 10 years, the Griffins Society pioneered the first after-care hostel for women, expanded it, established a range of community-based services for women prisoners and ex-offenders, and began the first experimental women's bail project. The Griffins appeared dauntless in their grasp of opportunities and challenges, setting a trend of innovation which would continue for a further 20 years.

> It was very much a period of growth and enthusiasm...It just felt that it was a 'can do' organisation. That's how I remember it. (Hostel manager)

There was always something. We were pioneering. We were asked to do all sorts of things by the Home Office in developing [services for] women within the criminal justice system...All these things that we got involved with...which was very challenging...There was a lot of activity. There was a lot of development. (Council member)

While progress was not always smooth, the Griffins seemed indomitable. Due to disappointments and delays over the search for, purchase of, alterations to and furbishment of a suitable building, the bail hostel did not open until September 1978. It opened with 12 bed spaces. Stockdale House reverted to its original purpose as an after-care hostel for 13 women; the Annual Report records unnecessary initial anxiety as to the continuing level of demand for such accommodation after the five year gap (Griffins Society 1978). The organisation began then to develop increasingly adventurous projects.

Stockdale House, up to this time, provided a self-contained flat for its warden. This tradition was finally broken when a resident warden chose to move out to independent accommodation after getting married. The empty flat was subsequently let to a resident who was making good progress in the hostel (Griffins Society 1979). Perhaps this opportunistic experiment provided the inspiration for another project: to develop a house for women moving towards independence who needed transitional, reducing support. Certainly, reflecting a now customary alacrity in seizing new ideas and opportunities, it was only two years before the Annual Report recorded a successful approach to a local housing association, 'who have been most helpful in enabling us to acquire a small house in West Hampstead with six bedrooms' (Griffins Society 1981:4). After conversion to bed-sitter flatlets with communal lounge and kitchen, Halfway House took its first residents in May 1983, letting one room to a 'responsible care-taker' who collected rents, reported house maintenance problems and otherwise led an independent life (Griffins Society 1983a). Meanwhile, the organisation was also negotiating for independent move-on accommodation. By 1986, Stockdale House boasted a total of 11 housing units per year committed by the Greater London Council, Borough of Camden and housing associations (Griffins Society 1986a); Halfway House claimed four flats per year (Griffins Society 1985).

During the same period, however, Stockdale House suffered financial difficulties. Annual Reports show that the Griffins twice successfully
asked the Home Office for help: a fourth staff appointment was funded in
1978 (Griffins Society 1978); an increase in grant was awarded the following year (Griffins Society 1979). The Society also approached a national
housing association with a view to forging a relationship which would
relieve it of the costs of structural maintenance (Griffins Society 1979). The
negotiation was finally concluded in April 1982, when the housing association took over responsibility for structural maintenance and staff salaries.
Thereafter, the Griffins Society was to manage the hostel as agents for the
housing association, having passed over to it the property's deeds to be held
in trust. The Annual Report observes that this 'has been a great relief to our
Society, which, like so many other charities of the same kind over recent
years, has seen its resources gradually reduced by inflation' (Griffins
Society 1982a:4). Thus re-invigorated, a plan for renovation and total refurbishment of the property was immediately prepared, which ultimately
would lead to temporary re-location of the project for 36 weeks in 1984.
The Annual Report recounts: 'we lived happily, but on a smaller scale in
somewhat shabby elegance, in a crumbling Georgian house in Guilford
Place, Bloomsbury' (Griffins Society 1985:3).

Plans for expanding the range of provision continued to develop
during these years. In 1988, there was exciting news:

> For some years it has been the aim of the Griffins to set up a hostel
> for homeless women who, having completed their sentence, could
> get their children back from Care if they were offered accommoda-
> tion. We now see a light at the end of the tunnel towards bringing
> such a hostel into being. [A] Housing Association has bought the
> house next door to Stockdale House for this purpose. (Griffins
> Society 1988:3)

The fate of the mother and baby project will be discussed below: the
premises, in fact, opened in 1992 as a second-stage hostel for nine
Stockdale House graduates who could cope without 24-hour support
(Griffins Society 1992). For now, we need only note the expansionist ideals
of the Griffins in 1988, declaring their ambitions to cater for the most chal-

lenging groups: 'Our future plans cover further second stage housing, specialised hostels for alcoholics, drug addicts and those with psychiatric problems: we believe that these are the areas of the greatest need' (Griffins Society 1988:3).

The Griffins had good grounds for confidence in their ability to grow. Their projects thrived. Halfway House secured funding for a part-time support worker (Griffins Society 1988). The Bail Hostel raised its occupancy level to 95 percent, due partly to effective liaison with Holloway to establish a bail scheme for remanded women. The happy coincidence of this success with a Home Office drive to expand bail provision resulted in a request to the Griffins Society to increase its bed spaces (Griffins Society 1989a). In August 1990, the first bailees moved into newly purchased, converted and furbished premises, with capacity for 24 residents. The Griffins were triumphant: 'This is a great coup for the Griffins Society to receive such substantial funding from the Home Office to open this new hostel and, therefore, we are in the forefront of providing a serious alterna-tive to custody for women on remand' (Griffins Society 1990a:3).

The Griffins barely paused after this climactic moment before again expanding its bail provision. In the following year they reported the success of negotiations with a private landlord for the let of 'a spacious flat on two levels, with four bedrooms, where four carefully chosen women from [the Bail Hostel] move-on *(sic)* to live together, essentially running their own lives and the flat. Supervision is minimal, still complying with bail condi-tions' (Griffins Society 1991a:4).

Serendipitously, vacation of the original premises of the Bail Hostel coincided with an invitation to the Griffins Society by the Special Hospitals Service Authority (SHSA) to establish a hostel for women discharged from the special hospitals at Rampton, Broadmoor, and Ashworth. Preparations, in partnership with the housing association already involved in the mother and baby project, for conversion and refurbishment of the house began in 1990. With hindsight benefit, it seems portentous that the first mention of this project in an Annual Report is to record 'a setback, due to an alteration in fire escape regulations. This has unfortunately delayed work on the building so that the project is now behind schedule' (Griffins Society 1991a:2). It would be, in fact, 1994 before Special Care House took its first referrals, following a whole series of 'setbacks.' Announcing readiness to take referrals at last, the Griffins succinctly recalled 'a great deal of work, a few serious disappointments and some moments of great satisfaction' (Griffins Society 1994a:5).

At that point, the Griffins Society ran five hostels: Stockdale House; Second-Stage House; Halfway House; Bail Hostel and its cluster unit; and Special Care House. In total, the hostels could accommodate 65 women. These milestones are charted in Figure 1. Yet, 1994 was the last year in which the Annual Report was produced as a glossy brochure and

FIGURE 1: SIGNIFICANT DATES IN THE HISTORY OF THE GRIFFINS SOCIETY

YEAR	EVENT
1965	The Griffins Society is founded from the funds of the disbanded Holloway Discharged Prisoner's Aid Society
1966	Stockdale House opens
1978	The Bail Hostel opens
1983	Halfway House opens
1986	Stockdale House has 11 housing units p er year committed for move -on accommodation by GLC; Halfway House has 4 flats per year.
1990	The Bail Hostel re -locates
1991	Cluster flat for the Bail Hostel opens
1992	Second-stage House opens
1994	Special Care House opens
1995	Decision taken: F ebruary, to close Second-stage House; June, to close Stockdale House; November, to withdraw from hostel provision
1996	The Bail Hostel, Halfway House and Special Care House are transferred to a larger voluntary organisation

celebrated, as was customary, with a public launch. Before examining its withdrawal from hostel provision, however, we should explore the characteristics which, in combination, made the Griffins Society a uniquely dynamic organisation during 30 'can do' years: it was maternal, 'hands on', and bold.

A Woman's Place

True to Joanna Kelley's ambition, Stockdale House, from 1969, provided a venue for women prisoners to meet their children outside the prison walls. This project achieved more than local success: during 1974, mothers from Holloway, Moor Court, and Askham Grange prisons visited a total of 98 children (Griffins Society 1975); in the following year, Drake Hall joined the list (Griffins Society 1976). The project became an opportunity for multi-faceted personal and professional support:

> We have continued to have the children's visits at Stockdale House throughout the year. This means that a woman serving a sentence may come out of prison, usually with an escort, to meet her children at Stockdale House. This obviates the necessity for children to go into the prison to see their mother, and the visit takes place in a more normal atmosphere. Moreover, if the children's social worker wants to talk with the mother, or with the probation officer, they can easily move to another room and do so quietly. The Sheriffs' Fund, through the Hon. Lady B-, pays for the refreshments which are provided for these visits, and they tend to be very happy, if noisy, occasions. (Griffins Society 1978:6-7)

> They were also giving lectures on child care and hygiene, because they ran a family day to allow women in Holloway to be released for an afternoon to be with their children. (Probation officer)

It is unclear precisely when, or why these family visits ceased. However, the history of the Griffins Society is infused with the ambition to support motherhood. The needs were all too obvious at Stockdale House.

21

> A number of the women...were mothers...When they came out [of prison], it was very difficult for them to get custody of their children. So they only had access. That, for some of the mothers, was very difficult. Therefore, there was a need to reunite mothers with their children as soon as possible. We also had women who had their babies while in custody...and...women who came into Stockdale House and then became pregnant. (Hostel manager)

Inevitably, children and babies featured regularly in hostel life at Stockdale House.

> We had a number of cots in the basement, so we could set up a cot...or we had some folding beds. There were about three children who were older...But the majority were usually babies...We had a number of babies born ...to parents who [stayed] until they moved on. (Hostel manager)

This reality of their residents' lives aroused an uneasy conflict of sympathies for some Council members: 'Most of them had children...We [weren't supposed to] have children, during *my* time, *living* in the hostel. I very often turned a blind eye if they stayed over the weekend.' The ambition for a dedicated project for mothers and babies flowed from the inescapable intrusion of the problems of thwarted motherhood.

> There were all too many women who, when they came out of prison, found it impossible to get their children back, either because [the children] had been—if they'd been lucky—with families whose mistrust of the woman was considerable, or [the women] had nowhere to go, most common of all. You don't just walk into a council house because you've got a baby and have just come out of prison. The children were in care because there was nowhere else for them to go. Social Services were very reluctant to release children to a homeless ex-offender. We wanted there to be somewhere people who came out of prison could...be with their babies. (Council member)

The prevalence of unfulfilled motherhood was thrown into stark relief by the gender specificity of the organisation's clientele. However, the opportunity to mother was only one female need exposed in this context. Gender specific provision 'meant we could focus on the needs of the women who came into the house. It wasn't diluted in any way' (Hostel manager).

> It was very woman focussed. They were very good at that. Certainly, as a man going in there, I felt very much that I was in a woman's place, that I had to respect that. That was fine. That was absolutely right. (Housing association officer)

To describe the Griffins Society as a 'maternal' organisation, then, implies more than a particular focus on providing for mothers, although this was the most obvious expression of the approach. It denotes a perspective that is not only sensitive to multi-faceted needs of women, but, moreover, which evokes responses that are also typically female. Thus, the maternal approach sprang from *both* the exclusive focus on female offenders *and* the female composition of the Council, creating an organisation which was 'much more aware of the family needs and the family involvements' (Probation officer).

This brand of maternalism has characterised many forms of female philanthropy and activism. Female philanthropists have traditionally favoured those aspects of social life which predominantly affect women, children and families in their charitable donations (Ostrower 1995), voluntary work (Prochaska 1980) and reform efforts (Freedman 1996; Koven and Michel 1993; McCarthy 1990; Scott 1990). Moreover, these activities draw responses which are themselves gender typical (Koven 1993; Koven and Michel 1993). Female penal reformers have similarly drawn on the qualities of female experience, most significantly that of motherhood, not only as foci for social change, but to craft a distinctive style of justice rooted in a feminine perspective (Freedman 1996; Kent 1962; Manton 1976). While the Griffins did not articulate their approach by explicit appeal to a maternal ideology, this perspective, arising naturally from their personal experiences, underpinned distinctive elements in their projects.

Hands On

The Annual Report for 1975 recalls that the Griffins 'in the early days considered that the rehabilitation of the women should be in professional hands and that they themselves had to be concerned largely with the alterations and furnishing of the House' (Griffins Society 1975:4). It records their change of view in 1967, when 'Committee members started involving themselves more with the women and began visiting the House on a rota basis—a practice which is continued today, despite several debates as to its value' (Griffins Society 1975:4). In fact, the 'visiting member' system endured, with modifications, to the very end of the Griffins Society's involvement in hostel provision. Staff recollected this approach with appreciation.

> [She] was an example of someone who didn't have a professional background in any relevant field, but took a real interest, visited and was very positive in her attitude to the hostel. (Hostel manager)

> Sometimes they would chat to the staff, see how things were going. Sometimes they'd sit in the lounge, chat to the residents, get things from their point of view. (Staff member)

Interviewees repeatedly advanced the expression 'hands on' in their accounts of the Griffins approach to the management of their hostels. This operational style became a crucial aspect of the Griffins' organisational identity. The Griffins acknowledged a certain eccentricity about their style of management, but maintained a staunch attachment to it, and, indeed, were convinced of its virtue.

> Well, it's unique. I've never heard of an organisation where the volunteers were really running it...Some of [the staff] might well say we interfered too much: 'We were the professionals. These women were just barging in. They didn't really know what they were doing'...I'm sure there was always this idea that we were a bunch of grand women, giving our time when we could, but the real work was being done—which it *was*—by the staff. But we had a continuation

of expertise which we'd built up. I felt that had a value. (Council member)

The Griffins' 'hands on' orientation involved them in both the drama and the desultory minutiae of everyday hostel life. Council members recalled:

I was very much—because I lived so locally—able and willing to arrive at the drop of a hat, [for example] if someone needed to be taken to a hospital appointment. We couldn't afford taxis for them...Then if we were suddenly and unexpectedly short staffed...I would be called upon to go down. I could man the phone, take messages, that sort of thing.

[In the early days], we had to go and do the shopping once a week. That sort of thing. Yes, we did. Two members of the management committee went down to the local Cash and Carry and got everything. Loo paper!

The incongruous image of peers of the realm shopping for toilet paper for a household of miscreant women distracts the observer from the deeper significance of this level of activity. Being 'hands on' demonstrated the volunteer spirit and personal commitment of Council members.

It was very much, in the early days, a question of *personal* interest. That's how it remained all my time. Everybody on the committee took a close *personal* interest in it, gave of their *own* time, their *own* energy, their *own* general experience. I don't think any of us had any kind of social work training at all. (Council member)

More deeply than individual commitment, however, the approach symbolised the ethos of an organisation which sought connection between women from different social worlds.

[My contribution] was the fact that I was local, available, able to put my head round the door and be recognised. [It] was really part of the ethos...They *wanted* [the women] to feel that it was run by people who cared, who wanted to help, rather than some distant committee who never got involved. (Council member)

Direct participation in the practicalities of service delivery has long characterised women's philanthropy. Prochaska (1980) records how increasing prosperity during the nineteenth century, by facilitating hiring of domestic labour, alongside poor educational and employment opportunities, fostered the emergence of voluntary charitable enterprise among middle-class women who found themselves with a surfeit of leisure time. The emergence of the social work profession itself is rooted in 'a long tradition of voluntary female benevolence in which middle-class women assumed social responsibility for the welfare of poor, sick, or delinquent women and children' (Freedman 1996:57). Biographies of female penal reformers, including Elizabeth Fry (Kent 1962), Mary Carpenter (Manton 1976), and the American Miriam Van Waters (Freedman 1996), testify to an involvement of women in the practice of welfare equally as intense as their intellectual contribution to its ethical justification. Indeed, in her biography of Margery Fry, Jones (1966) points out that while educational opportunities increased during the twentieth century, women, particularly those who remained single, found few alternatives to dedicating their intelligence and energy to philanthropic service to the disadvantaged.

The phenomenon of 'hands on' philanthropic volunteering, crucial to a full appreciation of the mission and social significance of the Griffins Society, will be examined in greater depth in the next and later chapters. For now, the point is that, whether they recognised it or not, the Griffins were extending a very old tradition of philanthropic activity by wealthy women of the leisured class.

Bold

Joanna Kelley harboured a particular ambition for the Griffins Society:

I very much wanted to have some help for what I call the *unhelpable*. In those days, women who went to prison often did not go back again, having learned the lesson...But there *are* people who—either

26

because they are so disadvantaged or they are so disturbed mentally—simply *cannot* cope with the complexities of life. I wanted to *help the unhelpable*.

The Griffins did not disappoint her. From the outset until the end, they refused to exclude a woman from residence on the basis of her offence alone, which was a common practice elsewhere. Indeed, an early Council member observed that setting *any* exclusionary criterion was self-defeating: 'We said we wouldn't have alcoholics or people that took drugs. But who *do* you have, then?' More recent Council members reflected:

> Overall, the Griffins was true to [Sir Edmund Stockdale] and Joanna Kelley...We *did* fulfil their wishes, offering an alternative to custody for women who had committed any degree of crime, any degree of severity. That was what it was all about.

> The biggest thing about the Griffins was that it was prepared to take those risks about who it took in and who it helped. It was filling a really important gap. It was a brave organisation to carry on with that policy. That's really, really good.

Professionals associated with the organisation confirmed that these were not false claims. A liaison probation officer from the early 1970s recalled:

> It's always one of the oddities, if you had a 'nice, quiet girl', you'd put her in [say] a Church Army Hostel and they'd say, 'Yeah, no problem.' But as soon as you mentioned anything like violent crime, [they] ran a mile...Whereas Stockdale House was actually *trying* to take people...with pretty severe problems.

Government reports emerging in the early years of the Griffins Society's venture deplored the failure of many hostels to provide for 'more than a limited category of homeless offenders. The large numbers of offenders who present the more difficult personal problems can be accommodated only to a very limited extent and may often be excluded' (Home

27

Office 1966:3; also Home Office 1967). The Griffins Society, however, was distinguished by its liberal access policies for thirty years.

> [The Griffins Society's] underlying ethos to deal with women with difficult backgrounds and mental health problems remained throughout...the '80s...Voluntary agencies, by their very nature...they're dealing with difficult people. When difficulties arise, they tend to re-jig their rules and controls, not to support the individual, but to exclude them and keep the higher function of the organisation going. Griffins didn't do that. Griffins *always* kept to the difficult women. (Probation officer)

> That was a really laudable thing for them to do. One of the problems that people who have multiple needs find is getting access to accommodation. It was a very laudable thing for them to do...because one of the big criticisms [of] a lot of direct access schemes is the exclusion criteria. It means that hostels aren't always helping the people who are in most need. They're in a position where they can cherry pick. (Housing association officer)

A probation officer, asked to describe an unsuitable woman for referral, reflected, with self-conscious irony: 'I can't, actually. Because if *my* client was suitable, then *everybody else* was suitable for Stockdale House. *My* view was that my client was unsuitable for *any* communal living, shared housing, full stop...But she was "suitable" for Stockdale House. She lived there, they worked with her, it worked. So *anybody* would be "suitable" for Stockdale House.'

Its anti-exclusionary access policy, however, did not define the organisation, but reflected a deeper courage. Each project upon which they embarked broke new ground in the field of penal welfare, yet the Griffins approached it in a spirit of adventure, apparently undaunted by the risks they were taking.

> It did feel *bold*, that you were doing something that other people would shy away from. [For example, Special Care House] was totally *new*. They had the *cheek* to try and do it in the middle of

London, without having all the support networks in place! The *audacity* is amazing. I liked that. (Hostel manager)

To be innovative and daring and imaginative. Which we certainly were. (Council member)

With hindsight, a Council member mused: 'Really, looking back, it took quite a lot of nerve...setting up [Special Care House]. We had one problem after another.' Perhaps the intensity of focus and energy spent on piecemeal problem solving in the development of their projects distracted the Griffins from dwelling too heavily on the enormity of their undertakings. Perhaps, too, they simply expected to get their own way in the end. As we shall see, the Griffins' courage flowed, in some measure, from their powerful social positions.

[They had a reputation] as mavericks, because they *wouldn't* take no for an answer. If they believed that something needed to be done, they'd pursue it. They would be so *persistent*. (Hostel manager)

I marvelled at the membership of the organisation and was bemused at its workings. It was a unique organisation in those terms...That's very, very strong in my mind...Linked with that was the *courage* of the organisation. Maybe because of their power and influence. They would just bluster in, get things done. Roll up the sleeves. Very matronly. Get it done. I liked that. It was different. (Senior probation officer)

I think they liked being bold. (Housing association officer)

RUNNING OUT OF STEAM

What misfortunes could trigger such a rapid spiral of decline that within two years a vigorous organisation, with five pioneering projects to its credit, would withdraw from hostel management altogether? The origins of its demise may be traced to events which, treated as isolated disappointments at the time of their occurrence, were not recognised as symptoms of any deeper malaise: the failure of the mother and baby project; and the closures of Stockdale and Second-stage Houses.

It Never Came Off

The Griffins committed considerable resources and energy to realising their ambition to develop a mother and baby project.

> It *seemed* like it could be a really good idea. They had it well worked out. [One Council member] did a *huge* amount of work on it. It was [the Chair's] baby, she wanted it really *badly*, she thought it would be good. Really, [they] did a *lot* of work. (Council member)

> We got a professional fundraiser...to help get the money. It was awfully *sad*, because it never came off in the end. (Council member)

At the outset, the Griffins clearly believed there was good reason to expect this project to flourish. Stockdale House, during the early 1980s, was regularly asked to accommodate women with small children: for example, one seeking phased reunion under supervision with a two-year old child from foster-care (Griffins Society 1982b); one whose three-year old child was discharged from care (Griffins Society 1983b); and one, with a ten-month old child, awaiting trial at the Central Criminal Court (Griffins Society 1984d). Moreover, multi-agency support existed for such a project, including local authority funding (Griffins Society 1986b:3).

Nevertheless, the project failed. Firstly, there were repeated problems in securing a suitable site. For example:

> We had a *great* disappointment at one point, because there was an old fire station just around the corner from Stockdale House...We were very anxious to take it over, make it into a place where mothers and babies could have flatlets and be given support...I was particularly involved with that. I was *very* keen that it should come about. It didn't. It was because of planning permission rather than any...inability on the Griffins' part to implement the idea...That was *very* disappointing. (Council member)

Secondly, when, in 1989, a property was eventually secured for the purpose by a housing association, there were, after all, funding problems. The Griffins Society's fundraiser was highly successful. However, progress stalled when it emerged that the Housing Corporation had 'run out of funds' (Griffins Society 1990b:1; also 1989b, 1991b).

> We went to the Housing Corporation...There was lots of dilly-dally-ing...After much negotiation, they said, 'If you raise [£60,000], we will match it.' We then went off and raised [it], through connections and various trusts, went back to the Housing Corporation, who said '*Oops*. We've run out of money now'...So there was a lot of egg on a lot of faces at that point, because money had been pledged to us or received. (Council member)

It was 1991 before records show confirmation of grant by the Housing Corporation and the start of property conversion (Griffins Society 1991c). Progress in this direction, however, exposed a new set of problems. The property to which the Griffins were now committed was, in fact, adjacent to Stockdale House.

> It's a tall [Georgian] house. It's got a lot of floors and half-land-ings...There is *no way* you can have mothers and babies. You need some communal space. You need staff on duty. You *don't* need people tucked away separately in little rooms with no staff. I could just see *endless* problems. You would have no control over who came into the house...You would also need a series of gates...Imagine eight, at *minimum*, small children...I had visions of disasters there. (Council member)

Reductions in overall funding and lack of local authority commit-ment in advance to fund each placement, forced revision of staffing plans to minimum week-day cover, which the Griffins came to perceive as dangerously inadequate. Nevertheless, the treasurer still projected a substantial annual deficit. A memo, summarising these issues, from the project sub-committee to the Council eventually conceded: 'Despite all the problems and indeed embarrassment that is entailed, we unanimously agreed that it would be unwise to continue as presently proposed' (Griffins Society 1991d). The Council abandoned the mother and baby project on July 11, 1991 (Griffins Society 1991e).

In their fierce attachment to this project, the Griffins appear to have failed to recognise warning signs that it was unlikely to succeed: signs, moreover, rooted in their own experience. In 1984, an apparently inconclusive discussion was opened concerning a proposal to take babies at Halfway House (Griffins Society 1984a; 1984b); notably, security and safety problems associated with an unsupervised house were arising at this time (Griffins Society 1984c; 1984d). That same year, the Home Office agreed to designate three beds for mothers with babies at the Bail Hostel: the facility was never used. Nevertheless, when the Bail Hostel was re-located, spaces were dedicated for mothers and babies. Records suggest that the facility was used only once.

> It was quite a hassle. [She] was a...drugs [trafficker...who] had come with her baby...She came with us for a long time. Some of these cases take a long time to come to court. That was satisfactory for a time. But only for a time, as the child got bigger, no longer a baby. (Council member)

The experience illuminated the tension between the organisation's liberal access policies and the need to protect children within a volatile milieu. A Council member, with hindsight, recognised the plan's naïveté:

> We then ran into the problem of women on bail who had done some horrendous things. We could not have *trusted* them with children in the house...It was *far* more complicated than we thought...We discovered early on that women, perhaps with children who had been taken into care..., perhaps they had abused them, or murdered them even, was *not* a good mix.

One interpretation of these accounts might argue that the Griffins made a disastrous error of judgement, propelled by their maternal instincts into a doomed enterprise. A more sympathetic analysis might press mitigation: the pursuit of their ideal reflected, as we have seen, some realities of practice at Stockdale House; and the original ambition found support from other agencies, which apparently withered. Moreover, there is a legitimate, but unfortunately unanswered question why the partner housing association condoned the purchase of an unsuitable property. The narratives above suggest that during the protracted development period ideas were changing rapidly, both as to the requirements of such specialised accommodation and as to the suitability of linking child care integrally to offender accommodation. Council members recall that the introduction of the Children Act 1989 brought the full realisation that their project was infeasible. Nevertheless, whichever reading of history is preferred, the enterprise certainly left a legacy extending far beyond disappointment.

> We were always full. We thought, 'Ah! We should expand.' We would have done better to have not had the mothers and babies idea. We thought that it complemented: we would have one [bail] hostel, one after-care hostel and a mothers and babies unit. No. In fact, it put the kibosh on it. (Council member)

A Huge Drain

Donors to the mother and baby project 'agreed that the Griffins Society could use the money donated as it saw fit for women offenders' (Griffins Society 1991f:1). As time ran out for claiming grant in 1992, the property was re-designated as an after-care hostel, 'as there was no time to think of anything else' (Griffins Society 1991f:2). Thus the Griffins launched into another problematic project.

Second-stage House never thrived. Its vulnerability stemmed primarily from its dependence for referrals on Stockdale House, which failed to provide sufficient recruits. The result was financial disaster.

> [Second-Stage House] closed first. It was just a *huge* drain on the charity's finances...But the trouble was the turnover in Stockdale House was just far too high. [Second-Stage House] had nine bed spaces. I don't think we ever, at any one time, had more than five bed spaces filled. (Staff member)

> The highest occupancy that [Second-Stage House] achieved was [about] 50 percent. It was really *poor*. It was *disastrous*...because the [Housing Corporation] would not accept such a poor perform-ance if it's putting in money. (Housing association officer)

Problems were also accumulating at Stockdale House, which, as a voluntary after-care hostel, did not attract the generous level of Home Office funding that was provided for the Bail Hostel. The difficulties of managing a volatile population of women, entrenched in seemingly intractable lifestyles of drug use, prostitution and abuse, will be explored in detail later. Here, it is important to note the impact that these problems were having upon occupancy. Attempts to clear the hostel of disruptive residents, or to restrict access to exclude potential troublemakers, became self-defeat-ing by increasing turnover and vacancies. Lowered income from under-occupancy resulted in inability to sustain staffing levels, which, in turn, exacerbated the problems of maintaining a safe house. The Griffins began to feel trapped in an irreversible cycle of decline.

> We were *trying* to avoid making the same mistakes again, but it was almost impossible to do so. Because anyone that we took in, on the terms on which we agreed to take people, would come with a huge drug problem. Or, if they didn't—this is terrible—they might *acquire* one...That was just too much really. (Council member)

> There was lots of pressure on the Griffins Society because of the voids. So, for them to think about introducing even more restric-tions [on eligibility] would inevitably cause even more problems with vacancies. (Housing association officer)

During the 1960s, government reports repeatedly called for increased hostel provision for discharged prisoners, identifying this as an important role for voluntary effort (Home Office 1963, 1966, 1967). In the 1990s, however, it appeared that discharged prisoners entertained different expectations of accommodation (Griffins Society 1994b).

> This was no longer what the people we were trying to attract and provide for *wanted*. They *wanted* a little flat. What they *got* was a

tiny room which was a posher version of the cell [they] had just left. All that money had been spent [on refurbishment] and it no longer fitted the bill. (Council member)

The physical standards that people expect these days, quite rightly, have changed...Very few people want to live in a hostel any more. They might want to live in a...shared flat. (Housing association officer)

More generally, housing policy was shifting in favour of supported housing schemes in smaller projects and self-contained accommodation. The financial consequences, for the Griffins Society, were severe. The probation service switched its financial support to alternative projects.

We transferred that money into a very different type of service for women offenders...The women will vote with their feet. They'll leave...Which is why the grant aiding was transferred into a very different type of project which was more dispersed, [for example] three women sharing a flat, more space, a lot more emphasis on privacy, support services brought in as opposed to [24 hour cover]. (Senior probation officer; also Griffins Society 1994b)

Central funding structures also changed.

I've worked in housing since 1987. When I started, it was so *casual*. It was so *easy*. You got 100 percent capital grants from the Housing Corporation...On the revenue side, you got Hostel Deficit Grant. It seems *bizarre* now, but basically the bigger your deficit, the more money you got...You could go back to the Housing Corporation for more and more money...Then in the early '90s it all changed. (Housing association officer)

The result was potentially bankrupting.

It got to the stage where, if I drew up a *realistic* budget based on the usage that we'd experienced in the previous two years, I couldn't get a budget to *balance*. There was an [*enormous*] deficit. There was

35

just *no way* that I could balance it...Despite doing everything we could, looking at every eventuality, [we were in deficit], unless the Society put in major fundraising from grants and trusts, which would be hard to justify when we couldn't improve the occupancy. It was Catch 22...The Society decided that they weren't prepared to see their reserves eroded at that rate. (Finance officer; also Griffins Society 1995a)

Indeed, since the Society judged itself poorly placed to argue for charitable grants to support an ailing project, it was drawing heavily on its own reserves to sustain Stockdale and Second-stage Houses (Griffins Society 1994c).

The decision to close Second-stage House was taken on February 13, 1995 (Griffins Society 1995b). Records show clearly a protracted debate about the future of Stockdale House, with many consultations with the housing association, probation service, and Home Office in a quest for a viable and acceptable alternative. However, the decision to close was finally taken on June 28, 1995 (Griffins Society 1995c).

The Griffins Society had already seen the failure of one of its dearest ambitions in the mother and baby project. Now, for the first time, it was closing hostels instead of opening them. The organisation's mood was changing fast.

I'm telling you...*feelings* that one had. One is not painting the whole picture. It *did* run. The rooms *were* nice. What I'm dwelling on is that it seemed to me it was running out of steam. (Council member)

The Griffins *were* prepared to review [the needs], work with others to look at what was needed...But they began to run out of steam. (Senior probation officer)

THEY WANTED OUT

Notably, the record of the decision to close Stockdale House is accompanied by the declaration that 'no consideration had been or was to be given to disbanding The Griffins Society' (Griffins Society 1995c:4). It is a telling inclusion. Why, after all, was it necessary to assert the point, unless, by the time the long deferred fate of its pioneer hostel was sealed, the Society's own fate was already in question?

In hindsight, it is all too obvious that Stockdale House's closure was a psychological watershed, with great symbolic importance for the Griffins. The procrastination over its demise appears, in this light, to reflect an unspoken awareness of its significance.

> We *owned* Stockdale House. We actually *owned* the building. That made a difference, because that was the *flagship* gone. So when *that* decision was made, the rest of it floated in very easily, to transfer the others...Everybody always looked sad at meetings after that. They really did. But the decision to transfer the others was an awful lot easier. (Staff member)

> I think we realised that if Stockdale House went, then it was the end...It was much easier to have [the Bail Hostel] taken over, or given back to the Home Office as a probation service hostel. That was no problem. We had problems with [Special Care House]...[Second-stage House] never took off. All in all, once we'd made the decision that Stockdale House...had to go...there wasn't a lot left. (Council member)

Two more issues may be identified as particularly influential in driving the Griffins to their final withdrawal from hostel provision: the floundering of Special Care House; and professionalisation of the voluntary sector.

Difficult, Complicated and Frustrating

The former chief executive of the SHSA succinctly described the difficulties associated with discharge from special hospital:

> One of the biggest problems...was finding the right combination of circumstances...to find the right collection of facilities and people which would provide the next destination for the patients...So you

might find a *hostel*, but you wouldn't find a *doctor* to accept responsibility for the individual, or you wouldn't find the *social services* to provide the back-up care. Very complex. And a lot of *hostility*, *prejudice*, *fear*.

The Griffins discovered the accuracy of this analysis the hard way. As work to develop the project got under way, they found the ground shifting beneath them: 'The whole funding changed. It all became local. Everybody started guarding their own patch. So instead of...all play[ing] happy families and reciprocat[ing], it became totally different' (Council member). They realised that the project had begun from a false premise.

> They had this idea that the tribunal would discharge somebody who'd been in [Special Hospital] for years. They would ring up the local authority in [say] Northampton, where she had lived most of her life and say 'Guess what? She is ready to come home, but you obviously don't want her at home, so we've found a nice hostel for her. This is what it's going to cost.' [But] Northampton would have a complete nervous *breakdown*...They would say, 'Well, she hasn't lived here for 15 years, so why on earth is she *our* responsibility?' (Council member)

Lewis and Glennerster (1996) describe the transfer of funding for residential care from the social security system to local authorities following the Griffiths' report (Department of Health and Social Security 1988) and Government White Paper (Department of Health 1989) in similarly acrid terms:

> [The reforms] were not primarily driven by a desire to improve the relations between the various statutory authorities...or to help those emerging from mental hospital. They were driven by the need to stop the haemorrhage in the social security budget and to do so in a way that would minimize political outcry and not give additional resources to the local authorities themselves. Most of the rest of the policy was, as the Americans would say, for the birds. (Lewis and Glennerster 1996:8)

For these financial reasons, and others to be explored more fully later, the project encountered strong resistance from the very professionals whose cooperation was vital to its survival.

> The biggest negative for the longest time was the *doctors*... Getting...the medical cover locally...the forensic psychiatrists in the local service. (Chief executive SHSA)

> We had lots of very *negative* comments, feedback, [and] reaction to us. Many, many social workers, nurses, psychologists, psychiatrists just felt that it couldn't be done. 'These are *dangerous* women. Do you *realise* what she's done? Do you *realise* what she's capable of?' As though we hadn't thought it through at *all*. (Hostel manager)

More problems followed the abolition of the SHSA.

> The Special Hospitals Service Authority was set up as a NHS quango in 1989, to manage the three special hospitals which provide high security psychiatric care for patients who are dangerous, or alleged to be dangerous...The SHSA quango disappeared [in] 1996. Then [there were] four organisations...The three providers became Broadmoor, Rampton and Ashworth, as single hospital authorities in their own right. Then a new concoction was created to be the purchasing body, which was based in London and had a very complicated title, the High Security Psychiatric Service Commissioning Board. (Chief executive SHSA)

The SHSA, having instigated the project's development, helped it to weather many storms.

> The SHSA backed the project, funded it, bought the house, paid for all the development work including the interior designer, under-wrote the expenses of the first year of [operation]. So [funding wasn't] the issue...We did run out of money, so [went] back to the SHSA for more, which we got. (Senior probation officer)

Funding became an intractable issue, however, after the SHSA's abolition.

> The *protector*...of the project was abolished. Although the SHSA had said, 'We can't continue to pour money into this project,' I have no doubt that we could have continued to get money out of them. The [SHSA] would have been a good patron of the project. It had put more pressure on the hospitals...for discharges to the hostel. So I [blame] the lack of responsiveness from the hospitals, the demise of the SHSA, its influence and money, then the project being...cast off on a very unsound financial footing. (Senior probation officer)

The SHSA attempted to construct a framework of future support for its projects. A direct link was forged between Special Care House and the social work department at Broadmoor Hospital. Nevertheless,

> I suspect there was less *high level* enthusiasm for the project in the new organisation...By 'high level', I mean people like myself, [the professor of psychiatry at Broadmoor], others, who really *wanted* this to happen. When it was transferred to Broadmoor in anticipation of the changes, there *were* people who supported it...But the *power* of support was reduced. (Chief executive officer SHSA)

As Special Care House searched for residents, the Griffins encountered further problems for which they appealed for support, while the SHSA's ability to provide it waned.

> We had to *beg* them to give us an extra grant, because there was just *no way* it was going to happen. The gestation period for getting somebody out was [so long]. We would have a selection committee...[and] say, 'Yes, this person seems fine.' Then next day the [patient] threw a pot of paint at somebody and it would be put back a year...It was not within *our* control. So we were saying to [SHSA], '*We're* ready to take this woman, but we can't, because your *psychiatrists* are saying *they're* not ready. Who's going to pick up the bill for this? We've got a bed waiting.' It was endless arguing. (Council member)

The chief executive of the SHSA reflected, regretfully:

> Like all re-organisations, there's a dislocation. Relationships that
> were established no longer meant anything, because people shifted
> off to other jobs or moved out entirely. That's...the mania for re-
> organising things as opposed to improving what you've got...It
> could have been quite disconcerting for the Griffins to see all this
> change. The key supporters, that they'd always felt able to rely on,
> suddenly they're gone.

He summarised the disappointments:

> [It] became a very difficult, complicated and frustrating
> project...*Everything* was complicated. *Everything* went wrong...For
> a long time I felt I was right out on a limb, because we'd invested in
> the property and it [took so long] before we got any patients in.
> There was trouble with the planning permission. There was trouble
> with the building. Then we had the same old problem [as] always
> with the special hospitals, that the staff will say, 'Yes, we've got *lots*
> of patients ready to move on if only you provide the facilities.' Then,
> when you provide the facilities, they say, 'Well, we haven't got
> anybody [who] matches *that* particular facility'...So I found myself
> jumping up and down with the clinicians, saying, 'I've got so many
> *places*! I've spent so much *money*! I expect you to *use* them!' So *all*
> those things went wrong.

These tribulations did not in themselves inflict a fatal wound on the
Griffins. Their impact, however, was, almost certainly, to reinforce previous
disappointments, with the result that the Griffins began, perhaps for the
first time, to question both the worth of their philanthropic enterprise and
the limits of their personal tolerance.

> When [we] started up [Special Care House], good God, [we] found
> *immense* problems...That was when we were *folding up* [Stockdale
> and Second-stage Houses], [yet] we were doing *that*. That made us
> furiously think, from our own point of view, because...it becomes a

41

self-perpetuating process, without anybody trying to measure whether really we're doing any good at all. (Council member)

Charities are Businesses

In some ways, the Griffins were victims of their own success. Expansion and diversification brought with them new demands. An early Council member noticed the difference between Stockdale House and the Bail Hostel: 'The Home Office ran the Bail Hostel, you had to have double staffing...and lots of funds. It was a different kettle of fish altogether. We ran Stockdale House on string and sealing wax. It wouldn't be allowed in subsequent years.'

As time went on, the transition from 'charity' to 'business' became a recurrent pre-occupation.

> They realised that they needed a serious business person. They'd seen the writing on the wall, that this has now got to be run as a serious business. It can't just be ladies who do good. This is *serious stuff* now. (Staff member)

> We did *try* to professionalise...get into the twentieth century before the end of it. But it had been—this is awfully *hard*—a vicar's tea party for too long. This is being *hard*, but life was changing very fast...It was going from the amateur to the professional. (Council member)

> It had been set up in a different age, when it *worked* for these wonderful ladies with their contacts to phone up [someone] in the Home Office to get something resourced. But those days had *gone*. Charities had to be far more pre-occupied with running themselves as accountable *businesses*...It just wasn't run like a *business*. I believe that charities are *businesses*. (Council member)

An early Council member identified another deficit in the Society's composition, again contrasting the Bail Hostel's special status:

We never...had an efficient financial controller. We always had sweet, kind, well-meaning treasurers, which wasn't what we needed [to] make a much more efficient, much stricter, much clearer budget. Because...we were all enthusiastic *amateurs*. We needed desperately somebody to say, 'You have this much to spend and only this much...' We lacked that terribly. The Bail Hostel, with its Home Office background, *always* had this.

In 1991 the Griffins employed, for the first time, an executive officer to administer their hostels' budgets centrally. Then, in 1994, a business consultant was seconded to them from a major financial institution, of which the chairman was, not coincidentally, married to a Council member: 'I didn't cost them a penny! It went down in the books as a nominal donation.' The initial expectation that this 'finance officer' would advise on developmental planning was thwarted by the departure, almost simultaneously with her arrival, of the salaried executive officer, who was not replaced. The finance officer, inevitably, became involved in the immediate practicalities of budget management. However, another problem loomed.

The difficulty the Society had was that...they couldn't keep me indefinitely. The [institution] wouldn't have allowed it...There *had* to be somebody to run it centrally...To pay a director would cost a lot...We also had to budget for rent, because we would no longer have the use of the office, which was in the basement of Stockdale House...To find enough out of each hostel's budgets to pay to run a central office was going to be more than they could support. (Finance officer)

It was also becoming accepted that the Society required more than financial expertise. It also needed someone to formulate and direct a developmental strategy.

It was transparently clear to everyone that there needed to be something strong at the middle...organisational direction, strategic management...The income the hostels were producing wouldn't fund it. (Council member)

43

The lack of an infrastructure to support the organisation with its three surviving hostels became a financial impasse. Ironically, the Griffins Society was now too small to compete in the 1990s world of professional bureaucracies. The Society certainly undertook a great deal of work to modernise its policies and procedures. Yet, this process itself forced Council members to a sobering realisation.

> We worked really hard, trying to get it into good shape, getting procedures in place. About that stage, [when] I really thought it was being licked into shape, into a modern form, it occurred to me that the only way to go forward was to *grow*. Any organisation is only going to survive as it grows. I used to go to hostel meetings through the probation service and I realised that all these other outfits were growing, because they needed a central office, because there was so much paper...It was *endless*...But, in order to fund that, they needed more hostels...So then we realised we'd have to get much *bigger*, start collecting hostels...Then [we] just said to each other, 'Well, hang on a minute, do we really *want* this now?'

The pressures to professionalise also had deeper implications for the Griffins Society, as will later be shown. Here, however, it is important to recognise the organisation's inability to tolerate the prospects of either the financial costs of stasis, or the psychological ones of re-expansion.

> It *couldn't* exist. It was too big to exist with a voluntary manage-ment structure...too small to exist as a charity with the right level of support...The [Council] could *see* the writing on the wall. They didn't *want* to carry on any longer. They'd had *enough*. (Finance officer)

> [I said], 'I don't think that's the only option here. We can look at other options.' But the truth was that they had decided they wanted *out*. It was winding down. (Hostel manager)

On November 16, 1995, the Council recorded its irrevocable deci-sion to withdraw from hostel provision.

[H]aving discussed every option, it was decided that The Griffins Society does not exist just to run hostels. The problem lay not just with money—all three remaining hostels are financially manageable. The problems of our management structure which are not conducive to modern day commitment and the need for a director, which the three remaining hostels are unable to fund, have led to this proposal to Council that another organisation should be sought to manage the hostels... (Griffins Society 1995d:1)

Everybody *knew* there was nowhere else to go. There really *wasn't* anywhere else to go. (Staff member)

CONCLUSION

This chapter has charted the story of the Griffins Society. In doing so, a number of issues have been seen to influence its fortunes. The Society began, almost as an act of defiance, in response to the absorption of prison after-care into the apparatus of state provision for offenders. Yet, the policy environment in which it was established was, nevertheless, benign in its support for voluntary sector provision for discharged prisoners. Moreover, the funding structures in place during the twenty-five years of the Society's expansion favoured supported accommodation of the types which it developed. Finally, the Society's members were particularly well placed to press their cause in influential circles.

During the 1990s, the Society fell prey to shifts in penal, community care and housing policies from which flowed crucial reductions in financial support for their projects, simultaneously with increased burdens of management. In this sense, the Griffins are unfairly blamed, by some of their critics, for failing to adapt to a complex, fast developing environment. As will be seen, these critics often prefer explanations for the Society's demise that appeal to an anachronistic style of operation derived from its Council's membership of a social elite. Yet, given these severe external constraints, how far this portrayal accurately appraises the organisation's failure to survive the twentieth century remains in doubt at this point in the evaluation of its enterprise.

What its history does reveal is an organisation which pioneered new types of provision for the most challenging groups of women offenders. In so doing, it crafted responses to needs which, in flowing from its own female composition, were acutely sensitive to the personal and social problems of its clientele. The Griffins Society's unique combination of maternalism, courage, and 'hands on' involvement of lay Council members in its enterprise underpinned its achievements in the field of penal welfare. These same qualities, however, contributed to many of its errors. The study now turns to a closer scrutiny of these qualities in the Society's mission, professional and lay personnel, and service delivery.

Chapter Three

Just Ladies Who Lunch?

I learned what clout really was. (Staff member)

‘Lady Bountiful’; ‘Ladies who lunch’; ‘Lady of the manor.’ These phrases were commonly invoked in reference to the women who comprised the Council of the Griffins Society. Indeed, Council members themselves frequently employed these and similar phrases self-referentially, revealing a sharp and humorously self-deprecating awareness of their social image. This chapter looks more closely at these women, as they described themselves and as others saw them, to uncover the reality beneath the epithets. We begin by clearing a path through the most impressionistic accounts of a minority of observers, which, while striking, proved to be an unreliable guide to the truth of their characters. We then move to consider the accounts that the Griffins themselves gave of their involvement in the Society, and the observations of those who became familiar with them as close colleagues in their philanthropic enterprise.

A DIFFERENT WORLD

> Lady Bountifuls...It just felt very odd to be in this place with women who'd been in care and came from poor families...These women would walk into the committee meeting...going ‘Rah rah’, very [posh]. I was [thinking], ‘Who *are* these people?’ All wives of important people. It's the upper class. They always made me feel really uncomfortable, because they don't talk like other [people]. So, that's my over-riding impression, that they were Lady Bountifuls doing good. But sometimes when they were making conversation— ‘Oh, my God, what on earth are you *talking* about? What *planet* are

you living on?' Oh, it's so *shocking* it's not clean—They didn't even know what dirty *was* because they all had cleaners. (Staff member)

This brutal assessment reveals, unconsciously, more about the appraiser than the appraised. As we shall see, the freedom to disparage the Griffins in such strong terms was exercised by a small minority of interviewees, who appeared, ultimately, to be wilfully blinkered in their perspective. Nevertheless, the force of their recognition that Council members inhabited an unfamiliar social world was etched into the memories of all who came across them. Only the coincidence of involvement in the Griffins Society's work brought them together.

For me, they were a group of very privileged women; the like of whom I'd never met in my life before and probably won't again. Who came from a different world from the one I came from. That is what I remember. (Hostel manager)

We begin, then, by exploring briefly a range of emotional reactions that such encounters inspired, since, to make any sense of the accounts of observers of Council members, it is important to be alerted to the complexity of their responses. This collision with a parallel universe in which privilege and prestige were normative could inspire deep internal conflicts, perhaps particularly for individuals who felt their professional lives were dedicated to challenging social inequality. Many interviewees were fascinated by the strange customs of the social elite.

I can remember going to a *soirée*, [the chair] held at her Hampstead home...which is a place I don't go to very often. But I was intrigued to walk around the avenues there, into a large house and be greeted by someone dressed up in a 'Lion's nippy' outfit—the black dress and the white pinafore—with a tray of champagne glasses, [the chair's] husband, Judge W-, in attendance, being very affable. (Assistant chief probation officer)

Their [Annual General Meetings] were always in *incredible* settings, usually...in one of the Guilds, in some City institution. It was worth going just for that. There was always plenty of wine. We always had good speakers [because, again, they pulled their influence]. So it was always an *event*...It was a good turnout, quite *significant* people. So you always knew you were going to bump into *someone*. (Senior probation officer)

As these remarks suggest, the majority of interviewees did not appear to begrudge Council members their affluence and, indeed, considered themselves privileged to have been afforded a glimpse of such lifestyles through their connections with the Society. A few, however, appeared to sense an obligation self-consciously to disparage a world they fleetingly brushed against.

Social events in various houses in Hampstead, would include the probation service officers. So I attended many functions and social events in their homes. The criminal justice system really requires that magistrates...come from the environment with which they're dealing. That's why there's a lot of political hoo-ha that most magistrates are middle and upper-middle class. They know *nothing* about the working class. (Liaison probation officer)

One hostel manager eloquently expressed the unease aroused by the social distance. She also, poignantly, confessed to the cruelty of her class-based judgement:

What I remember most about them? How *posh* they were...That communication thing—'I *know* you really mean well. I *know* you really want to help. I *know* you're busting a gut here. But actually we don't want that. *This* is what we need. But I don't know how to tell you that because I don't think you would understand.' That's *horrid*. It's *horrible*. I feel *awful* saying that because they'd find that really *hurtful*. People don't *feel* posh, do they? They just feel like they *are*...I have no comprehension of the lives *they* led. *I* don't understand.

This courageous self-appraisal was a frank confession of the complex feelings that many observers of the Griffins acknowledged, albeit more mutedly. Bitterness, however, erupted in some who felt excluded.

> Of course, *I* wasn't manager. So *I* didn't go to their houses with all the Titians on the walls. It was a class thing. Huge. *I'm* middle class. But *they* made me feel [*that* high]. Lady Bountiful. (Staff member)

Close examination of remarks such as these revealed a surprising consistency in their sources, emanating entirely from a small minority with limited, or even *without* personal contact with Council members themselves. This phenomenon was at its most striking in the words of one probation officer, who asserted adamantly several times that she had never met a single Council member, yet concluded the interview with a bitter outburst, in which segregation (and thereby ignorance) became a virtue:

> When you've made it, and you've got to a certain '*lady's*' level, you put yourself on committees so it looks like you're doing extremely good work for the community. [But] really and truly, how the people who are out there, living on the street, live and behave is *alien*. I *hate* that. I really do *hate* that…I just cut off from that. I weren't interested at that level. I weren't ready to get involved with Lady this and Lady that. I just can't be *bothered*. Give me the grass roots any day.

Within this minority group of observers, some appeared unable—or unwilling—to generalise from their personal experience of individual Council members. One staff member, who fondly recalled four Council members by name, applauding their ability to relate as 'real world people', derided the alleged social incompetence of the remainder, to whom she had rarely spoken:

> They were like cartoon characters of Lady Bountiful. They *did* talk to [the residents], but in that unreal [way]—'I'm not of your world.' *Huge* discrepancy. *Meant* well.

Another, who recalled the staunch loyalty to their project of those Council members with whom she had personal contact, remarked disparagingly:

> Yeah. They used to come by. [*She*] would come. She wouldn't park her car in front of [the hostel]. Didn't want to risk no resident going to see her really flash car. She parks it around the corner and she walks around. Of course, you can see she's *flash*. You can *see* it. (Staff member)

Thus, amongst this small group of respondents, personal accolades were awarded only to those few Council members with whom they had achieved a level of individual familiarity. Council members who remained unfamiliar were routinely attributed with class insensitivity, personal prejudice, ignorance and incompetence. This failure to generalise from experience, cleaving to the view that examples of genuine social warmth were exceptions to the rule of incongruity, smacks of a deep class prejudice. The speaker quoted above, for example, readily attributed motives of aloofness and mistrust to a Council member, who may, for all that is known in fact, have been trying to avoid an ostentatious display of wealth when she parked her car out of sight. These same professionals would not have dreamed of applying such stereotypes to the working class or minority ethnic women in their care. Moreover, it is remarkable that this minority group were no less likely than others to praise the achievements of the Griffins Society, even while they withheld acknowledgement of the role played by Council members. It is important to stress that plaudits for the Society's work were virtually universal.

A hostel manager mused on the paradoxical attitudes of project staff towards Council members:

> There *was* a distance between Council members and other staff…The staff said 'We don't feel we know them at all.' They were quick to make judgements because of the smart suits and the flash cars. It's funny, because [a colleague] says to me, '*Now*, I can really see that [our visiting member] was brilliant. But at the time, I thought, "*Who* does she think she *is*?"'

51

One probation service manager inadvertently revealed the extent to which this derogation was rooted in feelings of personal exclusion, repeatedly deriding the Griffins' *modus operandi*:

> The Griffins almost were *obsessed* with the Home Office. Who's your primary customer? They seemed *obsessed* with the Home Office. Well, it's *actually* Inner London Probation Service. I did feel they never really made the transition [to] thinking that they had to work closely with [us]…They *always* went to the Home Office, they *never* talked to us…That management culture continued right to the end.

Later, however, when invited to elaborate on his direct experience with Council members through committee meetings, this manager confessed bitterly:

> Can't remember. My bosses did more than I did. Yes. Well, I was *kept out*, because my bosses would go…Basically because the Griffins liked to talk to the *top* people, not to the *functionaries*…So my managers decided it was better *they* dealt with them, because it needed the *higher* management touch more than *my* level.

The vehemence of such remarks could too easily draw the eye from the truth that is exposed by examination of their origins, beguiling the listener into believing that they were expressions of *fact*, rather than, as close inspection revealed, of *prejudice*. Most observers of the Griffins, indeed, sensed a quality that restrained them from reflex hostility, drawing their attention more closely to the underlying, unwavering integrity of women who had volunteered to 'do good' in the hardest way, by direct engagement with one of society's least appealing groups of misfits.

> [What] I remember most is that they really had a strong sense of *duty*...They were *conscientious*. (Staff member)

> I was told that they're the ladies who lunch. That they were well off, very socially concerned, kindly, nice people who had a *real* social

conscience, who *really* wanted to do good, who were *really* aiming to do something very positive for women. (Probation officer)

It is to this quality that we now turn, in an effort to understand how these women embarked on a philanthropic endeavour which was quite unnecessary to their fulfilment of their social roles. They could undoubtedly have chosen an easier charitable enterprise, for example, by sitting on fund-raising or grant-giving committees, from which to 'do good' at arm's length from the recipients, or by directing their attentions to more appealing and rewarding beneficiaries. Chequebook sympathy was not the Griffins' style. Instead, they elected a much harder route, which exposed them directly to unpalatable realities of the society in which they were privileged members, yet from which they did not flinch in their practical immersion in their endeavour.

A FITTING PERSON

Clearly, an encounter with the Griffins was a powerful, if confusing, experience, even more startling because it interrupted an environment dominated by poverty and exclusion. How did Council members themselves account for their introduction to this alien world? Their explanations usually appealed to several interconnected factors, revealing at their heart a closely entwined social network in which women forged multi-layered relationships. Council members recalled:

> You want to know how I became involved? Well, I can tell you exactly, although it sounds—in this day and age, when things have to be so equal opportunities—very curious. My parents were friends of Joanna Kelley...One day, the chairman of the bench in Inner London came to have lunch with them—who Joanna Kelley also knew. Soon after that, I was asked to dinner...with Joanna Kelley. She...had got a nice chap there, who was the treasurer then. By the end of dinner, I was a member of the committee! The chairman of the bench was also there. Soon after that I was on the bench, too.

I was asked to become a member of the Griffins committee when I was [chairman of] Holloway Board of Visitors...I had known [a Council member] in Hampstead, as a girl. I met her again when...I asked her to come and talk to us at Holloway about the work of the Griffins Society...In return, she asked me to go on to the committee.

Some stressed the friendships within this network:

I'd given up the bar. I don't think I had time on my hands, exactly, because I started to do a variety of other things. But a dear friend of mine...[who] always spoke about the Griffins, said she hoped that one day I would become involved. [Two more of] my friends, who I also knew outside the Griffins, suggested that I should become involved. [So] I just got sucked into it, really.

I [joined] at the behest of a friend of mine...who was then chairman of Stockdale House. She said, 'Come on the committee, you would be useful'...She's a very old friend of mine; I've known her since before either of us was married.

For a few, contact with this social group was peripheral, until the Griffins claimed them:

When I was a single girl living in London, a flatmate said she gave her second-hand clothes to a friend of her mother's, who ran a hostel for women in North London. So, as I was getting married, I said to Sarah, 'I've got all these clothes. What shall I do with them?' So I gave them to Sarah. I had a very nice letter from [the chair] who thanked me for them. A year or so later, I said to Sarah, 'I've got more…What shall I do?' I rang the hostel. They said 'Come round'—they were having a Christmas party—'Bring whatever you've got. Join in the party.' So I went along.

The Griffins had a keen eye for kindred spirits. This last speaker, who was recruited on the spot as secretary, reflected:

I think they thought I was one of *them*. [One of them] rang the Foreign Office [where I worked] and said, 'Is she all right?' They said, 'You're lucky to have her.' That was, really, how I came to be involved. Very casually, through friends of friends.

Later, this woman proved herself equally adept at talent spotting and persuasion:

I found them a treasurer, too. Yes...You'd invite people to the annual meeting at the Mansion House. They'd be quite impressed. Then you'd twist their arm and say, '*You* would like to do a job, wouldn't you?'...You can usually point your finger at somebody...get them to take on some job for which they have a skill.

Similarly, another Council member recalled:

I had met [Halfway House chair]. We just *got on*. She thought, 'Here is someone who's younger than me, who's also a magistrate, who lives locally...It would be a bit of fresh blood.' So that's how it happened. We had a lot in common anyway...Her husband was Permanent Secretary to the Lord Chancellor, my husband's at the bar...We knew a lot of people in common. [The Council chair] lived across the road from me...So I seemed a fitting person, I suppose, from her point of view.

This casual approach to recruitment, summarised by one Council member as 'word of mouth', reflected the extent to which women were already known, or easily knowable by reputation, within a closely connected network.

Things were very much less formalised in those days. I can't actually remember who asked me. There was a very splendid lady, who was the wife of a leading judge, who...was the chair...She must have known somebody who knew me...There was no talk of an application...You just were telephoned, 'Will you be interested? We need another trustee'...That's how it worked.

55

The magistracy, in so far as it reflected common membership of this network, was a fertile recruitment ground.

> I became involved because a member of the bench on which I still sit was a longstanding member of the Griffins Society...It's her fault!...She backed me into a corner one day in the retiring room and said, 'Now you're retired, you're going to have lots of time, aren't you?' She said it would be a splendid idea if I were to become a member.

At this point in Council members' accounts, their explanations of the processes through which they became involved blurred with their motivations. For example, for a few women the salient network, or source of interest, was a professional one.

> I was a probation officer...from 1969 to '75. I wanted to go on in that field. In fact, I became a magistrate, which I didn't like very much...but I remained a magistrate until last year...But my real interest was on the probation side.

> In 1986, I moved [house]...I was then chief administrative officer with [the] probation service. Through my job, I was told that a couple of doors away the Griffins Society had a hostel, which probation used and valued. I [let it be known that if] there was any way I could usefully become involved, I'd be interested, as a neighbour, as it was local and linked with the probation service.

Many women supplemented their explanations with more personal perspectives. Some, like the last speaker, were attracted by the opportunity to contribute to a project that was 'local' in relation to their own homes. Some appreciated an extension of prior interests and sympathies:

> I had always felt that I knew a great deal about how women *got* to prison, from the Magistrate's Court, and I would have been interested to see what happened to them *afterwards*. I never have been particularly keen on the prison system, but I *was* keen on picking up the pieces.

I was one of the very first volunteers for Victim Support. So...having tried to assist those who had suffered, I was interested to see more of the perpetrators of that suffering...I felt a great deal of compassion for them, which surprised me, because I thought, having seen what some of the victims of crime had suffered, that I would feel very disappointed and angry. But I wasn't at all. Because one saw the *social* side—the deprivation of *their* lives.

Some women were pleased to offer a valuable skill:

I was chair of the National Council for One Parent Families. [Very often there] was a problem about young women who were pregnant or who had a small baby, who came out of prison, or...it was thought better for them to be in the community. But then they had to be given support.

So I went along to the party...[The secretary] took me to one side and said, 'We need a secretary...I'm expecting my baby shortly. Could *you* take charge?'...I'd stopped working. I said, 'Yes, I'd be happy to.'

An early treasurer described a unique blend of these incentives:

I was resident at Toynbee Hall for just over a year, which is a settlement in East London for ex-university people...to give them a taste of the East End, an opportunity for doing some sort of social service. I did poor man's lawyer work there for a time. [Another] resident...knew Joanna Kelley, who was looking for a professional person to be treasurer...So I showed some interest.

Finally, but importantly, several referred to a family tradition of philanthropic activity:

My great-great-grandmother was Elizabeth Fry. So I had been brought up very much with a Quaker background...When I first left university and came to London...someone wanted a descendant of

Elizabeth Fry to be on the board of the Elizabeth Fry Hostel...in Reading...So...when I met Joanna Kelley I was already on a probation hostel committee, which I joined at an extremely young age.

It was pure chance I got involved in it. I don't suppose I would have gone out of my way, except I've always had a feeling for, or interest in that side of things, which I suppose is because my uncle was a prison commissioner, in the days when they had prison commissioners...Yes, Alec Paterson, yes.

These references to family tradition reflected the women's membership of a sector of society characterised by a tradition of philanthropic service, particularly as a female occupation (Freedman 1996; Jones 1966; Odendahl 1990). These alleged 'ladies of leisure' in fact filled their days, between supporting their husbands and families, with energetic, often multi-faceted 'invisible careers' (Daniels 1988) of voluntary activity. An early member explained:

We all had *leisure*. Either enough money of our own or our husbands were supporting us...No, it wasn't a full-time *job*. But it *was* a full-time *interest*...I was a Justice of the Peace. [A former chair] was not a JP, but of course, she had a husband, a very busy lawyer. She obviously had to do a lot of entertaining. She had children growing up, grandchildren, and the normal life that you want to lead. It was a full-time interest, but you perhaps had a *lot* of full-time interests.

These motivational accounts largely lacked a feminist perspective. While some Council members did claim a particular interest in women's issues, these were not couched in political terms:

I like women's issues...I've always felt that women are particularly vulnerable. They're biologically vulnerable and are victims so often. I was very committed to that particular project.

The women we dealt with had very little power over their own lives, because they were, on the whole, not sufficiently educated, not sufficiently prosperous to take control...I always noticed, from my time in the youth court, that if you have very little in your life, you will take whatever falls into your lap. If it happens to be drink, or drugs, or any kind of behaviour which might lead you to prison, you're in a less good position to resist it. Also, they were, on the whole, very abused by the men in their lives.

Others protested that their membership reflected other interests, which coincidentally were served by the Society's work on behalf of women:

> I'm not a *feminist*...It was the court side of it, what you learned from the courts of the appalling difficulties that people were in. OK, it just *happened* to be women. No, I'm not a *fanatic*.

> I just thought it was a worthy and interesting outfit...[It] just seemed *worthwhile*.

> Of course I think it's important, but quite honestly I would have got involved if it had been old men or young people or whatever.

Two early members had given the issue no thought:

> That's an interesting question. I hadn't really thought of it that way. I just thought that it was a good idea...They were having a pretty difficult time at Holloway. I suppose *that's* the answer, that I was particularly interested in...trying to stop [women] going to Holloway, coming to our bail hostel instead.

> We were less feminist in those days. We took for granted that there were women's prisons and men's prisons, that nobody was looking after the women, so there was a slot for people who were interested.

These explanations for involvement in an enterprise that many might consider extraordinary for women who had no need to take such a literal approach to 'doing good' by immersing themselves in the problems of offenders, are remarkable for their mundanity. Council members might as well have been explaining their membership of a social club, or, at the most, a charitable aid organisation making few demands upon their time and energy. They made no claims, as might be expected in such circumstances, to be driven by ideological principles, although undoubtedly they shared a sympathetic concern for disadvantaged groups. Very few sought out membership of the Griffins Society. Most were introduced through contacts within their social sphere. Yet, this apparently casual approach belies the seriousness with which they viewed their commitment. Council members were deeply attached to their cause, not as an ideal but as a demanding, difficult and absorbing effort. In the words of one member: 'I *loved* the Griffins.'

QUITE TERRIBLY WELL CONNECTED

Their network of contacts was *extraordinary*...They reminded me a lot of a super-powerful [Women's Institute]...It's partly who *they* were, what *they* could do, *their* own skills, *their* own determination. But it was reinforced by this *hidden iceberg* of power and contacts which they possessed...It's a very *'establishment'* type of thing, isn't it? (Senior administrator)

The Griffins followed, albeit unwittingly, the example of a line of female penal reformers who have manipulated social status in pursuit of their goals (Freedman 1996; Jones 1966; Kent 1962; Manton 1976). Indeed, well connected philanthropists often assume this to be part of their role (Jones 1966; Ostrower 1995). Reflecting on what one senior civil servant called the Griffins' 'top drawer quality', observers were deeply impressed, if somewhat scandalised by the power of this social elite.

What do I remember about them? Powerful, influential women...They were very powerful individuals in their own right. But they were nearly all attached to very powerful men. They *used* that—used and *ab*used—in the most amazing ways, that power and influence...They were just amazing. People *knew* of their power. (Senior probation officer)

A housing association officer, whose unhappy encounter with the Griffins will be recounted later, mused:

> There was a class thing. They were very posh. I think they looked down on us as being a bit rough and ready...But they really were quite *terribly* well connected.

While observers of the Griffins were certain of their power and influence, they were often less clear *how* they achieved their results. Many understood this to be a product of their own exclusion from the venues in which such power was wielded.

> They would *never* deal with oily rags. They *always* wanted to go to the engineer. They always seemed to have a hotline to a minister or to very significant people in either Houses of Parliament or, certainly, the probation service. (Senior probation officer)

> They could get ministerial access like we could *never* get ministerial access...The committee moved in those circles. They'd be at a party or a reception. They'd run into Sir David Ramsbotham. Before you know it, Sir David Ramsbotham's coming around to [the Bail Hostel]...*I* was [only] a middle manager. But the higher managers never get *near* Sir David Ramsbotham. The Griffins have got him coming around within two weeks of meeting him! (Senior probation officer)

> Baroness S- was on Council...She would ask, 'Do you want a question asked?...Give me the question. No problem'...I don't know if it actually ever *happened*. But she was always *willing*. She used to say it *quite* religiously...'If you want that raised in the House of Lords...' (Staff member)

In fact, the minutes do record at least one occasion on which this last-mentioned opportunity was exploited (Griffins Society 1995c). The somewhat caustic tone of the senior probation officer's remarks (noted above) on the Griffins' access to powerful individuals should be considered with caution here. In part, at least, it appears to betray an aggrieved sense of personal powerlessness. Who, after all, would *not* go to 'the engineer' if they could bypass 'the oily rag'? Yet, the tone of these remarks implies a criticism of social attitude, when, arguably, the Griffins were simply deploying the assets that they brought to their enterprise.

Council members themselves, attempting to explain the mechanisms of their influence, could be irritatingly vague, partly, it seemed, because their social connections were, to them, normative and therefore unmemorable.

> I *do* recollect the Home Secretary, or someone frightfully grand like that coming. I can't remember who it was. It might have been Leon Brittan. Anyway, there was a tea party, it was all very exciting, the press was there...That, I'm sure, was down to a personal contact. I just can't remember whose, and I can't remember which Home Secretary it was, which upsets the story a bit.

> Frankly, I could walk into the House of Lords. My mother was then a peer. I knew an awful lot of people, had a lot of friends there. It was very *easy* just to walk in and say can you ask a question, can you do this, I want to meet so-and-so. Yes, it was very easy...I can remember *very* well going to somebody called—Well, you *must* know him...Lord—oh, his name's gone right out of my head.

One observed helpfully, if somewhat dismissively:

> Callaghan took a lot of interest in it. He came and visited quite often. But I do not think he would claim to be an expert worth interviewing.

Notwithstanding the inexpertness of Home Secretaries, everyone agreed that relationships at the Home Office were productive. Moreover, Council members' personal influence was bolstered by their membership of interconnected committees. The multi-faceted alliances forged in this context were particularly powerful.

> One of the strengths was that we all did so many things with differ-
> ent hats on...It all interlinked together, which made it, not just
> interesting, but actually much *easier*. We could all manoeuvre
> around, because we knew all the characters. (Council member)

For some commentators, marital attachment to a powerful man has
uncomfortable connotations with dependence, which overshadow female
achievements (Daniels 1988; Ostrower 1995). To the Griffins, it was an
opportunity. All family connections, but particularly husbands, were
brought into service for the cause.

> We had some good treasurers. [A Council member] always found
> people like that because...her father was...very important in the
> accountancy [world]. So she always found us good accountants.
> (Council member)

> I was loaned out for two years...But [her husband] got everything he
> wanted. It's water off a duck's back to an organisation like
> [that]...just to let me carry on working for the Griffins Society for
> an extra seven months. In terms of *their* projects, it's not very much,
> is it? (Finance officer)

Husbands could occasionally be persuaded to offer more than connections.

> It was reported that [a Council member's husband] had completed
> the recent London marathon, and had raised almost £5,000 for the
> Griffins Society from sponsorship. (Griffins Society 1991g:3)

A Council member, reflecting on a challenging moment, observed:

> When we came to move [the Bail Hostel], we had a lot of antago-
> nism against us going to [that] street. I went with a couple of others
> to the planning meeting, had to get up and speak to it to get it
> through. But we *did* get it through. One of the reasons...was that [a
> Council member's] husband was a local councillor. He did a lot of
> lobbying of the planning authority. Yes, we have always been fairly

lucky at finding people in the right place at the right moment. (Council member)

This ingenuous allusion to 'luck' does not reflect serendipity, but the normative connections of a fortunate sector of society. Yet, despite their wealth of connections, the interlaced social world of the Griffins often appeared surprisingly small.

Sir Edmund Stockdale was, coincidentally, a friend of our family. His wife was my brother-in-law's godmother. His sister-in-law was my husband's godmother. So there were very close ties. But that's *totally* coincidental. (Council member)

These insights yield a fresh perspective on the derogatory phrase 'ladies who lunch.' Voluntary work of this nature is *typically* conducted in social settings (Daniels 1988). There was no clear division between the Griffins' voluntary activity and their social life. Indeed, entertainment was a vital element in their campaign strategy for their cause. Staff members reflected:

The people they knew, met at dinner parties, chatted to—it was of *tremendous* benefit to the organisation. They got to know things, if there was any money available. Like...[when the chair] happened to be dining with one of the trustees of the Paul Getty Foundation: 'Yes, of *course*. Just put an application in'...You know— 'I'm having lunch with *her* next week', 'I'm going to so-and-so's for dinner and I know *she's* going to be there.'

It's just odd. Very *odd*. Because a lot of organisations pick people for *what* they know. So they might go to another housing association and say, 'He'd be good on finance' or 'He's good on personnel.' But the Griffins was very much about them knowing *each other* through lunching with each other, someone expressing an interest.

Council members cheerfully acknowledged shameless exploitation of social opportunities:

Money raising was always at the forefront...We never had enough cash to do what we wanted. So we were very blatant in asking people for cash, whether we were out to dinner or whatever it was. If we sat next to someone who ran a charity, they'd absolutely *had* it. I *certainly* remember doing that. We *always* followed up any lead we ever met...Oh, yes; I've done it at dinner.

Thus, Council members understood their social connections as an asset that they brought to their enterprise, to be deployed in its interests. In so doing, they displayed a remarkably robust, utilitarian attitude to their personal good fortune. Their voluntary effort was not, as some who had little opportunity for understanding their *modus operandi* assumed, segregated into a small compartment of otherwise untainted lives, and insulated from their personal associations. Rather, it was enacted within the very social circles in which they moved. Voluntary activity blurred into their social lives, inviting a further misconstruction amongst more distant onlookers that it represented a kind of entertainment. As we shall see, however, the Griffins deployed their connections to powerful effect in pursuit of their aspirations for their project.

A FORCE TO BE RECKONED WITH

[What am I most proud of?] Being able to put the Griffins Society on the map. Make it a force to be reckoned with in the criminal justice system. (Council member)

Records confirm that their connections enabled the Griffins to command impressive resources at little expense.

The Carpenters' Company had proposed charging their normal fee of £225 for the hall, but Sir Edmund Stockdale had succeeded in getting this reduced to £125, and had been informed that the Company were making an extra donation of £100 to the Griffins Society. (Griffins Society 1983c:2)

The Chairman said that she would send an official letter to Mr. Kilroy-Silk confirming his acceptance of the invitation to speak at the [Annual General Meeting]…Sir Edmund Stockdale had offered to pay for the sherry…[The Bail Hostel] would be responsible for…the £40 fee for the Mansion House. (Griffins Society 1984e:2)

Thus, while *processes* were often opaque, *benefits* from the Griffins' social connections and style of operation were visible and tangible. It was generally acknowledged that they commanded attention when other organisations might safely be overlooked.

The Griffins sometimes got a better service than other agencies. They had more assistant chiefs running round than other agencies. Basically because of who they were. (Senior probation officer)

I'm *not* a proponent of a system that means that you get preferential treatment over other projects. But, at the end of the day, I *did* come to see that, for most of the committee members, these efforts were directed at improving the facilities for the women, which *were* good. (Hostel manager)

An onlooker remarked charitably: 'In fairness to the ladies, they never, *ever* used their titles unless they thought it was going to be helpful.' Nevertheless, the Griffins were astutely aware of their influence. A Council member mused on the background to the Home Office's invitation to open the first Bail Hostel:

We had a proven record looking after women. We'd been seen to do a good job. Also —it sounds as if I'm blowing my own trumpet; I don't really mean to—we were quite a *well-known* committee. We had several judges' wives. We had people who were prepared to do something about women within the criminal justice system. We had got the ear of the probation service and [its] confidence as well. That was a lot to do with it.

One Council member recalled an instance of success:

> Years ago, when we were short of staff, the women were being diffi-cult...at [the Bail Hostel]. We needed more staff. So I picked up the telephone, rang the necessary man at the Home Office…to say, 'We need more staff. We need another as of *now*. So will you pay for another?' He was so *surprised* to be asked so *directly* that he said yes! So we got another member of staff. Just like that. I can remem-ber it to this day.

Staff who witnessed this spontaneous solicitation remembered it, too: 'She got on the phone to the Home Office and basically *told* them she was going to appoint [someone]!' Managers knew that they benefited from a style of liaison of which some occasionally disapproved in principle:

> We made a claim through the Home Office for redecoration. The poor hostel badly needed it...It got turned down. The next thing I knew, phone calls had been made, our hostel was painted. Now, I'm *not* approving of that kind of system, of *course*. But it *was* done for the benefit of the women.

> Somebody from the Home Office came to visit. He criticised some-thing that I had said—he actually misinterpreted [it]. He told a relatively senior civil servant, who reported it to one of the Griffins. He rang me to apologise, because he'd had a flea in his ear from a particular committee member. I can't *imagine* anyone in the senior probation service giving a senior civil servant a flea in his ear!

> Once, [a television company] were filming outside the building. The deputy ran out and said, 'What are you doing? You don't have permission.' She rang a committee member, who said, 'Don't worry, I'm having dinner with [the chair of the company] tonight.' The producer rang the next morning to apologise.

Ultimately, they were persuaded of the value of putting pragmatism before principle:

I'd never heard of the Griffins Society before I went to work there. Probably like most people coming new into the organisation, I couldn't help but be struck by the 'titled' nature of the committee. It would be very easy to attach the tag of 'the great and the good.' I came to see that the connections that they had would very often be used for the benefit of the women. For example, I doubt that we would have had such excellent psychiatric oversight. [The] senior registrar in forensic psychiatry at the Royal Free, was on the committee, but also *came to the hostel* every week. Similarly, the GP, who was an excellent doctor, used to *[hold] a surgery* in our hostel every week. Try getting *that* level of medical care for hostel residents anywhere else! The local police inspector was on the committee...any problems at all, you knew who would sort it out for you.

A probation officer recalled how a mentally ill offender directly benefited from the world in which Council members moved:

The judge was very concerned about her. He didn't want to imprison her...So he asked specifically that [the Bail Hostel] be approached to see if they would take [her]...The judge in the case had knowledge of [the Bail Hostel], obviously, or he wouldn't have asked for that. That comes [back] to the committee...That is where the *good* social awareness and links with the justice system...were permeating at many levels.

Thus, the Griffins were adept and admired manipulators of a system wherein personal and political influence was a persuasive asset.

The Griffins were *tremendous* at PR, getting the position of female offenders heard within the Home Office. That *cannot* be undervalued and understated. By and large, the Home Office looked at numbers of female offenders and said, 'There's so few, we don't have to really worry about them.' The Griffins turned around and said, 'But there *are* a significant number.' The legacy of [that] is bearing fruit now. There is much more interest in the Home Office about minority groups, including women. So it *did* have a lasting achievement. (Senior probation officer)

They were a *strength*, a force to be reckoned with, within the probation world and within the hostel sector as well. (Hostel manager)

LARGER THAN LIFE

My perception was that they came from the moneyed classes. They were very sure of themselves. *Extremely* confident. They knew how to gain access to people who had power. So they had influence. Any pipsqueak who came along from [the probation service], like me, telling *them* how to influence people and get things done, would have had little effect. It was quite *intimidating*...My abiding memory is of powerful, upper-middle class or upper-class English women—very *English* in the way they did things. But very, *very* sure of themselves. Who didn't stand fools gladly, would get on with the job. (Assistant chief probation officer)

The Griffins were, indeed, personally self-confident women, perhaps because, as members of a social elite, they had never been supplied many reasons not to be. One Council member reflected on this attribute, when describing how she took the lead role in developing Special Care House:

I needed a new challenge...I just thought I could probably do it...When I look back, I'm frightened of what I did, really. I just *must* have been *mad*, because it was a registered care home, about which I knew absolutely *nothing*. I knew *nothing* about mental health. It was an *enormous* learning curve. I had to jump right in...It only struck me how *absurd* it was...when [the hostels were handed over and]...we transferred the registered names and I saw her qualifications.

Whilst this story reveals personal self-confidence fanned by naïveté, the Griffins were more than sophisticated enough to appreciate the impact of their social status, with its connotations of invisible power. In

69

many situations, it is quite probable that what they passed off as ebullience was a self-conscious manipulation of the intimidating potential of class superiority.

> They were *formidable*...There were people who were fairly senior, who were quite in *awe*. I think the Griffins were aware of that. Maybe it wasn't conscious, but they would hammer away. They had this *way* about them; with people not wanting to upset them...They would just *know* which buttons to press. (Hostel manager)

However, supreme self-assurance and manipulation of class sensitivities could not alone account for the Griffins' powers of persuasion and their achievements on behalf of women offenders. Indeed, these qualities in isolation would probably have alienated many potential supporters. Those who worked alongside them recognised deeper qualities beneath the veneer of class. Firstly, they perceived integrity.

> There was something *sturdy* about them...They felt like a *strong* group of women. Obviously, they were very *privileged* women predominantly, which would normally have gotten right up my hooter...But...they *really cared* about the women...They *gave* a lot of their time, *understood* very well, *cared* a lot. (Liaison probation officer)

> No, I don't think they made any particular secret of the strings they could pull...They were quite open about it...They were very civilised, very pleasant, very straightforward...There are a lot of people with all sorts of hidden agendas, games to play...With the Griffins, I didn't get that impression. They had *aims*, there were things they wanted to *do*, they were *committing* themselves to this project—'Let's *do* it.' That was very refreshing. (Senior administrator)

Secondly, they applauded personal commitment.

> You could *not* fault their commitment. They were *very* committed. They gave an awful lot of their time. (Senior probation officer)

Those very hairy years [at Special Care House]...It was very uncertain, very demoralising for everyone...But they kept it afloat. Many organisations would have thrown in the towel. The Griffins kept going. That's to their credit. (Senior probation officer)

The Griffins' psychological advantage thus flowed from this disconcerting blend of upper-middle class aplomb and disarming sincerity.

It did seem like a real anachronism, the way it was managed. Its committee was the most *extraordinary* bunch of women, it was a privilege to come across. It's easy to be cynical about them. (Co-opted Council member)

They were larger than *life*. (Hostel manager)

Volunteer organisations discourage the assertion of individuality: achievements are attributed to group effort; lone stardom is discouraged (Daniels 1988). That Council members were moulded by these norms is illustrated in the common invocation of the collective 'Griffins', yet no-one ever claimed to be, or was described as 'a Griffin.' Nevertheless, they became individualised personalities to those who worked closely with them. One, in particular, was remembered for her glittering lifestyle.

[The manager] told me how one day [another staff member] had seen a picture of [her] with her husband in *Hello!* magazine. (Observation notes)

[She] would think *nothing* of flying to New York on Concorde. She'd bring in the free packs—shampoos and things for the residents. (Hostel manager)

Again, it would be easy to neglect the wider context in which such observations must be understood, and thereby to accord them undue prominence. These remarks, taken in isolation, obscure two important points. Firstly, the written words do not convey the *tone* of real affection and humour with which reminiscences such as these were related and the fond-

71

ness with which this Council member and others were remembered. Secondly, they omit important additional information. Close observers of the Griffins frankly admired their practicality—an attribute not commonly associated with the stereotypical upper-middle class lady. This Council member, for example, was remembered, amongst other things, for organising a successful fund-raising jumble sale. More broadly, these volunteers from the so-called leisured class demonstrated skills normally expected of paid, senior-ranking professionals. For example, a longstanding chair was remembered for her command of business.

> The *outstanding* person that I remember is [her]...She seemed particularly plainspoken, forthright, knew exactly where she was going, [had a] *no-nonsense* approach to how she dealt with things. (Assistant chief probation officer)

> A *lovely* woman...very *forceful*, very *straightforward*, always knew where you were with her. (Staff member)

> A complete star. Took meetings very efficiently, but very *nicely*. Nobody could ever take offence, but she didn't muck around. Meetings were very much to the point. She didn't let people wander on...I don't enjoy sitting on committees. They tend to be hijacked by bossy boots. That's why she was so *good*, because she was never that sort of person. She didn't allow that to happen. (Council member)

This chair was also noted for her willingness to confront unpleasant realities.

> It was realised that some sort of shake-up [of the committee structure] was necessary...It wasn't working...So there was a new constitution drawn up. It was [her] very *courageous* decision that all of the members of the committee were asked to resign...and reapply to be members of the committee. (Council member)

Moreover, she was remembered for her participation at all levels of activity.

> [She] was *very* involved. I could see at first hand how *hard* she worked. She took on an *enormous* amount. (Hostel manager)

[She] did *not* mind getting her hands dirty. When we moved back in [after refurbishment], it was very interesting which of the members of the committee came to help me. She was one. There would be no question. We'd do it together. That was *never* a problem. (Council member)

Similarly, the Council member who was earlier quoted confessing to her ignorance of a specialist field of expertise, in fact impressed observers by her astute grasp of complex issues.

[She] was *very* well informed, had a *very* good working knowledge of the project...She seemed to know who everyone was...I never felt that she was intrusive or that her being involved was inappropriate. But she had *incredible* knowledge of the workings of the project. From *who's who* to *what's what*. She just *knew*. (Senior probation officer)

This woman was a fearless defender of her project. A manager recalled with satisfaction the debasement of an unhelpful psychiatrist: 'He'd had [*her*] on at him. He didn't *like* it. He's a consultant psychiatrist. He deserves *respect*. Yeah.'

One Council member took special pride in being 'ordinary', setting herself apart from the elite social status of others:

That lot were all *so* well connected. 'I'll speak to the Lord Chancellor.' Well, in those days, I did *not* hobnob with the Lord Chancellor. I didn't *want* to. Because I grew up in...Brixton...*not* in a privileged environment, with kids at my school from every sort of background. You realise that people *would* steal for their children. There *isn't* a great-aunt who's going to leave them money, or who you can beg furniture from.

This woman believed her proletarian background was her primary asset, enabling her to offer a fresh perspective:

That was why [she] *asked* me. I was probably the only Labour Party supporter among the whole lot...If I'm honest, I really think I brought a bit of *middle class common sense* to it...We should *not* in the 21st century still be talking about this *ridiculous* class issue.

She was cheerfully—and deliberately—outspoken:

> I heard one of the magistrates saying, 'I had to send a woman to prison for non-payment of rent. She has three children. Her husband had left her'…I said '*Excuse me*, but you sent a woman to prison, a family has been broken up, three children have been taken into care…Why are we *doing* this?'

Nevertheless, she was most remembered for her abilities as a 'fixer' of all things practical. A Council member recalled, admiringly:

> She was very much 'in' with suppliers of Marks and Spencer. She was *wonderful* at fund raising. She organised the *whole* refurbishment.

She explained her technique with deceptive simplicity:

> I did the refurbishments…I'd get a budget. I had to work within the budget. I knew someone in those days whose company was a big supplier to the National Health Service. So I phoned him and said, 'Come on, Harry, I want a *big* discount on this. We've got a lot of hostels.' So it went a bit further. The linen shop across the road—I said, 'Look, I'm buying lots. What have you got?' They'd fish things out from past sales. If you know your way around, there are ways and means of doing it. That worked pretty well. We got good service.

This woman's talent, like those of others, was not an accident of fortune, nor should they be regarded as a mere extension of the female skills of running a household. The skills which Council members contributed were the product of learning and practice. For some, arriving without prior experience in the criminal justice system, this was a formidable, self-imposed task. Council members remembered others in this position:

[She] was a *tremendously* good example of someone who *grew* through it. She made the most of the experience…She didn't seem to me to know much about young offending women when I first [met her]. Although *personally* I liked her very much, I didn't feel that she was very *professional*. But she jolly well got her act together and *became* much more professional.

[She] obviously learnt as she went along. She was incredibly *knowledgeable*. What she didn't know about what was going on in that hostel, honestly, wasn't worth knowing. They don't make them like that anymore, they really don't.

Thus, despite their volunteer status, Council members learned and deployed relevant knowledge and skills at a level of professional competence and displayed a remarkably earthy practicality. These women may have exploited their social status when it served their purposes, but they did not rely on this attribute as their only tool in accomplishing their mission. To this extent, it was the absence of financial reward, rather than class difference, that distinguished between their 'careers' (Daniels 1988) in the Griffins Society from those of the professionals with whom they were joined.

POOR THINGS

Poor things. *That's* what [the residents] were to those women. (Staff member)

Could the Griffins cross the class chasm yawning between themselves and women in their care? Several respondents, who, again, were notably lacking in observational experience, dismissed the possibility.

It's OK to see it on paper, and say, 'Yes…the *poor things*, they've got all these problems.' But it's one thing to *live* it and to *be with* the woman all the time. It's another to be somewhere else, in your nice house, seeing it on paper. (Staff member)

While Council members did invoke such epithets when recalling the residents, their critics' imputation of incomprehension and shallow sentimentality shows a superficial regard to their meaning in so doing. The non-professional, sometimes outmoded vocabulary in which they expressed themselves probably exacerbated such misreading. Closer inspection of their accounts of the 'poor things' in their care reveals a deeply compassionate sense of miseries, which they knew themselves to have been spared. For example, in interview, Council members reflected:

> They used to go off with baskets, rather like Little Red Riding Hood. I used to say, 'Where are you off to?' 'I'm going to see my boyfriend in prison.' Always in prison…All this *sadness*.

> There were some lovely moments. Some of them were absolutely delightful. But…they got themselves into the most *awful* jams. It was life in the raw…They had an *extraordinarily* tough time and behaved accordingly.

> One did realise one was dealing with a sad portion of humanity…Because, you see, the women were very, *very* broken people.

A general practitioner, who held regular surgeries at one of the hostels spoke in similar terms, trying to correct the patronising impression of her words:

> My impression was that a high percentage were poor souls. I don't *mean* that in a condescending way. They'd had a rough deal.

In interview, Council members mused, with a self-deprecation that was typical of them, on the barrier to communication that social difference presented:

> Poor dears…We must have appeared from outer space.

In retrospect, I think the women probably thought it was a bit much…just thought we were do-gooders, as you might say.

Notwithstanding their social differences, the Griffins claimed a natural affinity with the problems of women offenders, rooted in their common gender:

> I don't know *anything* about male criminals. A lot of those people [in the hostel] could have been my *daughter* in certain circumstances. Your *daughter*, your *sister*, your *mother*. Women are so often victims of circumstances…That's what used to upset me.

> It was for *women*…Yes, yes, for *women* offenders…It was simply, *being* a woman myself, I felt that I understood them better.

Distant observers of Council members, attempting to conjure a vision of their likely interactions with residents, confessed themselves at a loss. Their remarks implied a personal claim to an affinity with the residents, presumed to be lacking among women of higher social status, which should be regarded with scepticism, given what will later be revealed about these offenders' personal histories.

> It was all *very* well intentioned. But what used to strike me about it was that the women on that committee would *never* have experienced the things that the women in the hostels had experienced. It was difficult to know how they'd be able to relate to them. But they really *did* try. They really, *really* tried. (Housing association officer)

Direct witnesses, however, were pleasantly surprised.

> They related very *well* to the residents. This is the *weird thing*. (Hostel manager)

> I *didn't* feel that they were patronising. I *did* feel that they were quite realistic with them…So they got their *feet* in it. They got stuck in with the women…Whilst on one level they did seem like ladies in

hats, old fashioned voluntary [workers], the flip side of that—when it came to it—there was very little patronage. They actually related very *well* to the women. (Senior probation officer)

How did the Griffins manage this feat? A number of qualities came to their aid. First was an ability to inhabit two worlds simultaneously: one pristine with the trappings of prestige and affluence; the other pockmarked by disorder and decay. No one, among either their supporters or critics, ever accused the Griffins of pretending to be other than they were. On entering the hostels, they made no false concessions to the squalor in their own appearance or to a parlance that did not flow naturally from their tongues. Nevertheless, they were unexpectedly imperturbable in these conditions.

They seemed to be quite *unfazed* by it. They were very *practical*. They were in close touch with the manager. They understood the needs of women in a hostel. It really was *impressive*. But at the same time, whilst dealing with things like the leaky roof, if there was an overall problem about provision for women offenders, they would talk about nobbling the Home Secretary! (Assistant chief probation officer)

These women would arrive. They would always be dressed terribly smartly. They were very well spoken. It was such an extreme [contrast] to the women who were being accommodated. So you'd have women effing and blinding, sometimes looking a bit of a state. Then you'd have a very *nice* lady turning up in her very *nice* car. Totally at different ends of the spectrum. But most of the Griffins never seemed *fazed* by things. These women from a different back-ground would come in and there might be something kicking off. There might be the most terrible language…[The hostel] was quite chaotic at times. You would have women running up and down stairs, quite distressed, boyfriends coming round, perhaps threaten-ing violence, the television's been nicked, this kind of stuff. They didn't seem *fazed*. It was almost as though nothing was happening. (Hostel manager)

Personal self-confidence enabled them to move easily in this alternative world, with an assurance unattainable by many who might attempt the transition from the other direction.

> Any residents that were around, they would have a chat…If they were passing the sitting room…they'd *always* stop and have a little chat. *Always*. [The residents] were always knocking on the [office] door… not even wait to be answered, pop their heads in. [Council members] would *always* say something. I can't think of *any* committee member…that wouldn't talk to the residents. (Hostel manager)

Undoubtedly, the argument that pleasant exchanges were possible precisely because they took place in the residents' living spaces has force. Extending the hand of friendship did not require Council members to expose their own private worlds to the inspection of those for whom they cared. Sociability was a one-way transaction, conducted on Council members' terms. Nevertheless, this judgement would be incomplete. Council members who overstepped the bounds of familiarity attracted castigation by staff for their amateur attempts at helping. Indeed, they were seen to be courting disaster by that very openness. Hostel managers recalled:

> There were a couple of occasions when we know that Council members gave out their telephone numbers to residents…Some of the naïveté was quite *odd*…They *weren't used* to developing relationships with offenders. And of course, they *did*. They got to *know* them. Then they became individuals, who they saw developing and progressing…I certainly pulled up my visiting member and said, 'You can't *do* this'…That's how *involved* they got. *So* involved that they lost the boundaries.

> I can think of a Council member who would say things about her own life to a tenant, which was really *quite* inappropriate. It wasn't good *modelling* behaviour…It's something lots of people do. You *bond* with someone and you *tell* them about *you*. But…how do you take that back?

79

They were a caring body. If someone was re-settled and couldn't get their grant through in time and a Council member knew that, she would go out to John Lewis, buy her a bed, and send it round. Now that's completely *inappropriate*. That's *discriminatory*…It's *inappropriate* because it doesn't go via the policy and procedure…But it would have been done because that Council member cared and felt that it was helpful.

These criticisms, however, belie a complexity that has, at its root, the fundamental difference between Council members, as volunteers, and professional staff. For all their quasi-professional ability and intelligence in the pursuit of their enterprise, Council members were acting in a voluntary capacity. When staff judged their behaviour against the professional norms to which they conformed, inevitably, the Griffins fell short. This alleged shortcoming was, of course, most striking in their direct dealings with residents. However, to accept these standards unquestioningly as the appropriate measures by which to judge them is to suggest that volunteer status was, at best, irrelevant, or, at worst, a handicap to fulfilling their role.

Yet, to understand the Griffins' powerful dedication to their project, the key is to appreciate the unique energy that is inspired by voluntary activity (Wuthnow 1996). Seen from the perspective of voluntarism, these allegedly inappropriate behaviours are transformed into simple acts of generosity and openness. Re-examining the examples above, we might question how inappropriate are these gestures in the context of voluntarism. Should a volunteer understand her behaviour as modelling for the benefit of tenants? Should a volunteer who can afford the purchase of a bed feel personal validation in withholding such a comfort to a woman in poverty, on grounds of procedural equity? In this view, the Griffins may be seen, not to be acting *un*professionally, but *non*-professionally, in accordance with their true status. To overlook their laity, because it occasionally led to behaviours from which professional staff would abstain, is to neglect the inspiration underpinning their overall effectiveness.

It is also worth noting, at this point, that the Griffins themselves were experienced in the realisation that professionals' ideas of appropriate help were not always above criticism.

It is unfortunate that, on some occasions, when a bail bed is requested by the courts not all the facts pertaining to the women are told to the person on duty who makes the decision whether or not to take her...One of the criteria for accepting a woman on bail at Stockdale House is that she is not known to be addicted to alcohol, but that did not prevent an ancillary worker with the Probation Service arriving with a very drunken woman whose luggage consisted largely of bottles of vodka. When assuring the supervisor that one woman was physically fit and well, a probation officer did not mention that the woman weighed eighteen stone and that her varicose veins were so bad that her legs were totally encased in bandages. In the first case we took the woman for the weekend and were able to cope until another arrangement could be made for her as we felt it would have been wrong to turn her away once she had arrived but the whole episode could have had disastrous consequences both for the woman and the other residents. With regard to the second instance, a bed had to be hurriedly made up for the woman on the ground floor after she had arrived and this, inevitably, made her feel that she was being a nuisance. (Griffins Society 1977:6)

Notwithstanding this insight into the selective opportunism of professional behaviour, staff, it seems, were venal. They could be persuaded to set aside their professional sensitivies in favour of an act of bounty. One Council member certainly found a way to offer a piece of her social world, with which staff were well satisfied.

One of the first women to move in had been in hospital for many years. She was fairly 'down to earth'; a stocky woman who pretty much shaved her head; she was scarred where she'd self-harmed; very low self-esteem. There was our visiting member who had her hair done regularly...The biggest advance was when she lent us her season tickets for Tottenham. Sal was a big Tottenham fan. She'd supported them for years. [We] went and sat in the Director's Box and watched a match with her season tickets. That was *marvellous*. (Hostel manager)

COMPLETELY OUTMANOEUVRED

> *Very* astute politically. They *completely* outmanoeuvred us in terms of getting what they wanted out of us. You have to take your hat off to them for that. Because, if you've *got* that kind of political power, you might as well *use* it.

Thus a housing association officer recalled a disastrous acquaintance with the Griffins. The relationship never thrived. The officer identified differences in perspective, which became entrenched obstacles to collaboration. On the one hand, this housing association did not identify with the philanthropic tradition of the Griffins Society:

> There was this sense of *noblesse oblige*, good works…As an organisation, we became quite *uncomfortable* with working with this attitude.

Discomfort became acute on occasions when pedigree surfaced:

> I do remember one time when we were having a very difficult discussion with them about a particular decision that the Home Office had made. *We* were saying, '*You've* got to *do* this, because the Home Office *say* so'…One of the committee said, 'Oh, that's *daft*. I'll talk to Douglas.' I didn't know who she meant. She meant Douglas *Hurd*, who was then Home Secretary! *That was the level that they were operating at.* We simply—*I* simply wasn't operating at that level. So, I don't think there was a meeting of minds.

Conversely, the bureaucratic approach of the housing association did not chime well with the informal style of Griffins Society management:

> For them, it was more about wanting to be free of the dead hand of what they saw was a very large bureaucracy…They had a point. We tried to superimpose our model of working on small agencies, with small staffing. It wasn't really helpful. We now have a much—I like to think!—lighter touch…We were monolithic…it wasn't particularly well thought through.

There was more to this culture conflict than bureaucratic anomalies. The Griffins' operational style, in which, as we have seen, personal and professional boundaries were indistinct, while enjoyable to those on good terms, fanned the antagonism in this case.

> It was the kind of environment in which it's perfectly OK to bring up something that had been dealt with six months before and start banging on about it again, having a go about it again. You'd never know when you'd won an argument.

Looking back, a Council member reflected regretfully on the personalisation of differences:

> It was always the same young man. I think that he was entirely out of his depth and *we* saw it as obstructive...You *could* say that it was partly *personality*. But there was probably *extreme* intransigence on *both* sides, which built up a wall over which *no one* could have jumped...I think *he* found it difficult to deal with all these enthusiastic, powerful women. *We* certainly found it very difficult to deal with *him*.

The housing association officer readily conceded faults on both sides.

> I'll tell you something they were absolutely *right* about. They felt that our maintenance service was rubbish. And it *was*. It was *awful*. The maintenance service at the time was in a very bad way. They never felt they got proper service from us, which they were paying for. And they were *absolutely right*. It was very difficult. [*We'd*] say, 'You really ought to be pursuing these equal opportunity policies.' *They'd* say, 'Well, why haven't you fixed our front door?' In a way, they were right. *We* needed to develop as a *service* organisation, *delivering* services to people. But *they* needed developing in a *corporate* way.

Despite the frustration, the officer admired a ruthless resolve in the Council's severance of relations:

To their great credit, when we said, 'All right. Fine. You go and be independent,' they just went and did it!…They didn't faff about. Once they'd made up their minds, they went for it.

Torn between relief and chagrin, the housing association embarked on a face saving exercise. The officer remembered:

I *was* quite pleased when [another housing association] came along. We got *thoroughly* wrong footed. In that situation, the only thing you *can* do is put a brave face on it. We put out some great press release, which said how pleased we were, how much we'd enjoyed the partnership…It was fine.

This cautionary tale is instructive for several reasons. Firstly, it reveals all too clearly the embarrassment that could ensue from attempts to challenge the Griffins on the grounds of their class. Such a venture was ill fated from the outset. Paradoxically, while this was partly because of the real irrelevance of class to the Griffins' dedication to their project, it was also because they would always emerge the victors in such a contest precisely through the personal and social assets of their class. Secondly, despite the apparent potential for such strife, this account of irretrievable conflict is unique. The key players appear to have been unable to see below the surface in the ways that, as we have seen, others who became closely involved with Council members came to do. The recollections of those others are uniformly complimentary, laced with affectionate humour.

CONCLUSION

We weren't doing anything *genius* quality. We were just doing a good job looking after some damaged women. I don't think it was more complicated than that…*All* of us felt that we were fortunate. Had *we* been presented with their set of circumstances, maybe we would be the same as they were. We were *all* aware of that. (Council member)

This comment reflects some important characteristics of Council members: appreciation of their personal good fortune; enthusiastic practicality; and straightforward commitment to their project. Indeed, their commitment was remarkably uncomplicated. Exposed to it, one could not help but feel that complexity was a problem constructed by the observer, the product of ill-informed attributions made on the superficial basis of class. As far as Council members of the Griffins Society were concerned, their involvement was simple, their motivations mundane. While all acknowledged at some level a common gender bond with the women in their care, few were spurred by feminist interests; those who were lacked the political edge that characterises much of the movement. None had solicited membership; all had been drawn into the Society by 'an idiosyncratic mix of personal experience, chance, and special interest' (Daniels 1988:69), prompted by their affiliation to a particular social grouping. Yet, having arrived, they wanted to do 'a good job.' Their social influence was one of the tools to hand for accomplishing that goal.

To observers, it was much more complicated. Depictions of Council members, at least at first glance, appeared to reveal an extraordinary mix of approbation, suspicion and hostility. That being so, it is worth repeating the essential qualities of their judgements when closely examined. Firstly, there was virtually unanimous agreement that the Griffins Society had produced an outstanding quality of care for difficult women offenders. Secondly, all those with a deep experience of Council members commended them for their intelligence, ability and personal charm. Thirdly, while those with limited experience often spoke highly of individuals, some failed to generalise from that to credit all Council members with such worthy personal qualities. Fourthly, a few, with little or no direct exposure to Council members at all, felt free to express vehement opinions rooted in class-based stereotypes. It is to these latter attributions that we now turn our attention, in an attempt to unravel the layers of misunderstanding that have distorted perceptions of 'Lady Bountiful' since her first appearance on the philanthropic stage.

The majority—particularly those who came close to them— admired the Griffins, were generous in their praise, and harboured affectionate memories. A number of them frankly admitted being surprised. Yet, these women were also the target of interwoven prejudices concerning

professionalism, gender, and class. Their *non*-professional status as volunteers could be confused with a perceived potential for *un*professional
behaviour. Professional resentment of volunteers has a long history, but,
when the volunteers are women, this tension is mingled with suspicions of
both feminine inefficacy *and* female presumptions to power. Thus, for
example, Kent (1962) recounts that an inspection of Elizabeth Fry's work at
Newgate Prison suggested that 'the Ladies were well-meaning, easily
exploited, and far too inclined to regard themselves as in *de facto* charge of
the women's side of the prison' (p.121). These gender prejudices run deep:
for example, Freedman (1996) describes the perception of even highly
educated and professionally trained female prison reformers as 'amateurs
who coddled women criminals' (p.319).

For distant observers, these resentments were heavily imbued with
class prejudice. As 'ladies of leisure', Council members could be seen to be
indulging, as one interviewee put it, in 'a little hobby.' This attribution
obscures the time and energy that they committed, as well as the skills that
they deployed on behalf of their project (Daniels 1988). From this perspective, denigration of skill and intelligence was compounded by the equation
of leisure and levity, which, in turn, was encouraged by the social contexts
in which the Griffins accomplished their goals. Again, there was a gender
dimension to this misperception of voluntary work as play. As Daniels
(1988) remarks: 'Businessmen's lunches may be understandable as part of
the workday, but ladies' luncheons and teas are more suspect' (p.199). This
scepticism was fuelled, for some, by a conflict of cultures. At best, for
professionals accustomed to protecting the boundaries between their working and personal lives, the Griffins' style of 'sociable bureaucracy' could be
disconcerting. At worst, for the housing association whose doomed
acquaintance with the Society has been recounted, it smacked of trivialis-
ing a serious social cause.

Perhaps their critics' greatest error was to view the Griffins'
exploitation of their social world as a flaunting of powerful connections.
For example, their adroit manipulation of the public relations and fundraising opportunities presented by their social circle was perceived by some as
'hobnobbing' and 'name dropping.' Yet, for these women, their social
connections were unremarkable. As members themselves of a social elite,
encounters with high profile personalities lacked excitement and memora-

bility. Indeed, for the Griffins, many of these interactions were not isolated encounters, but were an integral part of ongoing relationships.

To their severest—and, again it must be stressed, most distant—critics, even the humanity of these women was suspect. The ability to relate with empathy and on equal terms to women whose lives were disgraced and disadvantaged was regarded as a unique personality trait. To some, it was apparently inconceivable that instances of such genuineness could be representative of the group.

If the Griffins were aware of such harsh judgements, they appeared supremely unconcerned by them. In reality, of course, they posed little threat to secure, self-confident and powerful women. Nevertheless, Daniels (1988) suggests: 'Perhaps it is difficult for the women who come from this social group…to escape an uncomfortable awareness of the stereotype of the socialite and its undertones of frivolity' (p.:121). Certainly, the Griffins were aware of the stereotype. Discomfort, however, was not apparent. They observed its effects with humour, including a degree of self-mockery, at the same time as they exploited its power both to charm and to intimidate as a vital element in their campaign strategy.

Ultimately, the vehement reactions of a few respondents, based, as they proved to be, on superficial or indirect acquaintance with Council members, or on selective interpretations of such encounters, reveals far more about those onlookers than about the Griffins themselves.

Chapter Four

Pioneers on the Front Line

The staff were crazy. They were good fun. They had an amazing power. They certainly fitted the Griffins very well. (Senior probation officer)

Perhaps it is not surprising that the extraordinary women of the Griffins Council attracted staff of equally extraordinary calibre. This chapter explores the characters of the women who were employed by the Griffins Society, the dynamics of their relationships with Council members and its consequences, for better and for worse.

A LOT OF FUN AND VERY HEARTBREAKING

> Whenever you meet someone who has worked there, there really is something that brings you *together*. You really have a *lot* to talk about. There was an *ethos* that continued for the whole time they managed those properties that never changed. There was something very *special* about that…[My line manager here] and I will often talk about it. We talk about it in the same positive terms. Yet, she was there many years before I was. (Hostel manager)

Any analysis of staff contributions to the character and organisation of the Griffins Society would fail to capture its essence if it were dryly concerned with their performance of tasks and duties. Interviews with staff members, some of whom had left the organisation several years previously, unleashed a passionate quality in their reminiscences that brought their experience alive, as if it were still ongoing.

Staff developed an intense emotional relationship to their work. This did not simply reflect an ideology about gender specific provision, to which all subscribed in some degree. It also, as we shall see, sprang from the unusually strong ethos of the organisation itself, as the hostel manager quoted above suggests. Firstly, however, it is important to observe the extent to which this emotional involvement was an inevitable product of working conditions, which pitched staff headlong into the turbulence of residents' lives. Contact with residents was necessarily intense in an environment in which long hours were spent together under one roof. One staff member, who began as a volunteer, recalled:

> I moved to London. I was living in the spare room. There were some void rooms at the time, so they couldn't be used, and there was also a staff room that was separate…so they shoved me in the back until I could sort out some accommodation…It was a bit of a *shock*. Of course, everyone was very nosy and prying. All very *friendly*, [but] I never got a *break* from it. So I'd be asleep and people would say, 'Oh, [I've] come to chat to you.'

Opinions differed about the merits of the shift system, which varied over time and between hostels, yet everyone agreed that it ensured continuous exposure to the stresses of hostel life for substantial periods.

> We tended to do 24-hour shifts. It sounds *horrendous*, but it was much *nicer* to know that when you came in on a Monday morning, you were going off Tuesday morning. You had to come in on Wednesday morning, because Wednesday we had a team meeting. But then you'd be off all day Thursday…So when you were away from the project, you *were* away. You might have two days clear and then come back and do two days. But that's how the staff preferred it. (Hostel manager)

> When I started as an assistant warden in 1984…you worked one weekend in three…The weekend that you worked, you worked on your own, starting at 5p.m. on a Friday. You worked on your own for *65 hours*, till 10 o'clock on Monday morning, without a break. It was *appalling*. (Hostel manager)

Notwithstanding the mathematics of the shift system, the job pervaded the lives of staff in many ways. They struggled to combine conscientiousness, enthusiasm and protection of their personal lives.

> [The deputy manager] had come in, even though she felt very unwell, to make sure everything was OK. She said that she wanted the doctor to be called to the house to check on Sal, to advise on how contagious chicken pox was and what precautions they should be taking. (Observation notes)

> [The manager] had wanted to go [on the holiday]. 'I don't often get to spend any *fun* time with the 'ressies' now I'm managing the place. I came from the project worker background and I really miss spending time with them. It sometimes feels like the only time I spend with them is when I'm giving them a warning.' She told me that she makes an effort to spend some fun time with them every week or so, for example cooking a meal and spending the evening with them. (Observation notes)

Thus, the pressures of the job were, to some extent, self-inflicted. The intensity of contact with the women combined potently with the excitement, loyalty and pride inspired by involvement in innovation. An appreciable number of staff worked for the Griffins Society for several years, despite the fast turnover of staff that generally characterises residential work. Many former employees declared that they missed the positive emotional charge offered by the spirit of pioneering adventure.

> We talked a little about her future. She said, 'I *love* this job and all the women. It's hard work, but it's *incredibly* rewarding and sometimes a lot of *fun*. But this isn't the kind of job that you can do for more than a few years. It's just too much. There'll come a day when I need my life back!' (Observation notes)

> It was a lot of fun. Yeah, it was a lot of fun and very heartbreaking. I think we did a good job...No, I'm *proud* of what we did. I think it was good. We probably could have done *more* if we'd known more. (Staff member)

91

BY GOD, THEY'RE STRONG WOMEN

> I particularly wanted to work with women offenders. They had built up a good reputation of working with women offenders…I *know* they had a good reputation because I still hear it. (Hostel manager)

Unlike Council members themselves, it was common for staff to stress an ideological commitment to the gender specific cause of the Griffins Society. Indeed, while this provided the initial attraction to the job, it also offered a pathway to professional development in this area of practice.

> I had a particular interest in working with women…But I don't think, when I initially went into it, I had any clear ideas. But as I became more experienced and undertook training through the job, I developed a strong commitment to providing a service that challenged some of the discrimination that women met in the criminal justice system. (Hostel manager)

Commitment to an abstract cause, however, is not sufficient in itself to explain either the intensity of these women's relationship to their employing organisation or their thirst for the uncharted waters of innovative, stressful and sometimes dangerous projects. Part of the explanation lies in their individual and collective strength of character.

> By *God*, they're strong women. They really are. I'd never met such a bunch of *strong* women, who *knew* so much about women's place in society and how low they saw it. I didn't always agree, but, by God, I learned to keep my mouth shut. (Administrative officer)

This comment on project staff is perhaps indicative of the match between the robust personalities of both Council members and their employees. Individuality was tempered by some cohesive organisational attributes. Firstly, hostel managers demonstrated a rare gift for forging a collective among individuals who prized personal autonomy.

We're very *strong* women, *all* of us. Strong women are OK when they've got a good manager behind them. Put strong women with a bad management and they all fight…It's hard to cope with us because we are strong women, all of us. We're very *independent*, we're very *strong minded*, we've got our *ideas*. So, you've got to have somebody who is extremely *diplomatic*, with very good management skills. (Staff member)

She welded the staff together. She always managed that little bit of distance, but was tremendously charismatic, really good sense of humour, very bonding, very good like that. (Council member)

Secondly, hostel managers themselves formed a close-knit group from which they derived considerable peer support, in which context they steered a course between the demands of their management committee and the challenges of project staff. On the one hand, their management committee required careful handling. Here, managers exploited their capacity for mutual support.

Sometimes we [the managers] would have met beforehand. We'd have our plan of what we were going to do at the committee…We had that strategic plan beforehand. Sometimes we would agree on how we were going to raise an issue, because often we had the same problem in a different form, in a different hostel. So…we'd have prepped each other beforehand on who was going to say what. (Hostel manager)

Equally, managers knew how much depended on the cohesion of the staff group: 'because they're the ones, when you're not there, who are going to keep the place running smoothly' (Hostel manager). They generally pursued an open, democratic style that accommodated the views of their staff.

Sometimes it was difficult. I would say to them, 'This is the organisation policy. What we've got to do is try and work to the best possible within that.' If it was something I totally disapproved of, then I'd have a hard job myself working with it. But if it was something that I could see was workable to some extent, then I would say, 'Let's try it,' and if we can't, then we can go back to the management committee and say, 'Listen, we've tried it, it's not going to work. How can we change it?' (Hostel manager)

[I was] trying to monitor sickness and came in with: 'This is what needs to be done.' One of the staff members turned around and said, 'Well, actually I find that quite invasive.' So, I was able to go away and think of a different way. Still get the information I needed, but the team felt more involved in how we collected that information. (Hostel manager)

Thirdly, many staff members recalled with affection the spirit of camaraderie that thrived in these conditions. This was one of the keys to understanding the lasting emotional impact of working for the Griffins Society.

I *miss* my team and the way that really *felt* like a team. The team weren't the *same*—I started, a lot of old staff went, I got some new staff, I got rid of some staff, then we got some more staff. So, I didn't have *one team*. But the *feeling* of the team always stays with me. Even when there were some rough bits, and some staff that didn't make it, even so, it felt really *good*. So, I miss that. (Hostel manager)

At the time, if I had seen the job advertised, I would *not* have applied for it. That would have been my idea of a complete *nightmare*—an all-female resident group, an all-female staff team and mainly female management committee…*Being* there and *experiencing* it was incredibly important…There was a real *camaraderie* amongst all of us staff. It was women together. You'd get these female-type jokes. It's difficult to explain unless you were into it. But, to me, it was a very strong, *powerful* force…That was very *powerful*, a very *powerful* feeling of what we could *achieve* together…We would have the most *wild* nights out as well, which we needed. That helped. Yeah, it was very intense, very intense. (Hostel manager)

I THINK SHE WAS REALLY THE CLEANER

She was a *Godsend*. (Council member)

Several of these strong personalities were etched into the history of the Griffins Society. Three examples reveal much about how such women wove vital threads into the fabric of the organisation, helping to craft a unique character that thrived on deep qualities of individuals as much as on professionalism.

Despite the fondness with which Miss O- was remembered, nobody appears ever to have known her first name; indeed, even her surname is variously recorded in two versions. Yet, over the passage of years, Miss O-, like ghosts in old hotels, appeared to have become an institutional legend, in which symbolism was privileged over accuracy. In the best tradition of such legends, there was a romantic tale attached to her appearance in Stockdale House.

> This is what I was told; it may not be true. She was given early retirement on full pension from [the prison service], because she'd been given the appalling, stressful task of having to be with Ruth Ellis the night before she was hanged. (Council member)

As a former prison officer, Miss O- brought a certain institutional reassurance to many of the early residents.

> I can see her very clearly in my mind's eye. It wasn't difficult to put her in a prison uniform. What she wore was not far off—the blue dress and blue top jacket. If you had HMP stitched on there, you'd be home and dry. But she was *bloody* good. She was never going to be radical in her ideas, but she was a real *sheet anchor* for a lot of the women there. (Liaison probation officer)

Miss O- was the most *redoubtable* person. She *really* was. She knew *everything*. She looked after the linen cupboard. If you ever wanted to find Miss O-, you'd find her up sorting out in the storeroom. She knew *all* the women. They *all* talked to her. She knew *exactly* how to cope with them in a very, very quiet and determined way. (Council member)

Miss O-'s solid, no-nonsense approach influenced the quality of life in the hostels for many years. Arriving at Stockdale House in 1969, she later transferred her attentions to Halfway House. Her calm character, though unassuming, permeated the turbulence of hostel life. She also appears to have been physically indestructible. The Annual Report of 1976 recounts that 'Miss O- would like to retire completely as soon as it was convenient' (Griffins Society 1976). Her retirement is recorded in the following year (Griffins Society 1977), yet her presence is gratefully acknowledged in subsequent reports. This protracted retirement is last recorded in 1992 (Griffins Society 1992). During all this time, it appears that Miss O- gave of her time voluntarily, remunerated only in the form of a small honorarium and gifts at Christmas and other appreciative occasions, including when it was discovered that she had been feeding the hostel cat from her own funds (Griffins Society 1991h).

Equally memorable, to those who encountered her, was an early warden at Stockdale House. Between 1972 and 1976, in keeping with the convention of employing resident wardens at that time, she inhabited the private flat at the top of the house with her husband, two sons, and various pets. During those years, the family became central to the project's character. While her husband acted as handyman, the warden cared—in a very literal sense—for the household and its residents. This period was recalled by some as the heyday of Stockdale House's history.

She was *very* good. She had minimal training, but she had a real *gut feeling* for it…I think it was when she was there that it was working at its best. (Liaison probation officer)

This warden was so absorbed in the welfare of her charges that it was hard to discern the distinction between her personal and professional life.

During that period of the drop-in centre, I linked with the warden at Stockdale House. She saw an interest because her women [were] socially isolated…[She] used to come down regularly, every Wednesday, like a volunteer. But she wasn't a volunteer. She was a professional acting in a volunteer capacity. (Probation officer)

The Annual Report of 1976 recounts that 'the very nature of the work takes a heavy toll on the strength, mental and physical, of anyone who gives as much as (this couple) gave. In October [she] felt that she needed a rest and a change and left us' (Griffins Society 1976). The liaison probation officer from that time mused, regretfully: 'Suddenly it all went pear-shaped. Personal relationships went on the ropes. Very untypically, she became unreliable. It was really her saying, "I've had enough. I want to go".'

The [wife] and husband routine could *not* have gone on. She was a *unique* person, who I liked so much. But they don't come like that any more. (Council member)

Finally, a woman who worked at Stockdale House and later at the Bail Hostel was remembered over many years with strong affection, although her status was something of a mystery. Her first mention in Annual Reports asserts that she 'cooks the suppers at Stockdale, comes in to clean at [Bail Hostel] in the mornings' (Griffins Society 1978: 8). However,

She was there a very long time…I think she was really the *cleaner*, but she did do a bit of *cooking* as well. (Council member)

She was very keen to remind us that she was the *housekeeper*, she *wasn't* the cleaner. She used to remind me of this whenever I used to try and get her to clean. (Hostel manager)

This woman retired in 1992, after many years. In the recollection of one early Council member, her attachment to her job stopped little short of heroism:

She had a *dreadful* accident in the kitchen one day. She was getting a big container of boiling water, picked it up and it went all over her. She was dreadfully badly burned. She had on some sort of synthetic jumper. They ripped this off and ripped the skin off with it. Nobody knew how to treat it. She was in hospital for ages. But she *came back*…Some people have a vocation. They find their niche and they *stay*, no matter what the traumas.

Besides her stoicism, her value lay in her ability to relate to the residents, for whom she was a source of practical help and emotional comfort. Council members inclined towards a pragmatic view of her encroachment on professional territory.

They all could *relate* to her. She was a good Cockney, very warm and friendly. If they came back feeling very depressed because they'd been trying to get a job and they couldn't, or they'd got to face up to going to court, or they'd been on drugs, she quite often had her arm around them. She was very *good*. But, of course, that wasn't actually her *role*. But that's *life*, isn't it? (Council member)

Indeed, her popularity with the residents was valuable to the staff themselves: '[she] always knew *ten* times more than *any* of the rest of us, what was going on' (Hostel manager). With so much to contribute, her ill-defined status suited everybody. Notwithstanding nagging doubts about its professional appropriateness, the ambiguity allowed the organisation to reap the benefits of her many commendable attributes.

She was *immensely* popular with the residents. She had a blurred role. I know [my successor] struggled with the way that [she] inter-preted her boundaries. I think that, from the moment she started, she had always been included in the staff meetings. Perhaps there *were* some concerns about the way the information was sometimes used…But, on the whole, she was a *huge* asset to the project…For a large number of years, it *suited* the project for her to have that kind of role. No-one was particularly *questioning* it. If it *worked*, then fine. (Hostel manager)

GIVE PEOPLE A GO

> It was very *exciting*. I was probably too young to realise the respon-
> sibility I'd taken on. I was only 26! So, it wasn't nearly as
> intimidating as something that I'd be doing now, because I'd realise
> the *enormity* of it all. But I didn't think of it like that, as you often
> don't when you're younger. I just saw it as a very exciting opportu-
> nity. I was convinced that I could make some real changes for the
> better. (Hostel manager)

While, on one hand, they describe unique personalities, the above portraits
also reveal many important features of the relationship between staff and
the Griffins Society. Their main distinction lies in the maturity of the
individuals concerned, given the youth of the majority of staff, rather than
the eccentricity of their positions. The Society benefited on a number of
occasions from recruitment of trained and experienced staff. However, the
manner of staff appointments could at times appear casual, many staff
reported a fluid tenure in which they occupied a range of positions and a
number progressed rapidly into positions of responsibility, despite having
few obvious qualifications for the roles they assumed.

> I was employed initially there in 1982 as a volunteer. Three months
> later, they offered me a position as a project worker. Then I was
> made project deputy manager…Equal opportunities didn't exist in
> the same way then. I wasn't interviewed for the job. They just *liked*
> what I did. They *liked* me, felt I fitted in, the women liked me, so it
> was 'Would you like the job?' So I said, 'Thank you very much!'
> (Staff member)

This approach to staff appointment and promotion through seizing
the opportunities presented by individual drive, enthusiasm and observed
capability rather than formal qualifications and experience, was not, in
itself, unusual in the hostel sector. Housing association officers remarked in
interview that, in this respect, the Griffins Society was representative of its
times. For example, one recalled:

One woman...*was* a social worker...For her, it was a *shock* to work somewhere where staff who weren't qualified were expected to manage very difficult behaviour. But that's not *exclusive* to the Griffins Society by *any* means. That's true of the *whole* of the supported housing sector.

The Griffins were aware of the hazards of such an opportunistic system, but perceived themselves to be driven by constraints that precluded more sophisticated recruitment techniques. They were sometimes inclined to conclude that they should be thankful to have staff at all. In a working context of high stress and low pay, they seized on expressions of interest and were keen to reward good work. Indeed, strategies of staff retention assumed a high priority.

It was very difficult to get a stable person [as warden]...It wasn't *easy*. There wasn't a whole pool of people out there looking for jobs. So, you *had* to take who you could get. (Council member)

One early Council member recalled persuading the committee against confronting a warden whose integrity was in doubt, offsetting this against positive qualities that would be difficult to replace:

We had reason to think that he was helping himself to little sums— 25, 50 quid—here and there. The committee became very suspicious of him. I had a task to persuade them that we couldn't *prove* it...and that he was *very good* at his job with helping the women, was on good terms with them...The problems we had with staff were simply the problems you get. It's *exhausting*, *wearing*...dealing with women like that.

The scarcity of people who were both suitable for and willing to work in such an environment for low wages was one source of the Griffins' dependence on those staff who appeared equal to the challenge. One former administrative officer expressed scepticism about the ways in which this dependence could be manifested:

It almost seemed to be that whatever the social workers *wanted*, well, of course they must *have*, because they couldn't be *critical*…Somehow, criticism was not something you did. Everybody has to pat everybody on the back, saying what a wonderful job you're doing. Nobody—but *nobody*—could be criticised…Much as I liked *enormously* all the ladies…there were odd occasions where, when it came to meetings with just trustees and ourselves, they could be critical of individual people that worked for the organisation. But when those people were *present*, no criticism—*ever*.

While this observation may hold some general truth, it would be wrong to infer that the Griffins deferred at all times to staff. Indeed, Council members did not shy from asserting their authority when certain absolute standards were contravened.

We were prepared to give people a go and, sadly, it didn't [always] match up. It didn't work and that was that. You had too many people whose lives were dependent on it to allow it to go on. You had to make some fairly quick and harsh decisions. There were probably a lot of people who don't like me at all…[One employee] *slapped* one of the women. I dismissed her *on the spot*, because I said I wasn't having *anyone* who behaved like that at all. It's been held against me to this day. She always says that I didn't give her the chance…of explaining her side. I'm afraid there *is* no side when you hit someone as a member of staff. I *still* believe that. (Council member)

For the Griffins, relationships with staff did not only reflect a generally poorly qualified labour force, but were also a product of the pioneering nature of their projects. For example, their staunch attachment to a liberal access policy posed challenges in the management of Stockdale House that had not previously been confronted in more cautious establishments.

It was a very *laudable* thing for them to do. What they perhaps *didn't* think out—or *couldn't* think out—was that they needed a multi-skilled staff team to provide a service to people with that kind of offending history. (Housing association officer)

101

In fact, their remarks suggest that the Griffins thought about it often. They were struggling to strike a balance between their ambitions for their projects and the limitations of their raw materials. An early Council member recalled:

> It was a new venture. There was no established structure. The people that we employed as warden were largely people who happened to be *available* and seemed *possible*. They weren't from any structured service with recognised qualifications. It was a question of unprofessional, untrained, well-meaning people trying to run something [new].

During its last years, Stockdale House benefited substantially from a skilled manager. It's relatively poor funding, as a voluntary after-care hostel, however, perpetuated staffing difficulties that contributed to its ultimate closure. The Bail Hostel and Special Care House were able to improve on these conditions, by virtue of their more generous funding and, in the case of Bail Hostel, the negotiation of secondment of a senior probation officer to the post of manager from the Inner London Probation Service. Nevertheless, finding staff who were suitably qualified to meet the demands of unique projects remained a problem. A manager of Special Care House commented:

> I would *never* have applied for it if I'd seen it in the paper…It was something that was *unknown* to me. I hadn't really worked in mental health. I'd worked with ex-offenders, but not with women who'd been in special hospital. But, looking back now, whenever we advertised, there were very few people who *did* have that experience… This was *major* stuff. This was trying to get women out of secure hospitals into the community… It wasn't explained to me in that way, which would probably have been helpful. But at the time I thought it was *me*, because I wasn't a qualified psychiatric nurse… But you couldn't have gone *anywhere*, you couldn't go to one *book* and learn how to run (Special Care House).

Thus, project staff rapidly became experts in navigating territory that was uncharted elsewhere, an outcome that further enhanced their value to the Griffins. Indeed, given their unimpressive qualifications at the outset, it was surprising that these conditions presented an opportunity for inspirational practice and personal development.

> I always felt they gave me an *opportunity* when I changed careers…I felt they'd taken a *gamble* on me…and given me a *chance* when nobody else had. So, I had great respect for them. (Hostel manager)

> Working my way up from relief staff to project manager. Yeah, I'm really *proud* of that. People obviously recognised that I had the skills, enabled me to develop some other skills. Some of the management committee obviously *believed* in me because *they* were the ones who recommended me to become a [Justice of the Peace]…So, when I say the negative things about them…it's *not* all negative, because they saw some positives and worked with me to *push* me and *enable* me to become part of the person I am now. Yeah, so that's a real *positive*. (Hostel manager)

YOU COULD ACTUALLY SPEAK TO THEM

> If you are the worker and you're actually *dealing* with the problems, trying to *manage* the service, it's very difficult to convey to committee members what that's *really like* on a day-to-day basis. The committee *should* be there to deal with the *overall* policy issues and the *bigger* questions. *Exactly* the same was going on in other projects with staff and their committee, this feeling…that the committee wouldn't have a very clear idea of the practical difficulties of running the service. I just think that's common across the board. I don't think that there was anything special about the situation there at all. I really don't. (Housing association officer)

What contribution did the Griffins offer to the management and support of the women who staffed their hostels? The remarks given earlier illuminate the extent to which they were able to enthuse their staff with their mission, even while some, as we saw in the previous chapter, failed to connect their individual experience to its source in their Council. As the housing association officer's remarks above suggest, the belief of some frontline staff that Council members had a poor grasp of their problems is typical of such working environments, although the Griffins suffered the additional handicap of attributions made on the basis of their social status. Hostel managers, who worked more closely with Council members, offered appreciative accounts of considerable support, albeit constrained by the limitations that were posed by the Griffins' status as lay participants in the enterprise of offender rehabilitation. Indeed, in fairness to the Griffins, it is to be observed that they never pretended to be equipped to supervise professional practice.

> I didn't see my role as being involved with the residents at all…No. I have even less training and experience than the staff had and I didn't see that as the management's role. (Council member)

> I was quite conscious that we, as a bunch of amateurs, were trying to run people who had been trained, which, at times, must have been quite frustrating for them. (Council member)

The Griffins welded their potentially unruly workforce together through a combination of three qualities: personal accessibility, encouragement of professional development, and trust.

I Knew Who They Were

As a 'hands on' organisation, the distinctive support that Council members offered was of a personal nature. This was highly valued by staff at all levels, notwithstanding the failure of some, which has already been noted, to generalise from specific encounters to organisational ethos. A manager, who was a project worker at the time of the transition to another organisation, recalled:

The biggest difference is [that] I *knew who they were*. I'd *met* most of them, even if it was [just to say hello]…Yeah, you *knew* them. Not on a personal level, but you *could* actually *speak* to them on a personal level if they were in [the hostel]. They were *part* of it in that way. Whereas [with] most of the management committees in similar organisations, I've known them by name on paper, but they have their meetings and I see the minutes, but it's much more *removed*, much more at arms' length.

The frequent physical presence of Council members in the projects was remarked upon repeatedly by interviewees, who, notably, did not report that this level of contact was intrusive, but attached a value to the interest it conveyed.

Very often, they would drop in unannounced, which probably was a *good* thing, really…They would come in and see staff first, or sit with residents for a while, have a chat with [the housekeeper/cleaner], or otherwise some would just come into the office and ask for a run-through of what was happening, so that they had information for their report [to] the committee once a month. (Hostel manager)

The Griffins excelled at the human touch in their dealings with staff.

She *did* take time to speak to people. She *did* come in, sit down, have a cup of tea and a chat, would talk to *anybody*…So that was good…It was enough, it was great. So, if there'd been an incident, she'd phone up that person and say, 'How is it? How are you?' (Hostel manager)

One of the tenants died. [Our visiting member] came round. She brought cake and everyone sat and talked about how horrible it was. (Hostel manager)

An unusual aspect of this approach was the accessibility of Council members at times of crisis in the hostels. This 'on-call culture' was taken for granted by staff, despite its rarity in similar organisations.

[This organisation] has on-call…It's held by everybody, including the Chief Executive, Senior Manager…It's really known throughout the projects that it is literally for fire, flood and pestilence—only used for *extreme* emergencies. Whereas the culture that's always been around for the Griffins' on-call is that it is there if staff need it for *support*. Even if they've *managed* an incident and they're *not* looking for advice, but they've had enough, they're at the end of their tether…then it's been part of the *culture* of the Griffins that they can use the on-call. (Staff member)

Never Any Accusations

It was their *idealised* view compared to the difficulties of actually *working* with the women. There was a *schism* there in the experiences between staff and the committee. If they'd had professional people, that might have helped them to avoid some of their mistakes. (Housing association officer)

The Griffins had brought upon themselves the necessity of supervising and managing staff in a professional sphere in which few of them were themselves trained or experienced. As volunteers themselves, they were employers of women who identified with a particular professional ethos and expertise. Nevertheless, their status as lay people within this professional field did not absolve them from their obligations to maintain absolute standards.

I had *no* training for this at all. I've always [been] self-employed. There was no system, no line managing, no mentoring or counselling or training…You just do your job. If you don't do well, you don't do well. There's *no one* going to say, 'Perhaps you ought to go on a training course.' You just don't get employed. So, I…tried to find my place in the system, which was *not* to run the hostel. That's what *they* had to do…I was trying to be a support for them but also see that they did their job. After all, it was *my* job to do the hiring and firing of the staff. I was trying always not to intrude…I knew they knew *far* more about management structures and running

106

hostels. These are *professionals* and most of them were very *good* professionals. But still, *I* was the manager of the committee and a trustee of the Griffins. *I* had to try to ensure that we were carrying out our mission statement, which is to help women offenders. (Council member)

Managers understood this tension, were appreciative of Council members' willingness to assume responsibility for difficult decisions and generally approved of the outcomes.

The Chair was very *clear*. She was very *precise*. I didn't always *agree* with the decisions, but I could understand the *process* behind them. As long as you can understand the *process* of the decision, then it's *fine*. As a manager, you're *never* going to get everything that you want. I've been around long enough to know that. They are your employers and you have to deliver to them. I didn't have a problem with that. On the whole, the decisions were absolutely *fine*. I got on with them. (Hostel manager)

Nevertheless, staff were quick to recognise the gaps in the Griffins' capacity to meet their expectations for professional support. One hostel manager related this shortcoming to the solidarity between her peers:

Although I gained a lot from [my committee members], their skills didn't lie in staff management. I was lucky that I got that elsewhere. But, of course, that's not really what should have happened. The managers supported one another probably more than they would have done normally.

Certainly, managers were more sharply exposed to this issue than their staff, for whom they themselves were the primary sources of support. For themselves, they recognised a lack of clear direction for their professional practice and personal career development. The following reflection on a career path that both thrived upon and suffered from the fluidity of individual positions illustrates the tensions arising from Council members' dependence upon staff for professional leadership, their desire to support

107

creativity and the relative inexperience of some of the staff while enjoying a high degree of autonomy.

> I'd gone through so many transitions with the Griffins, I was quite [confused about] what was my post, what was I doing, what was my role, what was my responsibility. I don't think I noticed *at the time*...they kept re-formatting my post. Because I was *open* to that, because I just *wanted* the experience and the development, I kept saying, 'Oh, yeah, yeah. That sounds like a really good idea.' I didn't realise how much of an impact that was having on me...There was no management structure above me, except for the management committee. I was working on my own...So, although there was a very *positive* aspect to that, which was that I was allowed to develop my skills as I chose...I didn't actually take very good care of myself. Nobody from the Griffins really did say, 'Well, hold on a minute. You need some stability or support.' So that was a double-edged situation, whereby I was *benefiting* from what became *detrimental* to me...I feel *guilty* saying this, because I believe that [Council members] felt that they were doing their very best to line manage me...But...I really received no line management. That would be the truth. But that *wasn't* neglect. That was an *inability*, an *inexperience*.

There is clear evidence that the Griffins were generous in their efforts to support the professional development of their staff. Several mentioned in interview that the Council had financed their training. They also appear to have been liberal in funding external consultancies for staff support.

> None of us were trained as psychologists or psychiatrists. So I asked for external support from psychologists, once a month, so I could talk about more of the dynamics—things that I couldn't share with the staff team because it was up to me as manager to try to resolve them. They paid for that and that was very successful. That helped an enormous amount. I think that was quite visionary of them, because a lot of voluntary organisations expect you to just muddle

through. We also set up some clinical teaching through the Institute of Psychiatry…where we could learn more about the features of certain mental illness. (Hostel manager)

On several occasions, the Council sponsored personal counselling for staff members by independent therapists. For example, an independent consultant met staff at Stockdale House monthly and the warden fortnightly during much of 1986 (Griffins Society 1986). Following a suicide in the hostel during that same year, personal counselling was also made available to the member of staff who had been on duty at that time. Records also show that a number of steps were taken, in the light of a review of this incident, to reduce the potential for such events (Griffins Society 1986). This was also the case in 1985 following an assault on a project worker.

Staff were rewarded for initiative by the responsiveness of Council members to their ideas. As one deputy manager remarked in interview: 'They would certainly make the staff feel as if they had a voice. That went down very well.' Moreover, the Griffins were prepared to back ideas with resources.

If I had a proposal and put it to them, I always got a good response. When I was working at Second-Stage House, I said, 'We need more staffing in this hostel.' They listened to me and looked into how they could raise that money. That's how they got three-year funding from a foundation. (Hostel manager)

One manager recalled a particular feature of the Griffins' style of management:

If there were major incidents, the Society *always* spoke with the member of staff concerned. In the time I was there, there were *never* any accusations. So if something happened, it wasn't like you were to blame. It was, 'How did this occur? How can we prevent it from occurring in the future?'…When we had the instance with the young person who committed suicide, the management committee were very supportive to the member of staff who was on duty at the time. I *never* heard of anyone blaming her for this happening on her shift.

They Were Proud of Us

> The difference is that the Griffins *trusted* the staff more…It's a feeling that we were trusted more in some ways because we were a smaller [organisation]. (Staff member)

One of the strongest messages from staff was their appreciation of the extent to which the Griffins were prepared to trust them in the exercise of their duties. They, and particularly hostel managers, enjoyed a degree of autonomy that they knew was rarely accorded to those in other organisations. For those who could rise to this challenge, the advancement within the Griffins facilitated by this level of trust ultimately enhanced their broader career prospects. These women combined strong initiative with a clear sense of their accountability to their employing organisation. Many left the Griffins Society to develop successful professional careers.

> My overall, overriding feeling of them is that they were a very enabling committee. That they trusted me. That they gave me a lot of space to imprint my own ideas on the hostel. (Hostel manager)

The Griffins themselves seem to have taken considerable pleasure in the achievements of their staff. In interview, they often expressed frank admiration for their abilities. However, the clearest evidence for this lies in the appreciative comments of staff themselves.

> They were *proud* of us, of the work we were doing. It was like a mother looking at her children—'That's *my* kids!' We were a bit like their children. They were *proud* of us. (Staff member)

YOU MAY JUST HAVE A ROTTEN APPLE

> We asked an *enormous* amount of them, paid them very *little* and really didn't support them *enough*. (Council member)

The very qualities that evoked staff approval of the Griffins as employers carried the seeds of disaster within them. There is no doubt that the Griffins gave full credit to staff for their initiative, took considerable pleasure in their development and were at pains to support them. They went out of their way to be personally accessible and supportive to their staff and to encourage their professional growth. They were willing to trust staff with considerable autonomy. They may not, perhaps, have fully appreciated the unusual degree of latitude enjoyed by hostel managers, partly, as some comments above suggest, because, with a few exceptions, they were themselves not professionally trained either in social work or in management.

These strategies paid dividends in respect of many staff whose pioneering energy was tempered by the strong sense of allegiance and accountability that such treatment fostered. Nevertheless, they also rendered the Griffins vulnerable to individuals who were willing to exploit the potential for abuse created by the combination of professional autonomy with close and trusting relationships with their employers. One manager reflected that trust is a fundamental necessity in such working environments:

> It would have been possible, if one so wished, to carry out small deceptions without anyone knowing, just because of the way the hostel had to operate. We had to buy food every day. There would be other household items that needed regular purchasing—linen…travel…and so on. In that type of environment, it would be extremely [difficult] *not* to place trust in staff…You just can't put systems in place that will avoid small deceptions.

The finance officer agreed:

> That's the thing with not-for-profit organisations. There is an enormous amount of *trust*. *Enormous* amount. There *has* to be that trust. What you have to do is try and make the system…sufficiently *tight* so that the rules are not going to be abused, but then sufficiently *loose* that it doesn't stifle…But…if people *want* to defraud, they'll defraud…[My company] employed 80,000 people at one stage, and it didn't employ 80,000 honest ones!

Hostel managers were particularly exposed to such opportunities for abuse of their position. One former staff member recognised a potential flaw in the relationship between Council members and their managers, although, ironically, she was clearly unaware, in interview, of the exploitation of this very loophole perpetrated by her own manager, which came to light after her departure. Notwithstanding their generally accessible approach, Council members largely relied on the information supplied in regular meetings with their managers concerning the prevailing conditions in the hostels. To some extent, this was an appropriate reflection of managers' status and the Griffins' expectation that they themselves should support project staff through, rather than independently of the manager. However, as the staff member observed, this created a situation in which '[Council members] might have a nice little chat with [project workers]. But actually, it was only the *warden* that the committee talked to. So, if the warden *kept* power and *could* potentially have power and information, they *might* have withheld it.'

This weakness in the Griffins' self-protection was exacerbated by their dependence on staff for professional leadership. A manager, who remarked on the Griffins' dependence on the professionalism of their key staff, made a different point:

> [The Griffins] were quite heavily *reliant* on the project managers. If the project manager was not good, then a lot could go wrong. So, if they were successful, then it wasn't just down to them. That might sound big headed. But just *look* at the stuff that [we] used to do. We carried an awful lot of responsibility. But we *wanted* to. We *liked* it.

Perhaps more importantly, however, because of their own immersion in their mission, combined with the pleasure inherent in seeing its accomplishment in the efforts of creative staff, the Griffins underestimated the capacity of individuals to neutralise professional and personal allegiance to their cause.

> Because *they* themselves were so *committed*, they expected that *everyone else*—the staff—would be as committed…and be there for the same reasons that the Griffins were there for. (Housing associa-

tion officer)

They were very *trusting* of staff. So, they didn't put in some of the management functions of checking...It reflected on their *enthusiasm* for getting things done, *forgetting* sometimes that you have to have management processes because you just *may* have a rotten apple. (Probation service housing officer)

In hindsight, a Council member appeared to agree with this assessment:

We'd been a fairly *trusting* lot. Because we hadn't *met* any member of staff who'd *deliberately* set out to defraud the place and to get what they could, when we were trying to help women who needed something better than they'd got.

Lapses of staff integrity took a number of forms. Among a largely untrained workforce, the level of professionalism that staff generally displayed was perhaps more remarkable than its absence among a few. There were, however, instances of serious lapses of judgement. Some of these had become humorous with the passage of time, although there is no doubt that they created a deal of anxiety when they occurred. An early Council member recalled:

We took some men from Wandsworth Prison. I actually took them in my car to the house. They were supposed to be doing gardening on a Sunday...One of them was due for release very soon afterwards. Without a by your leave or anything, we discovered that [the warden] had taken him to live in the house! So, there was [the warden] with her man up in the flat and the other women downstairs. Well, you can *imagine*, it didn't go down very well. We had to get rid of *her*.

The Society's records reveal a number of occasions on which disciplinary action was taken against staff for unprofessional behaviour, including inappropriate relationships with and abusive behaviour towards residents. It is fair to observe that, as earlier recollections suggest, these incidents were dealt with robustly, including the taking of statements from resident complainants and with clear assertions of the organisation's stance against abuse.

As indicated earlier, petty dishonesty presented a periodic problem in conditions where trust necessarily prevailed, opportunities were frequent and staff were poorly paid. It was also, as one Council member observed, not always easy to distinguish deliberate dishonesty from incompetence among a staff group who were poorly equipped to handle financial responsibility:

> The management committee had maybe not been looking hard enough at a) the salaries and b) the amount of pressure that the person who ultimately had to run the place was under…The ones who I remember most clearly had great strengths, but there were also obvious weaknesses, particularly with regard to the financial side of things. Whether they were actually examples of dishonesty, or whether they were really not trained adequately in bookkeeping…and simply that was always on a back burner, because the pressure was so great. [We] appointed people for their communication skills and experience in the sector and didn't really…look enough at providing supportive training for areas they were weaker in.

During the history of the Griffins Society, there were two instances of serious embezzlement committed by managers. The Griffins' part in these events and their aftermath reveals much about their optimism in human nature. Perusal of records suggests several prior occasions on which the behaviour of the perpetrator on the first occasion was open to question, yet trust appears to have prevailed. Nevertheless, the Griffins showed considerable compassion towards this woman, who was in their employment for seven years and whose offences were properly identified only after her departure.

> I was really very *sorry*. I was really *very* sorry. [She] was a very nice woman…[who became] pregnant. After all, she didn't earn very much and she really wanted the *best* for her child. *She* was the one who said to me, 'Wouldn't *you* steal for your child?' (Council member)

[She] had [an illegitimate] child…I have *no* doubt that all the money she stole was for her child. I wouldn't be in the *least* surprised, because her child was very important to her. (Council member)

Nevertheless, they did not shy from the unpleasant task of prosecuting someone for whom they had both fondness and sympathy, regarding it as an inescapable obligation of their position.

We felt…that we would be sending a message which would be absolutely *unacceptable* to our residents, to the staff, to our funders, to the world in general, that we were prepared to allow people to continue when they'd committed offences, while saying to the residents that, if they offended, they would be thrown out. I didn't think that was *ever* acceptable. (Council member)

Given the background, however, the Griffins were disappointed by the sentence handed out to this woman. In the words of one:

She—to my mind, very foolishly—was fined. It seemed to me extremely *stupid*, since she'd *taken* the money because she *needed* it. Then to have £1,000—which in those days was quite a lot of money—slapped on top of her. I had been hoping, as had everybody, that she would have a suspended sentence.

In the second case, it is clear that individual Council members were naïvely trusting in allowing the circumvention of strict financial procedure in pursuit of expediency. Indeed, this incident brought about the only serious rift in relationships between Council members, when resignations were required from individuals whose service and commitment to the cause had been in itself unstinting. In some ways, this might be deemed the most tragic aspect of the affair.

Realising that she had been discovered, the offending staff member disappeared, leaving a recorded message on the telephone of the administrative officer: 'All I can say…is that I'm really, really, *really*, very, *very*

115

sorry for all of this and ask that when the time comes that you go easy on my friends and my relatives. Bye.' It appears that the initial response of Council members on discovering this message was to fear for the offender's personal safety. A subsequent scribbled note reassured them on this point: 'Well I really messed up this time. I'm truly sorry for the mess—so I quietly slipped away now it's all over. Thank you for all you did for me. Goodbye.' Despite their anger, and, indeed, humiliation at her behaviour, coming as Special Care House, for which she had assumed the manager's role, was entering a critical phase of its development prior to opening, the Griffins appear to have exercised forbearance.

> [She] very much let a lot of people down. We were all fully expecting that the Griffins would be lobbying to get her a really *tough* sentence, because they *are* on the network and they were *mortified*. I think she got [several] months imprisonment, and the Griffins were really *angry* that this had happened. But, from what I could tell, they hadn't done anything behind the scenes. (Hostel manager)

Rather less restrained, it seems, were former hostel residents. Legend has it that the offender was immediately transferred from Holloway Prison to a safer venue, to avoid the delivery of informal justice.

In both these instances, the Griffins, with hindsight, saw the consequences of the combination of their trust in and reliance on personal and professional plausibility:

> [She] was a very *bewitching* warden. We were all *bewitched* by her.

> We had a very remarkable warden, who was an *astonishing* personality. She *ruled* the place. She ruled *everybody*.

The Griffins' reaction to both these events testifies to their personal investment in their mission and their staff.

> It was like a *bereavement* for them. They'd placed *so* much *trust* in this member of staff and then she took them for an awful lot of

116

money at a crucial time...It was a big, big *shock*...But it was very much a sort of *bereavement*. They were *shocked* and *horrified* that somebody could have *betrayed* their trust—which was slightly unusual, in the sense that they were dealing with these women offenders all the time... (Police officer)

We were all very upset, because she was somebody who most of us liked enormously, *personally* liked and we felt *betrayed*. We *understood* why she did it, but we felt *betrayed*. (Council member)

It is impossible to judge how far these experiences could be described as defining moments in the history of the Griffins Society. Nevertheless, it is clear that they bit deep into the confidence of Council members. One staff member, reflecting on the impact of the second fraud, which involved substantial systematic embezzlement over a period of time, attributed a considerable legacy to it, given its occurrence at a time when the Griffins were beginning to find it hard to sustain their investment in their mission:

There was *enormous* disappointment. *All* these disappointments, they're all *cumulative* in the trustees' minds. It's just another nail in the coffin. Another reason not to enjoy running the organisation any more. It all became so much of a *hassle*. Nothing was *fun*.

CONCLUSION

The staff of the Griffins Society disclosed a remarkable passion for the organisation and its mission. Many felt an intense loyalty, pride and sense of pioneering adventure that combined to forge strong bonds to the organisation. Indeed, as the mediators through whom the Griffins' mission was translated into practice, staff exemplified that quality of 'rational non-economic behaviour' (Payton 1988), in which, while career and financial expectations were limited, ambition was realised through achievement of the organisation's goals. This emotional bond was to be found among those who, as seen in the last chapter, criticised the Council members on grounds of class prejudice as much as those who openly admired their commitment and abilities. While staff formed a close knit group offering camaraderie and support (as well as, at times, equally strong antipathies), it would be inappropriate to view their attachment as arising independently of the Griffins themselves, even while some staff clearly failed to recognise them at its source.

The Griffins took upon themselves the task of managing, as lay volunteers, the employment of professional staff. This was a sensitive distinction in status, which staff were often keen to stress, and which implied a degree of deferment by the Griffins to their expertise. There was a certain irony in this, since, in common with many residential care organisations, many project staff were young, untrained and inexperienced. Indeed, Manton's (1976) description of reformatory work in the nineteenth century as 'physically and emotionally exhausting, badly paid and unjustly low in social status' (p.138), with the inevitable consequences for professional integrity, rang equally true in the modern twentieth century age in which the Griffins Society operated. Nevertheless, it is also true that staff, by their intense exposure to an unusual client group within pioneering residential projects, rapidly became experts in areas of practice that were little understood, not merely by the Griffins, but by professionals in allied fields. While this accomplishment was certainly real in itself, it also enhanced the power of staff to influence the organisation's direction and ethos through their justified claim to special knowledge (Payton 1988).

The Griffins accepted their position within this somewhat ambiguous nexus with a humility that would have surprised their strongest critics, but also with an energy that might have surprised them even more. They themselves offered a curious mix of developmental enterprise, drawing on their connections at high levels of influence, as well as practical and emotional assistance, for which they exploited their reserves of common sense and human compassion. Recognising the gap in professional leadership that remained, their investment in external training, consultancy and, perhaps most strikingly, personal support for their staff was not only generous, but may have been ahead of its time in comparison with other voluntary sector organisations in a comparable field. Whether or not they fully endorsed some of the professional reasoning that informed the practices of their staff, the Griffins were driven by their ambition to provide high quality care for women offenders to seek, support, and enforce absolute standards of practice.

Thus, it is by no means clear that the Griffins Society was necessarily fatally flawed in its construction or, to put this the other way round, that fully professional agencies are self-evidently more competent employers and managers than this eccentric body of volunteers. The Griffins were rewarded for their efforts by a remarkable number of dedicated and skilled staff. Their reliance on these individuals sprang more from the weakness and instability of the available work force and their staff's thirst for pioneering than from deference to esoteric professionalism.

The Griffins' deepest vulnerability probably sprang more from an excess of trust in personal integrity, than of dependence on professional leadership. Seeing the expression of their own ambitions in the achievements of their staff, they assumed from this a level of personal integrity that some failed to attain. Thus, the manipulation of this vulnerability by a few individuals was deeply hurtful to them because of its simultaneous insult to both their personal accessibility and their mission.

Chapter Five

Dangerous Women or Women in Danger?

Impulsively Phoebe decided that she would not let him gradually destroy her home because she would destroy it first. (Case notes: arson)

We turn now to consider the residents of the hostels of the Griffins Society. This chapter explores the organisation's claim to be dealing with the most difficult offenders, who were often excluded from alternative accommodation. It also examines the connections between the personal distress and the high-risk behaviour of this group of women.

INADEQUATE RATHER THAN DANGEROUS

We begin by examining the histories of the 79 women whose case notes were available, making formal documentation on their criminal and social backgrounds accessible for statistical analysis. Results in tables show information for 19 women referred to Special Care House separately from that for Stockdale, Second-stage and Halfway Houses and the Bail Hostel, since this group was distinctive in several ways. Thus, the cumulative profile of residents at the projects is somewhat altered by the inclusion of these women.

Table 1 shows the types of disturbance experienced by the women during childhood. Evidence of disrupted families, physical and sexual abuse, and psychological disturbance of family members, revealed by much previous research, is confirmed in this data. Table 2 shows the frequency with which these types of childhood disturbance were recorded in each case. It reveals the extent to which such problems were experienced in

TABLE 1: DISTURBANCES RECORDED IN CHILDHOOD
(PERCENTAGES IN BRACKETS)

Childhood Experience	Stockdale, Second-Stage, Halfway Houses and Bail Hostel (n=60)	Special Care House (n=19)	All Projects (n=79)
Living in single parent household	18 (30)	9 (47.4)	27 (34.2)
Residential children's home	11 (18.3)	9 (47.4)	20 (25.3)
Sexual abuse	6 (10)	15 (78.9)	21 (26.6)
Physical abuse	10 (16.7)	5 (26.3)	15 (19)
Mentally ill parent	1 (1.7)	9 (47.4)	10 (12.7)
Alcoholic parent	3 (5)	4 (21.1)	7 (8.9)
Living with foster family	1 (1.7)	5 (26.3)	6 (7.6)
Mentally ill sibling	- (-)	5 (26.3)	5 (6.3)
Violence between parents	4 (6.7)	1 (5.3)	5 (6.3)
Living with extended family member	3 (5)	2 (10.5)	5 (6.3)
Criminal sibling	1 (1.7)	2 (10.5)	3 (3.8)
Drug addicted parent	2 (3.3)	1 (5.3)	3 (3.8)
Living with adoptive family	1 (1.7)	1 (5.3)	2 (2.5)
Criminal parent	1 (1.7)	- (-)	1 (1.3)
Drug addicted sibling	- (-)	1 (5.3)	1 (1.3)

**TABLE 2: NUMBER OF DISTURBANCES RECORDED IN CHILDHOOD
PER INDIVIDUAL (PERCENTAGES IN BRACKETS)**

Number of Disturbances Recorded	Stockdale, Second-Stage, Halfway Houses and Bail Hostel (n=60)	Special Care House (n=19)	All Projects (n=79)
0	27 (45)	1 (5.3)	28 (35.4)
1	17 (28.3)	3 (15.8)	20 (25.3)
2	9 (15)	2 (10.5)	11 (13.9)
3	2 (3.3)	1 (5.3)	3 (3.8)
4	4 (6.7)	6 (31.6)	10 (12.7)
5+	1 (1.7)	6 (31.6)	7 (8.9)
Total	60 (100)	19 (100)	79 (100)

multiple combinations, particularly in the case of women referred to Special Care House. Thirty-one women (39 percent) had experienced two or more of these disturbances.

Table 3 shows the psychiatric and psychological problems manifested by the women in adulthood. While drug and alcohol problems were predominant among the group as a whole, they were less significant among women referred to Special Care House than self-harming and mental illness. The two individuals at Special Care House who had never been diagnosed with a major mental illness were recorded as suffering from severe personality disorder, although they had at times displayed some psychotic symptoms. Table 4 again reveals the multiplicity of such problems among individuals, and again this is particularly pronounced among the women at Special Care House. Overall, 35 (44 percent) of the women were recorded as having suffered from more than one psychiatric or psychological problem.

This information has been summarised briefly, since it confirms the familiar and consistent findings of previous research into the social and personal backgrounds of female offenders (see, for example, American Correctional Association 1990; Baskin and Sommers 1998; HM Chief Inspector of Prisons 1997; Loucks 1997). These women were damaged by childhood experiences of turbulence in family composition and trauma in

123

TABLE 3: RECORDED PSYCHIATRIC AND PSYCHOLOGICAL PROBLEMS (PERCENTAGES IN BRACKETS)

Nature of Problem	Stockdale, Second-Stage, Halfway Houses and Bail Hostel (n=60)	Special Care House (n=19)	All Projects (n=79)
Drugs	29 (48.3)	11 (57.9)	40 (50.6)
Self-harm	8 (13.3)	18 (94.7)	26 (32.9)
Alcohol	13 (21.7)	11 (57.9)	24 (30.4)
Major mental illness	3 (5)	17 (89.5)	20 (25.3)
Depression/anxiety	12 (20)	4 (21.1)	16 (20.3)
Eating disorder	1 (1.7)	8 (42.1)	9 (11.4)
Learning difficulty	2 (3.3)	2 (10.5)	4 (5.1)

TABLE 4: NUMBER OF PSYCHIATRIC AND PSYCHOLOGICAL PROBLEMS RECORDED PER INDIVIDUAL (PERCENTAGES IN BRACKETS)

Number of Problems Recorded	Stockdale, Second-Stage, Halfway Houses and Bail Hostel (n=60)	Special Care House (n=19)	All Projects (n=79)
0	14 (23.3)	- (-)	14 (17.7)
1	30 (50)	- (-)	30 (38)
2	11 (18.3)	2 (10.5)	13 (16.5)
3	4 (6.7)	7 (36.8)	11 (13.9)
4	1 (1.7)	4 (21.1)	5 (6.3)
5	- (-)	6 (31.6)	6 (7.6)
Total	60 (100)	19 (100)	79 (100)

124

relationships, and struggled with psychiatric and/or psychological difficulties in adulthood. Parts of the case notes seem to capture the emergence of even serious offending as a product of the confusion and desperation borne out of turmoil, rather than deliberate wickedness:

> She has no history of violence and is regarded by my team as inadequate rather than dangerous. (Case notes: robbery)

> In the days prior to [her offence] Cecilia had described being 'in pain', feeling unable to do anything, as if all of her feelings had been drained away. (Case notes: abduction and attempted murder of child)

> [T]he predisposing factors were the financial and emotional pressures she felt...combined with the feelings the counselling may have provoked and her inability to cope with these feelings. She ultimately released them in an inappropriate and dangerous manner. (Case notes: arson)

We should not, however, rush to conclude, with Allen (1987), that professionals were 'painting out' the seriousness and intentionality of women's involvement in crime. The quotations above capture only a part of their explanations. As we shall see, these women presented complex portraits in which their entrapment in the legacy of disturbed histories and in immediate social and personal stress combined with motivations and decisions that promoted their criminal actions. In this nuanced understanding, they appear not merely as pawns pushed by external forces, but as individuals whose histories shaped both their priorities and their problem solving strategies, influencing their perspectives on the legitimacy of negative, antisocial and even self-damaging behaviour.

A SPUR OF THE MOMENT THING

> She said her intention wasn't to hurt anyone but it was just a spur of the moment thing. (Case notes: arson)

While this comment from a case file encapsulates the reckless culmination of multiple stresses, it nevertheless concerns a woman whose pattern of repetitive fire setting had endangered life on several occasions. Case notes capture the struggle to reconcile the gravity of women's offending with their immersion in misery.

Table 5 shows the offences for which the women were charged or convicted prior to referral to the projects. Dishonesty forms the largest single group of offences overall, although the women referred to Special Care House make no contribution to this, because their mental illness was associated with behaviour harmful enough to themselves or others to warrant detention in secure conditions. Indeed, the combination of offences causing, or likely to cause serious personal harm (violence, criminal damage/arson, sex and robbery) constitutes 44 percent of offences for all 79 women. This cumulative combination represents 37 percent of offences for those women referred to Stockdale, Second-Stage and Halfway Houses and the Bail Hostel, suggesting a strong proportion of high-risk offenders.

TABLE 5: TYPE OF OFFENCE PRIOR TO REFERRAL
(PERCENTAGES IN BRACKETS)

Offence Type	Stockdale, Second-Stage, Halfway Houses and Bail Hostel (n=60)	Special Care House (n=19)	All Projects (n=79)
Dishonesty	28 (46.6)	- (-)	28 (35.4)
Violence	12 (20)	3 (16)	15 (19)
Criminal damage/arson	5 (8.3)	9 (47)	14 (17.7)
Drugs	8 (13.3)	- (-)	8 (10.1)
No offence	- (-)	5 (26)	5 (6.3)
Sex	3 (5)	- (-)	3 (3.8)
Robbery	2 (3.3)	1 (5)	3 (3.8)
Driving	2 (3.3)	- (-)	2 (2.6)
Unknown	- (-)	1 (5)	1 (1.3)
Total	60 (100)	19 (100)	79 (100)

Table 6 shows the numbers of previous convictions of the women. Forty-three percent had previous convictions, including 22 (28 percent) with five or more, constituting a substantial proportion of recidivist offenders. Table 7 shows the types of offences involved in the women's previous convictions, revealing substantial prior histories of violence, criminal damage/arson, public order/affray and robbery (40 women, 51 percent). The 25 women without previous convictions are of interest, since their offences were among the most serious, including, for example, attempted murder (one), manslaughter (one), wounding with intent to cause grievous bodily harm (two), child cruelty (one), arson (three) and sexual offences (three). First offenders thus made a dramatic entrance onto the criminal justice stage.

Despite their extensive criminal histories and levels of personal and social distress, only 29 women (54 percent of those with previous convictions) had experienced probation supervision prior to their referral to the hostels, although nearly half (48 percent of those with previous convictions) had received prior custodial sentences (Table 8). Indeed, a custodial

TABLE 6: NUMBER OF PREVIOUS CONVICTIONS PER INDIVIDUAL (PERCENTAGES IN BRACKETS)

Number of Previous Convictions	Stockdale, Second-Stage, Halfway Houses and Bail Hostel (n=60)	Special Care House (n=19)	All Projects (n=79)
No previous	21 (35)	4 (21.1)	25 (31.6)
Has previous; number unobtainable	14 (23.3)	6 (31.6)	20 (25.3)
1 - 4	7 (11.7)	5 (26.4)	12 (15.2)
5 - 9	4 (6.6)	2 (10.6)	6 (7.6)
10 - 19	5 (8.5)	1 (5.3)	6 (7.6)
20+	9 (15.3)	1 (5.3)	10 (13)
Total	60 (100)	19 (100)	79 (100)

TABLE 7: TYPES OF OFFENCES RECORDED IN PREVIOUS CONVICTIONS (PERCENTAGES OF WOMEN WITH PREVIOUS CONVICTIONS IN BRACKETS)

Offence Type	Stockdale, Second-Stage, Halfway Houses and Bail Hostel (n=39)	Special Care House (n=15)	All Projects (n=54)
Dishonesty	29 (74.3)	8 (53.3)	37 (68.5)
Violence	11 (28.2)	6 (40)	17 (31.5)
Criminal damage/arson	6 (15.4)	8 (53.3)	14 (25.9)
Drugs	8 (20.5)	2 (13.3)	10 (18.5)
Public order/affray	3 (7.7)	4 (26.7)	7 (12.9)
Prostitution	5 (12.8)	1 (6.7)	6 (11.1)
Driving	4 (10.3)	- (-)	4 (7.4)
Robbery	2 (5.3)	- (-)	2 (3.7)
Other	13 (33.3)	2 (13.3)	15 (27.8)

TABLE 8: PREVIOUS SENTENCES OF PROBATION, IMMEDIATE CUSTODY AND COMMUNITY SERVICE ORDERS RECEIVED (PERCENTAGES OF WOMEN WITH PREVIOUS CONVICTIONS IN BRACKETS)

Sentence	Stockdale, Second-Stage, Halfway Houses and Bail Hostel (n=39)	Special Care House (n=15)	All Projects (n=54)
Probation order (with or without additional requirements)	21 (53.8)	8 (53.3)	29 (53.7)
Immediate custody	19 (48.7)	7 (36.8)	26 (48.1)
Community service order	7 (17.9)	1 (5.3)	8 (14.8)

sentence most commonly preceded the referral and, together with those who had been subject to detention under mental health legislation, comprised a large group of women who would arrive at the projects from a (sometimes substantial) period of institutionalisation (Table 9).

This catalogue of crime, which reveals the extent of the women's involvement in offences causing, or likely to cause, serious personal harm challenges the apparent spontaneity of many of their criminal actions. Indeed, the case notes, examined more carefully, suggest considerable complexities in their emotional and motivational state at the time of their offences.

Mysie was petrified, frantic and very angry. (Case notes: arson)

TABLE 9: SENTENCE RECEIVED FOR OFFENCE PRIOR TO REFERRAL (PERCENTAGES IN BRACKETS)

Sentence	Stockdale, Second-Stage, Halfway Houses and Bail Hostel (n=60)	Special Care House (n=19)	All Projects (n=79)
Immediate custody	34 (56.7)	3 (15.8)	37 (46.8)
Probation order (with or without additional requirements)	16 (26.7)	- (-)	16 (20.3)
Mental Health Act	- (-)	9 (47.7)	9 (11.4)
Combination order	3 (5)	- (-)	3 (3.8)
Community service order	1 (1.7)	- (-)	1 (1.3)
Unknown/no conviction/no sentence (acquitted, bailed or hospitalised)	6 (10)	7 (36.8)	13 (16.4)
Total	60 (100)	19 (100)	79 (100)

Maude was driven by vindictiveness and anger rather than by any reasons of mental illness in performing an act of violence towards [the victim] by startling him with petrol bombs…Her need to demonstrate her feelings and her misdirected anger are causes of concern. The victim was a man with whom she had an abusive and humiliating relationship, but others…could be at risk. (Case notes: violence)

She described 'wanting to explode'; she had had enough and wanted to get her own back. (Case notes: arson)

SHE'LL HAVE TO LIVE IN A SHED

The connections between the women's social and personal distress and their problematic behaviours are illuminated in their pathways to homelessness, which was their most common immediate problem at the point of referral to the projects (39 women, 49 percent). Research on the relationship between homelessness and involvement in crime suggests a number of explanations for the connection. Some of these are relatively straightforward, as, for example, in survival offences of theft or begging committed by the economically destitute. Others invoke more complex interactions between the individual and factors in the volatile environment of street life, for example, drug deals and strategies for defence against victimisation (see, for example, Baskin and Sommers 1998; Maher and Curtis 1992; Sommers and Baskin 1993). These analyses, however, often understate the personal agency of the homeless offender. The condition of homelessness, with its connotations of deprivation and vulnerability, can appear as sufficient cause in itself of criminal behaviour, impelling involvement in crime in spite of any good intentions of the offender. Here, a preliminary examination of factors underlying the women's homelessness informs deeper consideration of motivations and behaviours that enhanced the potential for their involvement in crime.

It is necessary first to note three points. First, there was a mixture of distal and immediate factors in the background to homelessness, which imply different kinds of causal significance in the problem. Second, the majority of women experienced multiple combinations of these factors. In

130

few cases, if any, could their homelessness be attributed to a single cause. Third, for many of these women, homelessness was a repeated and perpetuating problem. It was not easy to distinguish clearly between periods of homelessness and stability in the complexity of their lives. For example, being a hostel resident might suggest termination of homelessness; yet, hostel residency is a temporary condition. Even when they had a roof over their heads, many women's lives continued to be marked by instability. Moreover, both psychological and structural influences often seemed to impede their ability to capitalise on temporary respite from homelessness in ways that would render it permanent. With these cautions in mind, three varieties of factors contributing to homelessness emerged: problems in their close relationships; issues concerning the formal services of support and intervention; and broad conditions affecting their quality of life.

Endless Parental Rows

Relationships with significant others that are commonly assumed to be associated with stability were more usually sources of disruption for these women.

The parents of several of the women had separated during their childhood, on terms that damaged or severed the links with at least one of them. For example: one mother divorced on grounds of cruelty; another refused to reveal the identity of her daughter's father; and two fathers emigrated. Loss was a common theme: a number of women had lost parents through bereavement; some parents had left, or never resided in Britain; one or both parents of some women had not acted in a parenting capacity towards them due to drug, alcohol or psychiatric problems. Many of these losses were traumatic, involving long-term institutionalisation, violent or drug induced death or suicide. Similar losses often extended to other family members, including grandparents (who may have taken an important caretaking role), siblings, aunts and uncles. Many of the women had experienced difficult, distorted family relationships, including physical, emotional and sexual abuse, neglect, domestic violence, drug abuse and alcoholism.

Her parents were both substance misusers. Her mother had been using heroin during the pregnancy and Lorna exhibited narcotic withdrawal syndrome when born. This…led to her being raised by her grandparents…When Lorna was eight years old her mother died of a heroin overdose. Lorna had only seen her mother once ever before she died…Aged 12, her father was killed by gunfire. (Case notes)

Mysie dimly remembers sexual abuse by her half brother…Her father was a heavy drinker, [which] caused endless parental rows and the eventual break-up of the marriage…Her father beat her mother and occasionally the children too. They were out of contact for many years…Her mother remarried several times and cohabited with a number of men. (Case notes)

Continuing relationships with family in adulthood could be severely destructive, undermining prospects of progress when opportunities arose. In some cases, parents sabotaged the woman's attempts at rehabilitation, although withdrawal from a programme would include leaving accommodation that was tied to it. Family members often expected support, although they offered little in return. Moreover, some encouraged the self-damaging behaviours that rehabilitation sought to modify. Given that many women were ambivalent about treatment, including residential options, they were vulnerable to these types of influence. Some women were unable to resolve these destructive relationships, remaining locked into a self-defeating cycle of attempts at rehabilitation weakened by family opposition.

One of the staff told me that Davina's father said, in front of Davina, 'We don't want her back here. If she comes back, she'll have to live in a shed in the garden'…Davina told me, 'My Dad said I should try and wind the staff up as much as possible so I'll get thrown out.' (Observation notes)

Tara was on the phone to her father about her grandmother, who is very ill. She was saying that of course she was going to visit her that afternoon, but that she had things to do first: 'I'm just *trying* to get used to having more freedom. Really, it's *hard*.' (Observation notes)

Turning to adult intimate partners, some women had lost relationships on which they had apparently built ambitions for a settled life. Termination of these relationships was followed by deterioration in the woman's coping abilities. Yet, for many women, relationships with partners were characterised by abuse, excessive control and intimidation, drug and alcohol misuse. In several cases, relationships with partners damaged prospects of successful rehabilitation. For example: one woman was pursued to a drug rehabilitation project, kidnapped and assaulted; one woman avoided contact with her only supportive relation after leaving Special Care House to live with her lesbian lover; and a number of women were effectively compelled by partners to choose between their rehabilitation and their relationship. Thus, for many women, intimate relationships threatened their rehabilitation.

> CID came with a search warrant…They had got June's boyfriend in custody for burglary/car radio theft…June's [college] course was confirmed today. She said she is looking forward to it. She also said that it might be good thing if Graham is remanded, so she can get herself together. (Case notes)

> At the age of 15, she came to London with a man whom she claims introduced her to prostitution…She describes her relationship with this man as violent, which often resulted in her reception into a Women's Refuge. (Case notes)

Disrupted or severed contact with children was the second most pressing problem confronting women at the point of referral to the projects (16 women, 20 percent). A number of women had lost children permanently through bereavement, adoption or removal into local authority care.

> At the time of applying to [Halfway House], permanent adoptive families were being sought for her children. Sandra found this very hard to cope with, especially when the frequency of her contact visits was reduced to help her children settle in to their foster families. (Case notes)

[Her partner] dropped one of his children whilst drunk, causing a frac-
tured skull. This led to the children being taken into care and eventually
adopted…She had two more children with another cohabitee. These
children were also taken into care following the death of their father.
(Case notes)

While others retained contact, this was often tenuous or unsatisfactory,
and unlikely to lead to reunion. These women frequently felt excluded from
their child's upbringing. Some perceived all options for their children's care
as unsatisfactory, forcing a choice between local authority care or placement with a former partner or relation for which there was inadequate
support.

> Alison was arrested when James was just a few months old, so his
> father had taken him and the grandmother looked after him. He's
> nearly five now. Alison is very worried about James' welfare. His
> father has started using crack again. His grandmother's health is
> very bad. So, James is never taken out of the house, 'to the park and
> stuff', unless Alison takes him. She's worried that he's not getting
> enough stimulation. His interaction with other children [at nursery
> school] is very poor and he's often violent. The primary school he's
> due to go to is concerned about his behaviour and has said he can
> only attend on a part-time basis. James refuses to eat…His grand-
> mother has become very possessive of him and is refusing her
> access, or, if Alison can visit him, she won't allow her to take him
> out of the house. [The manager] suggested that if Alison was so
> concerned, she needed to think seriously about the possibility of
> involving the Social Services…Alison was very reluctant to do this
> because she felt it could be very damaging to James. He was loved
> and received a lot of affection…The situation at the moment is far
> from perfect, but Alison felt that at least she has some contact with
> her son. (Observation notes)

Their guilty knowledge of the fragile circumstances in which their
children were being raised led women to compromise between the demands
of their rehabilitation programme and their felt need to prop up a weak

support system. Thus, for many of these women, the motivation for stability with which having children is commonly associated was absent, impaired, or contradicted their own rehabilitative needs.

> Alison said that her son's grandmother was in hospital. She hadn't been told: 'I had to hear it on the street. A friend told me. They didn't even tell me that.' She had spent most of the night with her son, trying to calm him down. She was exhausted and obviously upset. Her voice was very hoarse: 'I do feel bloody stressed out.' (Observation notes)

Distal factors in the women's histories, such as parental separation and early abuse, did not *cause* their homelessness in adult life. They did, however, have several repercussive effects on their subsequent experiences that are relevant to understanding the intractability of their accommodation problems. Firstly, they constituted a progressive atrophy of the familial and wider support networks that individuals commonly rely upon in an accommodation crisis. Secondly, they provided a social and emotional learning environment in which relationships were understood to be unsafe, conflictual, and without promise of stability. Thirdly, women perpetuated abusive, exploitative and hostile relationships in their adult lives, which disrupted the stability generally associated with intimate connections. Several failed to draw on the experience of motherhood as the opportunity for change that it has been portrayed (Graham and Bowling 1995). Close relationships, therefore, were no guarantee of safety or stability.

A Very Scarce Resource

Support and intervention from a variety of formal agencies had the perverse effect of exacerbating the women's vulnerability to homelessness. Many had spent time in local authority care, often with unsatisfactory results in terms of resolving the problems associated with their removal from home and planning a stable future. Drift and indecisiveness, rather than positive planning, characterised the response from social workers in many cases. Thus, for example, women had been returned to parental care with little support for any improvement in the quality of their experience, and a number experienced successive placement breakdowns while in care. These early experiences also contributed to women's lasting suspicions of, and antagonistic relationships with those agencies charged with the duty of their protection.

> Davina describes her childhood as being an unhappy one, with periods of her trying to run away but always being brought back home by the police, from whence…she developed an intense dislike of [them]. She describes this dislike as taking an intense form of anger, which she still holds to this day. She says that she could never understand why they always took her back to the place where she experienced such unhappiness. (Case notes)

> When her mother was evicted…[Candice] was abandoned with six of her siblings, with her mother informing Social Services that her children were their responsibility…[Thus,] Candice was made the subject of a 'place of safety' order at nine years of age…Perhaps regrettably, she only remained in a children's home for a short period of time, despite seemingly, like her siblings, making good progress when away from home. (Case notes)

For some women, the cumulative effects of imprisonment and/or hospitalisation were increasing difficulties in accessing accommodation, exacerbated in some cases by the legacy of unpaid rent from previous tenancies, which militated against another tenancy award, or the refusal of a local authority to acknowledge a housing responsibility. Many of the applications to the hostels reveal that the lack of alternatives is closer to their core than commitment to a programme of self-development. Yet, prior experiences of hostel provision, including probation and bail hostels, were often unsatisfactory due to inadequate support for women with multiple problems and a volatile mix of disturbed residents.

Professional risk assessments had resulted in several women being detained in custody or hospital while refused community-based placements. A number were seen to require a package of very high support in the community that was difficult and expensive to provide. Thus, women experienced the revolving door syndrome of passing between prison, hospital, and unsatisfactory community placements, with progressive deterioration in their opportunities to break out of the cycle of institutional care. For women with mental health problems, their typical responses of self-harming or fire-setting in inappropriate placements merely further exacerbated their rejections.

> She was originally bailed to D- Bail Hostel, but was moved to [the Bail Hostel] because she failed to return following an argument. From [the Bail Hostel] she was moved to C- Bail Hostel because it was felt she would benefit from their links with the Portman Clinic. She was transferred from C- Bail Hostel back to [the Bail Hostel] for her own safety. (Case notes)

> Due to concerns about the risk of self-harm and suicide and her mental health, the Court refused her bail a number of times…A solicitor's letter to a psychiatrist states: 'Normally the alternative to prison would be a bail hostel but we feel it highly unlikely that any bail hostel would take Mysie. Therefore the only alternatives would be either a hospital or a home of a relative'…She was bailed to [the Bail Hostel] after five months on remand in Holloway. (Case notes)

Ironically, in several cases, the women's lack of settlement arose in the context of a failure of the services upon which she was dependent. Hospitals disputed their ability to provide appropriate treatment, hostels declined to accept referrals, funding authorities refused to cover the high costs of a suitable community support package, and probation officers found themselves unable to offer constructive sentencing alternatives to imprisonment. Equally, women were left with a complex emotional legacy of their experiences of social work and treatment interventions that included disappointment, anger, grief and hostility, rendering them disinclined to view further involvement with the formal agencies of social support with any expectation of a positive outcome.

> Her frequent acts of deliberate self-harm mean that she might indeed succeed if only by accident…Concerning risk to others, her history of fire-setting could be considered a high risk

137

behaviour…[O]ver and above Kerry's ambivalence to engage in a sustained therapeutic relationship, her history of fire-setting may well preclude her from therapeutic communities…Most medium secure units would not offer the type of psychotherapeutic/therapeutic community, preferably in an all female environment, which might have some chance of success. (Case notes)

It is worth noting in this context that, despite their difficulties, some women failed to access treatment services effectively, or at all in many cases. Table 10 shows the previous psychiatric, drug and alcohol treatments recorded in the case files of the 79 women. Clearly, the numbers of treatments do not match the frequency with which these particular problems were recorded. Table 11 shows that no evidence of any previous treatment was found in the records of 37 women (nearly 47 percent). All of these were among the populations at Stockdale, Second-stage and Halfway Houses and the Bail Hostel, since those at Special Care House had all received psychiatric treatment by virtue of the severity of their disturbance. Thus, of the primarily 'criminal'—rather than mentally ill—women, nearly 62 percent never accessed treatment for their most prevalent problems.

Sabrina has a severe personality disorder rather than a mental illness…I doubt whether her condition is treatable, either as an out-

TABLE 10: WOMEN RECORDED AS HAVING PREVIOUSLY RECEIVED PSYCHIATRIC, DRUG AND ALCOHOL TREATMENTS (PERCENTAGES IN BRACKETS)

Treatment Type	Stockdale, Second-Stage, Halfway Houses and Bail Hostel (n=60)	Special Care House (n=19)	All Projects (n=79)
Psychiatric	11 (18.3)	19 (100)	30 (38)
Drug	10 (16.7)	3 (15.8)	13 (16.5)
Alcohol	4 (6.7)	5 (26.3)	9 (11.4)

TABLE 11: NUMBERS OF WOMEN WITH AT LEAST ONE PREVIOUS PSYCHIATRIC, DRUG OR ALCOHOL TREATMENT RECORDED

Previous Treatment	Stockdale, Second-Stage, Halfway Houses and Bail Hostel (n=60)	Special Care House (n=19)	All Projects (n=79)
Previous treatment recorded	23 (38.3)	19 (100)	42 (53.2)
No previous treatments recorded	37 (61.7)	- (-)	37 (46.8)
Total	60 (100)	19 (100)	79 (100)

patient or an in-patient...The hospital ward provides an environment in which she can behave in a disruptive way with a great deal of attention being given to her which reinforces bad behaviour. I appreciate that she will continue to behave in a disruptive way, however I believe that eventually, if this behaviour is not rewarded, it will be gradually extinguished; this may take many years however...Obviously long admissions to hospital would remove the effects of her behaviour from the community but would probably merely transfer the disruption to the in-patient environment. I do not think it is justified to use a very scarce resource in this way. (Case notes)

The accuracy of women's personal accounts of their treatment by formal social support agencies cannot be entirely judged from these records, although, as we have seen, there is evidence that many programmes failed. Nevertheless, whatever their objective reality, it is certain that these complex, and recurrently disappointing encounters left a legacy of grief and rage that would infect all subsequent interactions with such agencies.

Alison became very distressed when she was talking about James and cried a lot...She is very suspicious of Social Services because

139

of the way she'd been treated over her daughters, who were taken into care. The social worker had, by Alison's account, 'betrayed' her, failed to work with her and respond to her earlier requests for help. Alison feels if she was given this support, she may have been able to keep her children: 'I'm an intelligent black woman. If I *ask* for help, then it's because I *need* it. This woman just spent five minutes in the house and said I didn't need help.' (Observation notes)

She had a boyfriend who was an epileptic...He had a seizure and drowned in the bath in hospital. Gloria was devastated by this and had thrown herself off a multi-storey car park...She was visibly angry and upset when she talked about his death...'They should have looked after him. They knew they had to, but they didn't. They just didn't *care*. They don't *care* whether you live or die. *I've* been treated like rubbish too.' (Observation notes)

One hostel resident bitterly recounted the following tale:

They actually *told* me that they didn't think that I should be in that ward and that it was unsuitable for me. But they wouldn't let me leave or transfer me somewhere else. I wish they hadn't told me that, because it makes me feel even *worse*...When they told me that, I started self-harming more seriously...*Then* they told me, just as I was about to come here, that there was a unit next door, which would have been suitable for my needs. *Why* did they have to tell me *that?...Why* tell me? It makes me so *angry*...Did they think it would make me feel *better? How* can it make me feel better to know I was in the wrong hospital and that I should never have been sectioned in the first place?

No Money, No Clothes and No Possessions

Structural realities in most women's lives militated against a secure future, including the prospects of safe, stable accommodation. Firstly, the majority had very poor prospects of economic advancement, largely because of the degree of disruption to their education in early life. Several had negligible employment experience. Most had worked intermittently, in poorly paid, unskilled and casual positions. Thus, the expense of establishing an independent home of any desirability was prohibitive.

> She attended a residential school for the 'maladjusted' and left with no exams. She worked as a dental nurse for six months and hasn't worked since. (Case notes)

A minority of women had developed promising career opportunities, but lost their employment in difficult circumstances. For example: one woman used private money to set herself and her husband up in business, which he ruined through alcoholism and neglect; another was dismissed without notice from her post as manager of a pub when the owners decided to sell the business; another suffered a mental breakdown only months after qualifying as a nurse.

> She passed 10 O-levels and two A-levels…She went on to attend B-College of Art to undertake a course in Art and Photography. Following this she started an HND course in Photography at P-College of Further Education. Tilly said that she never wanted to undertake photography as a career as it was very competitive and she didn't want to take photos for money. She did not complete this course…After this she did a number of jobs, including shop work and auxiliary nursing. The longest period of employment was three months. (Case notes)

Women regularly discovered that affordable tenancies were hazardous. Several were harassed by landlords. Some had trouble sustaining a tenancy after a relationship breakdown, but believed they would be seen to have made themselves intentionally homeless and refused alternative accommodation. Several were forced into a choice between their tenancy and a residential rehabilitation opportunity.

> Alison was living in her own accommodation with her husband (now divorced) at the time of her sentence. Although she has a strong case to hold on to her tenancy, she wishes to make a fresh

start elsewhere…Her ex-partner lives there with his girlfriend now. She's happy to sign over the tenancy to him, but is concerned in case this would make her 'intentionally homeless' in Housing Benefit terms. (Case notes)

Most women had been reliant on friends at various times, including on release from prison and after a relationship breakdown. Several had lost accommodation as a direct result of violence perpetrated against them, usually by partners, or harassment by landlords. The circumstances in which some women arrived at the hostel can only be described as bereft: they were without shelter, family or material resources.

My living arrangements at present are very temporary. The daughter in the house is due to have a baby in April at which point there will be even less room than there is now and I will be forced to move. With no job at present I have little hope of attaining private accommodation without a deposit. (Case notes: application statement)

Marina was released from a one-year prison sentence in Rome. She arrived with no money, no clothes and no possessions. She is currently homeless, but is temporarily staying with an acquaintance who is on welfare benefits herself and has four children. (Case notes)

Thus, for many women, the combination of disadvantages accruing from their personal and social histories offered little expectation of a substantial improvement in their quality of life. The promise of residential rehabilitation as an opportunity to rebuild lives that were pervasively insecure may well have appeared hollow.

ALMA WAS THEN VERY TRYING

It is clear from the foregoing, much of which is familiar from earlier research on homeless and criminal women, that a wide variety of factors beyond the women's control played a substantial part in their homelessness.

However, within the context of their plight, women made decisions and behaved in ways that frequently both militated against successful resolution of their homelessness and enhanced the likelihood of continuing involvement in crime. Their contributions to their difficulties clustered into four groups: severing supports, self-harm, offending, and lifestyle.

It's Me That Won't Let Them

Many women had childhood histories of absconding from home, school and residential care. Some retained this pattern in adulthood by absconding, for example, from psychiatric care or probation hostels. These behaviours invariably had the consequence of worsening their situation by further fragmenting the quality of care, education and accommodation available to them, even when other actions suggested a desire for such opportunities.

> Three days after being released from prison…Sal was arrested for making further [hoax] telephone calls. Having made the call, she waited near the telephone box to be arrested. Three weeks after being remanded to Holloway, a place was arranged for her in a bail hostel in Reading. However, rather than travelling there, she took a train to East Grinstead to visit her friend. (Case notes)

Some women sought to break from their past, for understandable reasons, yet in the process isolated themselves further from familiar networks of support and, in some instances, increased the likelihood of exposure to crime. For example: one young woman left an apparently supportive home in search of independence, moving to a hostel that was poorly supervised; another entered a problematic marriage in order to escape her home life; one could not obtain employment appropriate to her skills, having severed all connections with her past life and thus being unable to provide references.

> Kerry currently has no contact with her parents and changed her name by deed poll some time ago. She does not wish to make contact with her parents or most of her siblings in the future. She currently has contact with one brother, who she finds overprotective and demanding of her time. She feels that when she moves to the

community she will tell him that visitors are not allowed, enabling her to have some space from him. (Case notes)

Several women repeatedly withdrew from treatment programmes and severed contact with community support services. In some of these cases, records amply demonstrated that professionals had made strenuous attempts to retain a supportive connection with the woman. The failure of many to access treatment for their primary problems, noted earlier, must also be considered in this context of a group of women who were poorly disposed towards formal support services.

> She was admitted informally to [hospital] in an agitated state and later detained on a compulsory order because of her reluctance to comply with the assessment. She was paranoid against her neighbours and believed that the television and the radio were referring to her. She gradually settled down on the ward on anti-psychotic medication and obtained her discharge with the help of her husband, whom she threatened with a divorce if he did not collude with her. She refused psychiatric follow-up. (Case notes)

A hostel resident, in interview, explained:

> A lot of the time, I feel as if I don't belong here anyway. I don't know if it's because of the place or it's the way I am. I think it's me. Yeah, it's because of *me*. It's not them. You know, they do offer me a lot of support, but I don't feel I can *accept* that support. Yeah, I don't feel I *deserve* it most of the time. I feel I should be saying to myself, 'Pull yourself *together*. You don't need to be here.'

Similarly, another reflected:

> Isolating myself, the depression, talking to people, getting out…But it's *me* that won't *let* them give me the support…I just stay in my room. When they come up—for keywork sessions and that—I just refuse to go. So, it's basically up to me…I'm just used to being on my own all the time. I'm not used to getting the support that I'm getting. (Observation notes)

Winding People Up

Their disturbed histories had produced serious self-harming tendencies among a number of women, particularly those with psychiatric problems. Some of them appeared to use their habit of self-harming deliberately to undermine attempts to help them. Some discovered that their methods of self-harming contravened eligibility policy in residential programmes and secured their eviction by demonstrating their habit. One woman secured a placement in a residential project that, unusually, enabled residents to maintain existing tenancies, but felt dissatisfied there:

> She stayed for two weeks, but had to leave following an incident that led to her readmission to hospital. She jumped off a first floor balcony in front of the other residents. This appears to have been an impulsive act with no easily identifiable trigger, though Nadine states that she did intend to kill herself. She had cut [herself] several times over the previous week and talked about jumping. (Case notes)

Case notes show that one woman explained to her social worker:

> The most gratifying part of cutting herself is gaining other people's attention and seeing their reactions. Alma told me she most enjoys seeing other people become angry: 'It's a laugh, winding people up.' She expressed considerable fascination in observing the reactions of others to her self-harm.

Before Any Permanent Harm Was Done

The offending behaviour of the women frequently contributed strongly to their accommodation difficulties. Several women had histories of aggression and/or violence towards staff and other residents. Indeed, some had been previously refused placements in secure psychiatric hospitals on grounds of their violence, with the further consequence of making community-based placements extremely difficult to find. Some had been barred from community services because of previous aggressive or assaultive behaviour on the premises. Some women had lost accommodation, a few repeatedly, because of a habit of fire setting. These backgrounds also had the effect of excluding them from a variety of residential placements.

> She had her own flat and returned to hospital for one or two nights a week. She had community support in the past from a day hospital and a drop-in centre, although she had been asked not to attend these services because of her inappropriate and aggressive behaviour…Tilly has no previous convictions. She has a history of assaulting staff, but these incidents have been dealt with internally. (Case notes)

Finally, for some women, homelessness was triggered by the offence itself. In some cases, this was necessitated by the need to protect the victims of their offences. For example: a woman who persuaded someone to throw a firebomb into the house of a former partner was made subject to a probation order excluding her from her home county; women who set fire to property, endangering the lives of neighbours, were required to leave their tenancies; some women who had committed offences against their own children were removed from the household. In other cases, accommodation depended on employment. For example, a woman who defrauded the property company which supplied her accommodation was dismissed and evicted.

> Alma was then bailed to her maternal grandmother's address. It seems Alma was then very trying, and eventually set light to her grandmother's curtains…She then had to be found alternative, bed and breakfast accommodation prior to her eventual trial. (Case notes)

> Thankfully, Collette's behaviour was discovered before any permanent harm was done to her child. As a result of this [she] has now been taken out of the environment where there could be any further threat to life. (Case notes)

Revolving Around Drugs and Alcohol

A focus on the underlying causes of women offenders' homelessness risks obscuring an appropriate consideration of their lifestyles, bearing in mind that temporary, insecure accommodation and, for a number, living rough or semi-rough was a pervasive aspect of their lives. For some women, this lifestyle took primacy over other parts of their lives. This was particularly noticeable in their subordination of parenting obligations to expenditure of time and money on drugs and fast living, but also reflected on other responsibilities, for example, for rent payment and respect for the privacy and safety of co-residents and neighbours.

> Alison said that she was concerned for Katie at the moment—e.g., Mary doesn't get food in, so Katie isn't being fed properly when she stays at the weekend. (Observation notes)

> She moved to London aged 22. This marked the beginning of her lifestyle revolving around drugs and alcohol. She financed this by prostitution and begging. She slept rough and in temporary accommodation. (Case notes)

Such a lifestyle carried considerable risks, particularly for women. In a number of accounts of events in women's lives, the close connection between victimisation and offending was abundantly clear. Many had been involved with aggressive and exploitative men, as partners, pimps, punters and drug dealers, who contributed to their victimisation at the same time as encouraging their participation in crime.

> After leaving home and living rough on the streets of London, Davina describes numerous incidents of being sexually propositioned and indecently assaulted. She describes these events as happening daily and often involved people she thought she could trust. (Case notes)

> She is adamant that she had no prior knowledge as to the dealers' intentions and that she obtained no financial recompense for her

part. Indeed, she says she was threatened and physically forced to co-operate [in the robbery]. (Case notes)

Women's criminal convictions often reflected this lifestyle, including offences of carrying offensive weapons (often for self-protection), begging, bilking, drunkenness and soliciting. Several women participated in a street drinking culture, which attracted police attention for a variety of associated behaviours, including drunkenness and begging. Some had developed skills in obtaining money from neighbours and members of the public by feigning a domestic crisis.

Women accustomed to street life often displayed ambivalence towards it. Despite its risks, it carried a number of connections and attachments, which they continued to value. For some, the connection was simply geographical, in that in order to visit family, they had to return to the neighbourhoods in which they had lived, made drug and criminal connections and offended. For others there remained ties that continued to pull them back to the streets. Equally, aspects of settled living appeared at times more problematic than the street life to which they had become accustomed. For example: one woman continued a relationship with an exploitative, abusive male partner while in residence at the hostel, becoming increasingly resistant to staff requests that she spend significant portions of the day on the premises, which were made in an effort to protect her. Some women, even while attempting to sever connections with their street lifestyle, found themselves recognised and approached by previous acquaintances, thus perpetuating relationships and drug connections. For these women, there was a continuing struggle for primacy between the conventional lifestyle to which they might aspire, yet was an abstract ideal, and their previous lives, which, though difficult, were real and familiar.

There was one man in particular that Davina wanted to find: 'He was good to me when I was on the street. He looked after me—no funny business, though. He was the one who persuaded me to go back to hospital when I ran away…I just want to find him and say, "Thanks for being kind, a friend".' (Observation notes)

AFTER A WHILE SHE FELT HATRED

> Nina describes her childhood as being dominated by her mother's alcohol problem, which has affected the whole family. Over the years, she has had to take responsibility for her mother and, in recent years, their roles have been reversed to a great extent. Her mother is described by Nina as a reasonable person when sober and an abusive, intolerant, demanding person when under the influence of alcohol. Nina cares a lot for her mother, she has always been supportive and hoped that her mother would curtail her drinking. (Case notes)

How might we understand the psychological transition from a caring, responsible daughter into a woman who would attempt to kill her mother? The foregoing examination of the connections between women's personal and social problems and problematic, often self-damaging, yet purposeful behaviours facilitates a richer insight into their offending. As we have seen, their offences often appeared to erupt spontaneously from chaos and confusion in their personal and social experiences. Nevertheless, it is possible to understand how they offered apparently viable solutions to their problems.

Revisiting the accounts of women's turbulent histories, several distal themes that appear repeatedly in the women's histories can be seen to have potential explanatory value for their offending. One of these, as indicated in the above extracts from Nina's case notes, concerns the long term impact of severely distorted relationships during childhood on subsequent relationships, lifestyles and perspectives on self, others and events. While it does not follow that such experiences *caused* their offending in adulthood, one consequence may have been to blur the boundaries, in the women's perceptions, between normal and egregious behaviour. Some records suggest that trauma assumed the status of normal experience in women's lives.

> Alma has made several allegations of sexual abuse against her own family, and also against foster parents. Subsequent investigations were unable to establish that in these instances any sexual assault had been perpetrated. However, there have long been concerns that

149

Alma puts herself at risk sexually. In 1991, a man was convicted of indecent assault on Alma and sentenced to a term of imprisonment. Of this period in her life, Alma told me, 'I was just experimenting, finding out about life.' She seemed to find nothing remarkable in her experiences. (Case notes)

Thus, these women had been subjected to experiences in which they had learned that violence and trauma was a normal part of existence, and, moreover in which role models of caring and responsible behaviour towards others were largely lacking. In this environment, they failed to acquire the habit of considering the welfare, rights and feelings of those who would become their own victims.

Grace's overwhelming preoccupation is with her own needs and experience and her own perception of herself as the victim…This, together with her apparent lack of comprehension about the suffering and damage caused to her son, can probably best be understood in the light of her own very damaging life experiences. (Case notes)

Maude has been convicted of two very serious offences, the consequences of which could have been devastating. It is concerning that she minimises her involvement and the consequences of her behaviour, seeking to blame others and taking the 'victim' role for herself. (Case notes)

Their failure to connect with the perspectives of others, combined with their prioritisation of personal needs, produced the apparent recklessness of many women's offences, which, understood from this vantage point, now appear as problem-solving strategies.

She states she set fire to her own mattress in an attempt to draw attention to her predicament and she had not thought through the consequences of such actions in terms of endangering life. (Case notes)

The impact of abusive, coercive relationships in adult intimate partnerships, can also be seen both in direct relation to offending, as well as in the psychological precursors to it.

> She took an overdose and when she realised that was not enough to kill her, she cut both her wrists…This also, she realised after a while was not proving fatal and she wondered why. 'I'd said my prayers for my children, taken my razor, seen the blood everywhere, said I'd got to a better place than this. I'd vomited and thought that was the end of it, but it wasn't.' She wondered if that was because she had not taken [her son] to the 'better place', but left him to go through the hell she had been through with a drunken father and the dreadful prospects he had, as she then thought, in store for him. 'I thought, if I was going to a better place, I ought to take my child with me.' (Case notes)

> She was 'worn down' by his persistence and violence. He broke into her house when she refused him entry. He 'ordered' her to commit the offences and assaulted her when she refused. He drove her and parked out of sight, telling her which house Mary should approach…When she returned home without the money he assaulted her; he put her in casualty at least once. He also began to insist that her 10-year old daughter stayed with him to ensure her return. (Case notes)

A further theme to emerge in the histories of these women was traumatic, sometimes serial loss. Again, these experiences did not in themselves cause the onset of offending, but poorly resolved grief or shock led some women to adopt maladaptive coping strategies that heightened their vulnerability both to criminal lifestyles and to victimisation. This theme appeared strongly, but not exclusively, in the backgrounds of women whose criminal careers commenced relatively late in life.

> She became pregnant aged 18. Her daughter had to undergo a number of operations and died aged three after another major operation…Sonia found it hard to cope with her emotions. Many of her

friends were using heroin so it was easy to get hold of. She used it to help dull her feelings. (Case notes)

When the baby was three years old, his father hanged himself. Ada was shaken by this and began to drink heavily—up to two bottles of vodka a day. During this time, her father began to come to her flat, bringing alcohol. It was at this time that sexual intercourse took place. She said that this stopped when she was 32, and that she despises her father and blames him for her drink and drug problems. (Case notes)

As we have seen, these women were frequently isolated from support networks other than those acquired through substance misusing and street lifestyles, leaving them with few alternative sources of help during times of particular stress. The following accounts suggest that risky, damaging or illicit behaviours learned under pressure could become central coping strategies at times of crisis, increasing exposure to and involvement in criminal lifestyles:

'I was forced into loitering years ago. When I got into rent arrears, I went back into it. Last year I did it again because I stayed at a hostel where they wouldn't take housing benefit'…She has no previous convictions. (Case notes)

Indeed, the following narratives suggest an affinity between self-damaging and antisocial behaviours, indicating that some women perceived no clear boundaries between them:

Candice…said that she had a drink problem and that when she drank she became a lot more violent, boisterous and aggressive. She used to drink with a friend. They [would go] on a spree of smashing anything they could get their hands on with hammers…She said that she virtually always got this way when she drank, never getting happy off alcohol but getting down and upset, which led to her cutting up and then drinking more. (Case notes)

152

Between 1994/1997, Davina admits to receiving numerous cautions and convictions for being drunk and disorderly, self-harming [cutting arms], causing minor damages to property and being aggressive towards the police whilst under the influence of alcohol. (Case notes)

Similarly, anger was a diffuse, perpetuating emotion for several women, and was vented independently of the specific events and individuals that provoked it, or was fixed on inappropriate targets.

[She] had been drinking cider when she suddenly felt very angry. She attributed this anger to the association of the flat itself with a recent experience of sexual exploitation and she decided to set fire to it. She put papers on foam filled armchairs and lit them, which in turn led to the chairs bursting into flames. This relieved her angry feelings and she described pleasurable fascination by the sight of the flames. (Case notes)

Ilona bore considerable resentment towards her father for his behaviour towards her mother when she was a child, and for her perception of him as a cruel and dangerous man who had abandoned her and her family. She also developed a powerful dislike of her stepmother and began to make connections between the presence of her stepmother and her mother's death...[She] broke into her father and stepmother's flat and ransacked it, flooded it and broke up furniture. (Case notes)

Anger, combined with despair of any relief from unhappiness, gave rise to powerful motivations to end it through destruction. Even for women who generally restrained their anger, the presentation of an easy opportunity could remove the last barrier to its expression.

The offence was not planned...When [her mother] [who had been drinking excessively] asked her to help her 'end it all', she was reluctant to do so, but after a lot of persuasion, she gave [her] the blades. After further discussion, [her mother] lay down and put her wrists out for Nina to cut, which she did. (Case notes)

153

She said that when trying to look after him, 'I was afraid of going under. It was like being in a dark room. I couldn't cope. I couldn't stop crying. I was too proud to admit I could not cope and I wanted to stop him crying.' After a while she felt hatred towards her son, because she was so humiliated when she could not stop him crying, but he would stop instantly when either her father or mother picked him up…Collette does not say that she actually wanted to kill her son, although I think her meaning is fairly clear when she says she knew that, if she did hold her hand over his face for long enough, he would die and that she did want to stop him crying permanently. (Case notes)

There are indications in some accounts that some women dissociated themselves from their behaviour, in a manner that may have been a learned response to childhood abuse (Herman 1992).

She set fire to her incontinence pads and plastic bags on the floor. They did not flame, but she ran out of the room…She states that there was damage to three feet of carpet and that she left the premises without checking to see whether the fire was out and without mentioning it to any of the other residents…She stated, 'It was as if it wasn't me, but someone else inside of me.' (Case notes)

She told me that she does not regard herself as having done the offence and is hurt by being told that she is not a good mother and by her son turning against her…[S]he said that she had no recollection of committing the offence…Grace says that when shown the video of the offence by the police she did not recognise herself and that she thought what she saw was disgusting. (Case notes)

Indeed, in some cases the offence appeared to offer a mechanism for generating an emotional charge among women who were chronically detached from their feelings.

The offences for which she is serving this custodial sentence involved forging signatures on credit card receipts and cheques. She described having feelings of a sense of achievement when she committed these offences and elevation...The moments of highs she experienced while offending were anomalies in her otherwise depressed state. (Case notes)

CONCLUSION

This chapter has exposed the complexity of the relationships between women's experiences, survival strategies, lifestyles, offending and rehabilitation. The women passing through the Griffins Society hostels were multiply disadvantaged in ways that enhanced their vulnerability both to homelessness and to crime. Distal experiences contributed to this in a variety of ways: weakening the potential for family and kinship support; providing a social learning environment in which stability through relationship was not to be expected; blurring the boundary between normal and egregious behaviour; and disrupting the capacity for empathy.

Early relationships continued to threaten progress in rehabilitation in adult life. Similarly, adult intimate and parenting relationships were poor guarantees of security. The formal services from which these women might have expected support had frequently failed them. The women had relatively small prospects of substantial improvement in their quality of life, in which poverty, homelessness and insecurity were pervasive features.

Within this context, women developed a variety of survival strategies, which, while they may have achieved short-term success in alleviating painful and distressing experiences, also had longer-term consequences that weakened their capacity for self-advancement. Moreover, these behaviours interfered with their motivation and ability to succeed in rehabilitation opportunities. Yet, they were not easily abandoned or unlearned. Indeed, self-damaging behaviours could be transformed into tools for manipulating the environment and relationships to achieve specific goals. Thus, women's responses to rehabilitation services, even when these were of high quality, often appeared as acts of sabotage.

The women's offences similarly reflected the behaviours and perspectives that had developed in the context of a toxic environment of recurrent turbulence and trauma. They frequently represented the pursuit of short-term goals to relieve immediate pressures, in which consideration of

155

the impact upon others was submerged in the prioritisation of personal needs. In this way, women for whom victimisation had been formative developed the capacity themselves for cruelty towards and endangerment of others.

Thus, the women experienced a complex mix of contradictory ambitions, both to extricate themselves from their plight and to retain what remained of the familiar relationships and positive features of their lives. Successful extrication would also require huge effort in developing alternative coping behaviours from women with few personal and social resources. Rehabilitation opportunities did not provide an easy route out of difficulty and, in some respects, offered further losses as their price for success. These losses of relationships, coping strategies and familiar environments were frequently more obvious and tangible than the promise of advancement to follow. Thus, a hostel resident reflected, in interview:

> All the things that I thought I wanted when I was in hospital…, like independence and the opportunity of going back to work—I wanted it *all* the second I moved in. Now I realise it's nowhere in sight and probably never will be. That was the *worst* day, [when] I realised that this is only the first step, isn't it? Just moving in. I wanted it all the next day. Now that reality's hit me. That was my *worst* day.

Chapter Six

Rehabilitation in the Real World

*Davina was drunk and cutting her arm in front of staff in an aggressive manner, asking, 'Is **this** deep enough for you?' (Case notes)*

This chapter draws on what has been already learned about the staff and residents of the Griffins Society hostels to illuminate practice within the projects. As we shall see, while dramatic events are graphically described in the accounts of staff, good practice as it was enacted on a daily basis had a more modest, understated quality. It thus requires careful, appreciative analysis. Moreover, rehabilitation has commonly been portrayed, through evaluation studies of special programmes, as the delivery of measured, specific, pre-planned inputs (Farrall 2002). Yet, the reality within hostels is that the rehabilitative enterprise is, paradoxically, both continuous, occurring throughout each and every day, and piecemeal, drawing its inspiration from immediate, often unscheduled contingencies for the material from which to craft the change effort.

We begin by examining the influence of the legacy of residents' prior experiences, described in Chapter 5, on hostel life. We then move to consider the rehabilitative endeavour, in the context of both mundane and egregious events.

I'VE GOT A WICKED STREAK IN ME

Nadine explained to me that she still wasn't sure whether she wanted to be at Special Care House or not: 'I know that if I'm in my own place, I can get lonely and get in a bad way with the drinking and all. But it's *hard* being here. If you're used to having your own place, it's *hard* having staff telling you what to do and when to do it.

157

It's *hard* living with some of this lot [other residents] too.'
(Observation notes)

We begin by exploring the everyday environment of the projects in terms of the emotional tensions that underpinned women's behaviour within them. These tensions arose in great part from the legacy of women's prior experiences of personal relationships, social problems, and rehabilitation attempts. Indeed, the ambivalence that characterised their perspectives on their rehabilitation opportunity permeated many aspects of hostel life. The women simultaneously resented their placement and feared failure. Nadine, whose doubts are recorded above, refused to relinquish her tenancy of a flat, not only because of her reservations about the project itself, but also as a safety net in case she was unable to sustain her efforts there. Women did not enjoy their dependence on hostel staff, seeking constantly to distance themselves from processes of—as they perceived it—infantilisation.

Simone was not happy about having to go to staff for her medication. I have heard her say, 'I feel like a bloody *kid*, having to come to you asking for what's mine.' [Staff] think that she has particular problems because she is so much older than the other residents and the staff. [Staff] talked to her about the 14-day trial of coming on time and not refusing any medication, but Simone was still unhappy, feeling she was being treated like a child. (Observation notes)

Sal was in a quiet mood today. When [a staff member] asked her if she was OK, Sal got annoyed. She complained to me that the staff will always ask her if something is wrong when she's being quiet: 'Sometimes I'm just not in the *mood* for talking. It doesn't mean anything's *wrong* with me, but they don't leave me *alone...Why* can't they just *understand* I don't always feel like talking?...How would *you* like living here? You get no privacy. *Questions* all the time.' (Observation notes)

A disconcerting manifestation of the resentment inspired by the women's dependence on external resources for their survival was an unnecessary frankness about the public labels applied to their status, or about their personal difficulties, intended to embarrass the listener.

I was in the garden with Sal and Gloria, talking about haircuts, as Sal was about to visit the hairdresser. Gloria told me that she used to have very long hair and showed me the photo in her travel card…Sal said, 'We get free travel, you know. It's because we're officially *disabled*. Anyone with mental health problems, like us, gets a free travel card, because they think we're *disabled*.' She looked directly at me, which is something she doesn't do very often. (Observation notes)

We talked a lot about her going horse riding…Davina also told me she had fed the birds in the square outside the house earlier. I said, 'You really like animals, don't you?' Davina turned and looked directly at me (which is very unusual): '*Why* did you say that?' I said, 'Because you often feed the birds. You've been talking about the horses that you like, how you think they deserve treats when you've been riding them…You seem very fond of them.' Davina looked away: 'Oh, right, yeah. Well, yeah, OK then. But I've got a *wicked* streak in me. But I ain't gonna say no more.' She paused for a matter of seconds, then told me how she used to harm animals if she got angry or upset…She had done things like shut chickens in a hot oven. She gave a small laugh when she told me this and gave me a sidelong look: 'I *did*, you know. They'd run about inside and stuff.' But, she said, she wouldn't do it now, partly 'cos someone did something similar to me and it made me think about how they felt'…The conversation moved on to something unimportant like whether there was enough milk to last the day. (Observation notes)

Davina's confession of cruelty was perhaps only partially motivated by an urge to shock an unsuspecting listener. Such unnecessary disclosures were also linked to a poor appreciation of personal boundaries. Despite their resentment of staff intrusion, women often displayed a lack of concern about their privacy that could discomfit the onlooker. For example, at Halfway House, residents used a payphone situated in the hallway, where it was common for conversations about personal affairs to be conducted audibly. This lack of personal boundaries reflected the normalisation of trauma within the women's experience. It often appeared that they perceived little distinction between a discussion of mundane trivia and of deep dysfunction. Light conversations were often infused with candid disclosures of personal problems.

> We talked about clothes. Nadine said, 'I suppose I'm lucky, really. Because I'm so small, because I'm anorexic, I can fit into children's clothes. So, that makes it a lot cheaper. I *do* eat. I just don't eat very *much* and I tend to eat the same things. I'm on Pot Noodles at the moment. Are you hungry? Would you like one?' (Observation notes)

> I was sitting with Gloria, Kirsty, Nadine, and Davina in the kitchen. Davina was waiting for her medication. They started talking about their medication. The pattern and tone of their conversation was idle chatting: 'What are you on at the moment?…Oh yeah, I've had that. I put on loads of weight with that, have you?…I didn't like that, it made me feel really dozy. How many milligrams are you taking?' Gloria saw me looking from one to the other of them and joked, 'If *you* tried to take my meds, you'd be *dead*! You wouldn't be able to cope with the levels!' I felt that Gloria was trying to find a way to include me in the conversation. Nadine said, 'I knew a bloke who tried to top himself with [his medication].' Davina asked, 'Did it work?' Nadine replied, '*Nah*, of *course* not. *Kate* here might be out of it for a while if *she* took what he did, but it wasn't enough to kill *him*. He did puke all over himself, though. Maybe he didn't take them all in. I don't know.' The tone was still chatty when they went on to talk about their own suicide attempts. Nadine asked, 'Have *you* ever tried to top yourself, Davina?' Davina said, 'A while ago. I saved up some pills, but it didn't work. I wouldn't do it now, though. There was this woman I found when I was in hospital—we shared a room. I'd *told* staff she was really bad, but they didn't do anything.' There was a chorus of 'when do they ever?' Then, Davina continued, 'I found her. I thought she was dead, but she wasn't. So, I called the staff. It was difficult, though, because she *wanted* to die. She *asked* me, before she did it, to turn my back. [But] I thought I might get in trouble if she died. *I* wouldn't do it though. Not now.' Gloria

160

said, "No. I wouldn't *now.*' Nadine asked if she'd tried before. Gloria said, 'Oh, *yeah*. When I was younger.' The casual way in which she said this was very sad. Nadine said, 'What, pills?' Gloria said, 'Yes.' Nadine said she'd tried in the past, but didn't think she'd do it now. Then she looked up and said, 'Unless you count *anorexia* of course. They reckon I may kill myself with *that*. But that's not quite the *same* now, is it!' She laughed as if she'd just told a joke. Davina said, 'I'll see if they're ready for me *yet*.' The others all joined her in complaining about having to wait around for staff. (Observation notes)

Yet, on other levels, women were deeply afraid of having their difficulties exposed. Many lived with the constant embarrassment of having their incompetence displayed in public.

Tara was anxious about cooking a meal. She explained that she hadn't cooked in years. She didn't know what to cook or how to do it. Also, she didn't have much money, so it couldn't be expensive. She wanted to buy enough for the meal [for her boyfriend] and for the day afterwards, but didn't want anything that would spoil as she was going away for the weekend. She asked my advice. At one point, she ran upstairs to get a file from a pre-release cookery course she had done in prison. We looked through it to get some ideas, wrote out a menu and a shopping list. I also wrote down how to prepare and cook the meal. We had nearly finished when Debbie came down. Debbie was going to take Tara shopping. Tara had tried to go shopping a couple of days before, but 'just *couldn't*. I just *couldn't*. I had to come away again.' She felt overwhelmed by the supermarket and had no idea what to buy…Tara kept apologising for what she saw as her incompetence: 'This must sound really *stupid*. I'm sorry.' (Observation notes)

In this context, rehabilitation was experienced as a device for the exposure of weakness, rather than constructive help.

Deanna was a frequent visitor to the duty office. She was generally quite boisterous, but would also come to voice complaints. She resisted joint interviews with the two deputy wardens. When we did have a meeting with her, she found it very painful and withdrew into herself. She claimed that two of the female staff could 'see straight through' her and this made her wary of contact with them. (Case notes)

Whilst rehabilitation required honest self-disclosure in order to achieve its purpose of enabling the women to tackle their problems, they were nevertheless anxious that the effect of exposure would be to jeopardise their placement. Thus, they struggled constantly between the options of self-disclosure and concealment, in situations where the appropriate choice often seemed unclear.

Whilst we were waiting for the firework display, a man came over and asked Kirsty, 'Do you know what crack is? Someone just asked me if I wanted some, but I don't know what it is. Do you know?' Kirsty glanced at [the staff member] and said to the man, 'I *don't* know what it is. Even if I *did*, I wouldn't *want* any of it. I've been told to *stay away* from things like that now.' Her comment seemed to be very much aimed for [the staff member's] benefit. The man persisted…Talking to me later, [the staff member] wondered if the man recognised Kirsty from the streets, as he had gone straight up to her and directed all his comments at her. (Observation notes)

One mechanism for dealing with fear of failure was for residents to predict it openly, inviting yet rejecting staff members' attempts at reassurance.

Simone then said, 'Don't be too concerned about me, I'm just having a good moan!' [The manager] joked, 'Well, at least you're honest about it!' Simone replied, 'Oh, I'm *always* honest. When you kick me out of here, you'll be saying, "Whatever else you say about Simone, she was always *honest*".' [The manager] immediately challenged her: 'When we kick you out? That's *not* going to happen,

162

Simone.' Simone replied, 'Oh, it *will*. You just wait and see. I won't mind too much. I'd rather live on the streets than here, anyway. You've got your freedom on the streets, haven't you? Not like here.' [The manager] asked her why she thought they were going to kick her out. Simone replied that they were bound to, it was just a question of time. [The manager] continued to challenge her by restating that they had no intention of kicking her out...[Moreover]: 'Living on the streets wouldn't really be a good alternative to living here, would it, Simone? Think of the cold. It's *cold*. It's *wet*. It's *November*.' Simone replied, 'Well, yeah. I'll give you that. The weather's not great. But in Spring, I'll be out of here. If I'm not kicked out already, I'll be leaving.' (Observation notes)

Women often reacted precipitately under such stress. The potential for inducing a crisis that would ensure their eviction, noted in the last chapter, was an ever-present opportunity that could later become a source of regret.

Davina went home [one] weekend and did not return. Her care team said that, as she was a voluntary resident, she was not required to stay at Special Care House, so they could not force her to come back...Staff still have some contact with her: she phones up and says that she made a mistake and wants to move back into Special Care House. (Case notes)

Anxiety about incompetence also contributed to an apparent lethargy in residents' demeanour. Their scarce personal and material resources for self-generated activity, however, also fed their apathy.

Debbie said that she always wakes up about 8-9 a.m. Unless she has to go out and do things, she stays in bed until 11 a.m.-ish, thinking about what to wear etc.: 'But if I haven't got anything to do, I'm not going to go out and wander the streets just for the *sake* of it.' She's having her wisdom teeth out soon. She said she never got around to making appointments...She smiled and said she guessed she *could* register with the doctor [a couple of roads away] when she didn't have anything else to do, but doubted she'd be bothered to get around to it. (Observation notes)

Some women connected their inactivity to the legacy of their institutional experiences.

Tara talked to me about how bored she was. She has no work, no money, nothing to do. She said that her room was a tip, but she couldn't be bothered to tidy it up: 'It's hard to get motivated when you're feeling like this…Prison makes you *lazy*.' (Observation notes)

At a deeper level, however, inactivity appeared to be linked to an inability to envisage a positive future.

Tam…has now been offered two opportunities by the Court to demonstrate her motivation to change and her willingness to accept the help and support that is available to her…[S]he has not yet been able to take advantage of [them], remaining deeply fatalistic about both her short and long-term future. (Case notes)

Joleen experienced some difficulties coping emotionally with her new situation—she often appeared overwhelmed by the thought of her whole life stretching ahead, with little idea of how she wanted to spend it. Joleen was able to make friends, visit her GP and local DSS office, but, on the whole, found it difficult to structure her day and to pursue possible pastimes independently. (Case notes)

Pessimism and lack of personal agency have been observed among recidivist offenders (Farrall 2002; Maruna 2001). In this context, much of the appearance of apathy might be more usefully understood as a manifestation of both immediate and long-term stress.

At about 12 noon, Alison knocked on the office door, wondering if she had any post. There wasn't any for her. She wasn't dressed and didn't look very good—tired and drawn. (Observation notes)

Sal's review panel meeting ended. Initially, I wasn't sure whether or not Sal had been in the meeting, because she was wearing her pyjamas. She often doesn't get dressed until fairly late in the day. (Observation notes)

Unfortunately, the agencies upon which they relied for their rehabilitation often fed the women's lethargy. For example, attempts to overcome anxiety about specialist treatment were not guaranteed a favourable response.

Lorna was being referred to a drug resource, but she was apprehensive because of all the other people there. She said that she would prefer to have in-house sessions with [staff]. She attended the drug project, but they decided they were unable to offer her anything, due to her mental health needs. (Observation notes)

There was a perverse incentive to remain unemployed during residence at the projects, built into the inevitability of low wages.

Tara explained to me that she needs and wants to work, but she can't, because of the high rent at Halfway House. She said that she needed to work to give her motivation to get up in the morning and to give her day a structure. She was concerned that she would end up drifting through days without doing much if she wasn't working. Several of the other residents have expressed very similar feelings. (Observation notes)

Moreover, the bureaucratic inertia that characterised a number of such agencies frequently left even highly motivated women with little option but to await changes that were beyond their control to instigate (see Farrall 2002).

Melanie was nominated, in November, for rehousing…She was allocated a one-bedroom flat, but there have been long delays waiting for it to be redecorated. She doesn't want to request different accommodation, in order to move out of Halfway House more quickly, because she would risk being allocated a bedsit instead of a flat…Melanie's resettlement was 'imminent' before I came to Halfway House. [She was still waiting one year later.] (Observation notes)

[The manager] felt that custody might well be the safest place for Mary just now: 'At least she'll be able to access support services such as the [drug free] wing at Holloway.' People in the community have to wait a long time: the drug project that Halfway House uses has a waiting list of two months. Mary was referred, but relapsed long before the first appointment. (Observation notes)

Despite their own reluctance to venture beyond a narrowly circum-scribed sphere, residents took what opportunities presented themselves to vent their frustration at enforced idleness. Inevitably, staff offered the easi-est targets for their impatience.

I waited with Sal and Gloria in the kitchen. They were impatient with staff. Sal kept checking what the time was. Gloria was up and down, knocking on the office door, asking when they were leaving. They were also waiting for their entertainments money. As usual, they were impatient to have their money. They disliked having to hang around in the kitchen being kept waiting. It was common to hear comments such as 'What are they *doing* in there?' and 'Are we *ever* going to leave?' (Observation notes)

Women's moods could alter unpredictably. Within the hostels, this undercurrent of turbulence, induced by volatile mood swings, was a constant source of uncertainty. As we shall see, their capacity for anger was not to be underestimated. However, their rage could dissipate equally rapidly. Women seemed at times to recover their equanimity as quickly as they lost it.

I was alone in the office when Simone came in. She had come to check her post. I asked, 'Are you glad to be back after the long jour-ney?' Simone shouted back, '*No*! I'm fucking *not*! Cos this place *stinks*, along with everyone in it!' She pushed past [the manager] who had reappeared…Only half an hour later, Simone came in with a letter about her Disabled Living Allowance claim. She seemed happy enough and smiled at me. [The manager] said, 'Kick her out while you make your call.' Simone said to me, 'Go on, then. I'm officially kicking you out!' (Observation notes)

Maude was often a little distant with me. [The manager] explained that if Maude was annoyed with one professional, she would often take it out on any authority figure available. This fitted my experience: Maude would often ignore me one day, the next she'd be offering me bacon sandwiches and cups of tea, wanting to chat for ages. (Observation notes)

A manager who intervened in a violent encounter between residents, also remembered the aftermath:

She bought me some silk flowers, which I have in my house to this day. She bought them the next day to say she was sorry. I always keep them and think: 'This is the person who would have *killed* me!' But then the next day, she realised it wasn't me that she had [the argument] with. She said afterwards, 'I don't know why you got in the way.' But I said to her, 'I couldn't allow you to stab somebody else'…Three days later, they're friends!

At times, women's mechanisms of conflict avoidance were as problematic as their open rage. This was particularly true in Special Care House, where self-harming was a routine strategy among the women for stress management. Isolation was a common strategy, yet carried negative consequences.

Davina said that she is being pestered by two residents for loans of money, and is finding it difficult to refuse. She expressed her annoyance at the situation, and said that recently she has been handling it by isolating herself in her room. [She] then came to the conclusion that this will not work as one of the residents came to her room the previous night to ask for money…Davina expressed her worry that if she does refuse requests, she will suffer consequences. (Case notes)

Women struggling with problems that, subjectively at least, threatened to overwhelm them at any moment sought immediate solutions to stave off disaster. For example, a relapsing drug problem posed constant challenges to financial solvency:

Alison knocked at the office door…She said that she wanted to pay £10.00 towards her rent. I explained that I did not work for [the organisation] and could not take her money. She pleaded with me: 'If I don't give it to someone *today*, I *know* I'll only spend it. Then I'll be *fucked.*' I repeated that I did not know the procedure for taking rent money. She looked tearful and asked me again, saying she knew which drawer the receipt book was kept in. I replied that I could not go through the drawers, as I did not have the authority to do this, but that I would take her rent money. I explained that…I was only doing it this time because I knew she was under a lot of stress and because she had expected [the manager] to be there. (Observation notes)

Women's stress management strategies also included methods for coping with symptoms of a mental illness. This was not an issue confined to Special Care House, although it was, of course, most concentrated in that setting.

I offered to help Davina cook, but she wouldn't let me near any of the food. 'It's better if *I* cook, because then I know what's gone in it. I know that no-one's trying to poison me.' She was putting the food onto two separate plates: one plate was for her, one was for everyone else. (Observation notes)

These observations offer crucial insights into the women's notions of effective problem solving. In the volatile environments in which they learned their coping strategies, short-term remedies were not only effective in removing immediate obstacles or threats, but were the only type of solution available. Long-term strategies for avoiding abuse, for example, are unavailable to children without independent resources. Similarly, safety on the streets for homeless women depends on quick responses that seize upon immediate situational opportunities for escape, deflection or pre-emption. Survival itself, under such conditions, demands maximisation of immediate opportunities and resources. In such conditions, it is perhaps small wonder that offenders may possess few suggestions for strategic resolution of chronic problems (Farrall 2002). Thus, women became strongly attached to their self-management strategies, notwithstanding their inappropriateness in the rehabilitative environment and their ultimately self-damaging effects, because they achieved short-term goals. Longer-term considerations bore little relevance to their needs and priorities, having rarely provided solutions to urgent problems. Their shifting moods further reflected chronic exposure to volatile environments in which pain and pleasure arrived in unpredictable bursts.

Thus, daily life in the hostels was interwoven with the emotional and behavioural legacies of women's prior histories. The result was a mixture of contradictory responses to rehabilitative efforts, in which the emphasis was constantly shifting: dependence versus resistance; self-disclosure versus concealment; attempts at change versus predictions of failure; impatience versus passivity; and knowledge of self-damage versus attachment to learned coping strategies. A hostel resident, in interview, illustrated an aspect of these paradoxes in her own experience of the liberal self-harm policy at Special Care House:

> [Cutting] makes me feel *good*. I feel I'm in control of the situation, although the extent of my cutting has probably got worse since I've had control of my blades in my room. But I don't have so many *desperate* times now, when I could *really* do some *damage*. Cos I know that I can cut whenever [I want to]. But it doesn't make it easier for me to want to stop. Because I *don't* want to stop. I've *dealt* with it for so long, why change?

POISON DRIPPING DOWN THROUGH THE HOUSE

> Suddenly, [a staff member] started laughing. She pointed to the monitor. We all saw Gloria waving her arms about frantically. A bee or a wasp was obviously pursuing her. Then she turned around and ran off. It was a minute or two before she reappeared. She rang the bell to be let in. [The staff member] pressed the intercom button and said, 'Hey, Gloria, bzzzzzzz!' When Gloria came down into the office, she told her we enjoyed her show and laughed some more. Gloria laughed, said the wasp chased her all down the road before she managed to escape. This episode made me think how relaxed the relationship between staff and residents is at times. They often tease and play around with each other. (Observation notes)

Staff revelled in opportunities such as this for light-hearted interaction with residents. This dimension of their relationships with residents was important. Cheerful informality played a crucial role in cementing bonds with women whose moods could be exhausting. Moreover, levity within the projects had a vital significance in affirming everyday normality, in which the irreverence that typifies ordinary human interactions was enjoyed.

> Sal was in a lively mood, being quite playful. She asked how they were going to get from the train station to the Butlins camp. [The manager] told them that [a former manager] might pick them up from the station. Sal joked, 'Great! I liked [her]. She was a really *good* manager. Not like the one we've got now.' She looked at [the manager] and grinned. [The manager] play-acted hurt feelings. (Observation notes)

Similarly, but more consciously, staff capitalised on every moment of success.

> [A staff member] came through the kitchen, gave Simone an envelope: 'Here you are, love. This is for you.' It was Simone's certificate of completion for [the] alcohol users' group meeting. Simone was very pleased with it: 'Oh, I'll have to put it up some-

170

where. I've worked hard for that, you know.' As she opened it, [the staff member] sang 'Congratulations' to her. (Observation notes)

They joked that if they got a large grant, they would go to the Caribbean for their next holiday. [The manager] said something about aiming high: 'If you don't try, you never know what you could achieve.' Sal agreed with her and offered herself as an example. It was her three-year anniversary at Special Care House that day: 'Broadmoor said I wouldn't last three *months.*' [The manager] said, '*Exactly.* You've worked really *hard, despite* what other people told you was possible. You've come a long way and you're nearly ready to be moving on from here. *Congratulations*!' There was a round of applause for Sal and her achievement. Sal then told us that she'd sent a card to Broadmoor saying simply 'I'm still out here!' (Observation notes)

Women accustomed to chronic failure may need to experience success before they can envisage personal change (Maruna 2001). Success was, however, often an expansion of very small achievements, generously reconstructed with hindsight.

As soon as we were off the bus, Gloria started talking about the journey home…She wanted to make sure we didn't leave it too late to get home…We went over to where the firework display would be. There was quite a crowd already. The women stopped behind a few trees. I suggested moving around a bit, as the trees were obviously going to block our view, but they wanted to stay where they were. [The staff member] said, 'I think we'd all be happiest not in the crowds'…Ten minutes into the display, they all started making moves to leave. We walked to the bus stop and waited. I pointed out that we could still see the fireworks from where we were, but none of them was interested. The display was still going on whilst we were on the bus home. I was quite bemused by all this. Before we left, everyone was excited by going to the fireworks. The next day, all the women talked about how much they had enjoyed the display. (Observation notes)

In this context of the need to maximise all opportunities for small successes, apparently simple scenes at the projects are revealed as highly complex.

> [A staff member] was sitting in the kitchen with Lorna and Gloria. She was asking them if they fancied a trip up to town to see the Christmas lights: 'Why don't we make a notice about it? Get *every-one* along.' She got some paper and pens and set them down in front of Gloria: 'Can you write it out for me, Gloria?' Gloria was hesitant to begin with, but [the staff member] encouraged her. She dictated what Gloria should write down, asking Lorna every now and then, 'Does that sound right to you, Lorna?' Whenever Gloria said she had made a mistake or it was messy, she assured her it was fine and complimented her on how neat it was. While Gloria was doing this, [the staff member] asked Lorna to draw a Christmas tree with presents underneath it on another piece of paper. Lorna insisted that she couldn't draw, but [the staff member] said, 'Just do what you can, Lorna. It doesn't have to be a masterpiece. We're all allowed a few mistakes.' She smiled at Lorna. When they had finished, she held up the papers admiringly and asked Lorna to pin them to the notice board. Gloria got up to help her find pins to fix them up. (Observation notes)

> [A staff member] was helping Davina cook. Lorna came in and she said, '*Just* the woman I was looking for! Fancy chopping some vegetables up for us, Lorna? We could *do* with your help.' Lorna was reluctant to join in: 'I'm not very good at cutting. I'm not usually allowed knives. I'll probably just mess it up.' [The staff member] said, 'Well, if you're not very good, then you could do with some practice! *Now's* your chance. Sit down, Lorna.' She gave her the board and vegetables: 'Off you go!' Lorna asked how she wanted the vegetables cut: 'However you want, Lorna. I'll leave it to your choice. They'll taste the same whatever shape they are. Cut little heart shapes if you like!' Lorna grinned and started chopping. Her face was fierce with concentration: 'I've left the ends of things, because I'm a bit shaky. I didn't want to get too close to my fingers.'

[The staff member] said, 'That's *fine*, Lorna. Thanks. Now, Davina, do you think we're ready to put them in?' Davina said, 'Well, *I* don't bloody know! *You're* the one who knows what we're cooking. I'm just standing here stirring. I'll probably mess *that* up and ruin it all.' No matter how many times [the staff member] assured her that she wouldn't ruin the meal and was doing very well, Davina would always criticise herself again. [The staff member] ate with them. Davina ate very little food, pushing it around her plate, saying, 'This is too *much*. What do you think I am – a *pig* or something? I *can't* eat all of this.' [The staff member] merely said, 'Well, eat what you can, Davina. Leave the rest. It doesn't matter if you can't finish it.' Lorna was pleased with the meal and offered me some to try. (Observation notes)

Within these domestic scenes, staff were simultaneously engaged in several different tasks: inclusion; encouragement; education; challenge; reward; conflict management; de-emphasising the dominance of psychological problems; and role-modelling social behaviour. In this context, activities that appeared to be play, or leisure pursuits, were, in fact, demanding work for staff.

She recalled the Christmas before last when they took the women on a trip to the theatre. The residents chose the play and they had a meal afterwards. [A staff member] raised the money to pay for this from charities. [The manager] organised cheap tickets by telling the theatre that they were from a hostel for 'disadvantaged' women - she omitted to tell them that they were offenders. In retrospect, they had a great time, but it was a lot of work…One resident gave a running commentary on the play. They could do nothing to shut her up. After the interval, the seats around the party were all empty. (Observation notes)

At about 2 p.m., the staff came back from the holiday. They all looked shattered! [The manager] asked [a staff member] if they had a nice time: 'Well, I don't think "*nice*" is the word that *I'd* use to describe it!' None of them said very much about it other than it was

173

very demanding and a great deal of work…[A staff member] said that Sal and Gloria were fine, but Simone was very difficult at times. She had walked away from them a few times: 'I think she found it hard being in quite a large group. But I think she enjoyed herself some of the time'…[Later,] I asked Gloria if everyone had enjoyed themselves. She replied: 'Well, *Sal* and *me* did, but I don't know if I'd say *everyone* had a good time.' [It transpired that this holiday brought into focus feuding between residents that was to prove irresolvable.] (Observation notes)

Staff were thus continuously involved in a complex process in which practical and bureaucratic tasks mingled with the need to be responsive to women's personal support needs.

Once the police had gone, I helped [the manager] to clear up the mess in the office. In the middle of our tidying, the phone rang: it was someone wanting to make a referral. Yet again, I was amazed by how [the manager] switches so seamlessly from one issue/task to another. She was perching on the fridge, because her desk was covered in glass, with a dustpan in one hand, yet was still able to give the call her full attention…At about 3.30p.m., the glaziers arrived, after a great deal of persuasion by [the manager], who was very concerned that leaving the window boarded up over the weekend would attract more trouble. Tara arrived back and told [the manager] that she needed to speak to her: 'I had a *shit* day at that social services place.' They went to the lounge to talk. (Observation notes)

Such 'multi-tasking' demanded immense reserves of patience.

[The manager] was evidently snowed under, trying to sort things out for the holiday and to make sure everything would be OK at the project whilst she and other staff were away. Sal knocked at the office door and came in: she wanted to know when the entertainments and food money would be sorted out. [The manager] said, 'I'm working on that right now, Sal. But I've also got other things I have to do before we leave. I *know* it's frustrating for you, but I really am *trying* to go as quickly as I can. So could you just hang on a *little* longer? I'll come and let you know when I've done it.' Sal grumbled a little, but went out. I was impressed by [the manager's] self-control: I'm sure, if I'd been asked the same thing for the umpteenth time, I would have been short with Sal. (Observation notes)

Flexibility was also required for staff to shift pace with residents' mood changes in order to sustain rehabilitation efforts. This could include crisis management until a woman was able to continue with her programme.

28.3.96: Abigail had a few drinks, called the Bail Hostel, was upset and said she felt let down by people, particularly concerning voluntary work. Abigail returned for the pre-arranged meeting with her PO and myself. Abigail was very emotional, obviously under the influence and the meeting, which lasted one and a half hours, was fairly chaotic and difficult. We tried to calm Abigail and create some order to her thoughts and emotions.
29.3.96: We sat and discussed what happened yesterday and the way forward from here. Abigail is much more able to speak about her problems and the help she needs—we agreed a plan of action between now and keyworking. Abigail will write down a list of all the issues she wants to discuss/look at, plus all the practical things she wants to achieve, such as get a passport. Then we can look at the most urgent and tick them off as they are achieved. (Case notes)

Dogged persistence was also a feature of the work over the longer term. There are several examples of staff continuing to work with women, in the face of failure, to attempt to generate alternative placements.

Sadie was a chaotic drug user whilst at Halfway House. She became pregnant and was to be evicted because of this. So, she decided to terminate her tenancy voluntarily. She was very disorganised, kept missing appointments with the Homeless Persons Unit…She was

175

still staying at Halfway House after her tenancy finished, with staff permission—was even staying there the night before a new resident was due to move in. (Case notes)

Equally, residents' contributions of positive help could not go without remark.

> The three of them talked for a while about the broken toilet. Water had been flooding out of it last night. Debbie and Maude had bailed water out. Maude had been concerned about it affecting the electrics, so she called in the emergency maintenance company…[The manager] thanked them for sorting the situation out. (Observation notes)

> Early evening, Davina made pancakes. Most people had one or more. Davina asked if someone would take some up to Sal: 'She'll be pissed off with me if she doesn't get some.' [A staff member] said, 'She *wouldn't* be pissed off at you, Davina. But it's a really *nice* thought that *you* remembered her, when none of us did.' (Observation notes)

A Stockdale House manager reflected on the importance of acknowledging residents' requests for attention in the midst of competing responsibilities:

> Residents who are talking about suicide: this could be day or night. If we don't acknowledge it and spend the time with them, then what they tend to do is go up into their room and do something. I've *never* known of a case *not*. If you say, 'Go away, we're having a team meeting', you can *guarantee* ten minutes later the team meeting will have to stop, because we've got to go to the hospital. They're going to cut their wrists, take an overdose, set the alarms off. So, *why* then let them go through all that process, when you could just *give* them the time, which is what they're asking for? It's inappropriate, because we need to teach them to ask for time appropriately…But, on reflection, when *I* need time is when I *need* it. You can't say to *me*, 'You can't be vulnerable at three o'clock in the morning.'

Such responsivity demanded constant vigilance, as well as rapid changes in focus and emotional tone.

> Davina came into the office for something. [Her keyworker] asked her if she was going to be about in the afternoon. Davina asked, 'Why do you want see me? Have I done something?' [Her keyworker] assured her that she had done nothing wrong: 'I just thought it would be nice to spend some time together.' Davina laughed: 'Why do you want to spend time with *me*? Are you my *allocated* worker today?' This, and her tone of voice, suggested that she didn't believe [the staff member] wanted to spend time with her and thought she had been assigned to keep watch on her. [All the] staff picked up on what Davina had said. They all made sympathetic noises, while [her keyworker] asked Davina to sit down and said: 'We don't work in that way here. It's not like hospital. I wasn't trying to watch over you. I just thought it would be a good opportunity to spend some time with you and get to know you. But if you're busy or don't want to, we don't have to.' Davina said, 'Oh, right. Yeah, I'm about' and left the office. [Her keyworker] went after her. I was struck by how all the people in the office suddenly stopped what they were doing and focussed on reassuring Davina. The atmosphere flipped from general office chatting to addressing Davina's needs instantly. (Observation notes)

For many of these women, such reassurance was required repeatedly. Staff were frequently required to demonstrate considerable persistence in the face of intractable psychological problems, for which there was little hope of substantial improvement.

> [The staff member] estimated that Carla will need stitching every 10 days or so. [The manager] said, 'Her mood swings aren't going to change. They may be lessened a bit by being here, but they aren't going to change significantly.' (Observation notes)

In the end, she deteriorated into a psychotic state and was readmitted. I *tried* to keep her out in the community as long as possible, because she was the sort of person who, once she came in, I thought she wouldn't get out again very easily. That's proved true…The hostel were very *good* about that. They *coped* with her when she was getting worse and worse. It was only when *I* threw in the towel that she came back to hospital. (Psychiatrist)

To work at this level of intensity, in a constantly shifting emotional atmosphere, day after day is a demanding enterprise. Staff, at times, felt drained by the emotional charge that infused mundane activities.

Davina often puts herself down or points out that she is ignored or her views aren't important. Most of the staff challenge her: some-times they will let it ride and say nothing. [Her keyworker] told me how wearing she could be. Other staff have said the same thing either directly or jokingly: e.g., when [a staff member] said she was going to spend the afternoon with Davina, the others laughed and said, 'Good luck!' and 'Rather you than me!' They don't let this atti-tude come across in the way they interact with Davina. But [her keyworker], who appears to me to be very conscientious, admitted to me that sometimes, if she's tired, she will avoid spending time with her alone, because she is so demanding. (Observation notes)

Whenever anyone came into the room, Gloria would ask them if they're all right. She would also ask whoever was in the room. She asks everyone: me, the staff and other residents, [repeatedly] …Gloria was spending a lot of time downstairs in the kitchen. [Her keyworker] thought she was needing to be around people and want-ing company. Staff wondered if it might have something to do with Kirsty having just arrived and Lorna due to come soon: maybe Gloria was feeling threatened, that staff might not have enough time for her. [Her keyworker] said that Gloria has been asking for a lot of keywork sessions and it was becoming quite wearing for her. (Observation notes)

Managing such behaviour required team and individual effort.

> Simone targets one person at a time: they can do nothing right. She'll complain about them to other staff and residents. Then something will happen and she will move on to targeting someone else. This behaviour was discussed in handover, as Simone is complaining about [a particular staff member] at the moment…Simone had said she was annoyed with [the staff member] over medication, complaining that she was being very authoritarian. [The staff member] said the only thing she could think of was that she would read out all the details of the medication, if Simone did not, before she took it. This is something they are obliged to do. [The staff member] asked if everyone else was doing the same thing: 'We've *all* got to be doing meds in the *same* way. We've got procedures we should *all* be following. If we don't we leave ourselves open.' (Observation notes)

Managers constantly encouraged staff to persist in their efforts.

> On a number of occasions I have heard [the manager] ask, 'What has Kirsty got planned for today?' Often the answer was not what she wanted to hear: staff were unsure—'Can you check the diary, then, please?'—or nothing was planned. A few times, I saw her look quite frustrated—but keeping very calm!—saying things like, 'We really need to keep on *top* of the weekly plans. I want them very *tight*, particularly for Kirsty at the moment. I don't want her having time to *drift*. It's very *important* that when they first arrive we're working *closely* with the women.' (Observation notes)

Thus, life in the projects was an emotional roller-coaster that might speed unpredictably through humour and warmth, grief and misery, challenge and hostility throughout the day. Many apparently conventional activities performed by staff were complex and sustained attempts to infuse rehabilitative effort into this volatile environment. At times, however, the impact of a woman's damaged personality evoked strong emotional reactions that permeated staff's responses to her, despite their efforts to suppress or overcome them. A manager from Special Care House recalled:

179

There was one woman…who would *not* let us in at *all*. She would block us out as much as she could. We became the whipping boy. Special Care House is bad, Rampton was good. She'd become low, she'd drink, she would really *worry* us at times. But you couldn't reach her a lot of the time. So we just had to be there for her, talk to her. She'd snap back. But we just had to keep on *trying*. But that's blooming *hard*. One day we were in our staff support meeting. This woman was in the garden having a cigarette. The windows were all closed. One member of the staff said, 'I really, *really hate* her.' Another member of staff said, 'She sits up in the top lounge and her influence is like *poison,* dripping down through the house.' Somebody else said, 'I fucking *hate* her. She's a fucking *bitch*.' That *happened*. There was an *outpouring* of anger and frustration. Then, people said, 'Yes, she *is*. But how are we going to *work* with her?' That was incredibly *releasing*…Thank God, it came out in a supportive environment. It sounds *dreadful* to someone who wasn't part of it. But it was very *releasing*.

I COULD HEAR HER SCREAMS WHEN SHE'D GONE

No change in A-, usual self. Was abusive to staff during the week. (Griffins Society 1990c)

Despite its removal from most of our notions of mundane normality, the foregoing sections describe the emotional tone and its practical conse-quences during everyday life in the projects. The extract above dryly reflects staff's resignation to these conditions. A few examples of incidents recalled by staff as extraordinary clarifies the extent to which their 'base-line' expectations of conventional existence were altered by their experiences. Invited to recount incidents in which they were afraid, or were obliged to call the emergency services, staff offered graphic accounts that are reproduced verbatim here for the emotional impact that they convey, despite some cost to narrative clarity, lost in the dramatic re-living of the moment.

Crises took a rich variety of forms, illustrated in these examples. Perhaps the most predictable, to the outsider, were confrontations between staff and residents. While there is some humour in the following account, the spontaneous invocation of the present tense betrays the lasting impact of this encounter with an aggressive resident on an inexperienced staff member. This 'historic present' featured in many such narratives.

> My *second* day at Stockdale House, a resident came in and said to me that she could use the telephone. I said, 'No, you can't. Cos no-one had told *me* that residents were allowed to use the phone for personal calls'…She said, 'Phone the project manager.' I said, 'No. It's a Sunday afternoon. I'm not going to do that.' She went outside, she got a crash helmet, came back in and said if I don't fucking let her use the phone, she's going to put my head through the window with the helmet. I said, 'OK. Go ahead. Cos when you put *my* head through there, make sure *yours* is coming with me.' She looked at me and thought I was a bit crazy. I said, 'You're damn *right*. If *I'm* going through there, I'm not going without *you*.' As you can see, I was quite small. She was really *big* built…I'm [thinking] if this is a test, then I'm not going to let her get away with it. She *effed* and *blinded* and *fucked* and *sweared*, walked out, threw the helmet down on the floor and says, 'I'm going to *get* you.' I said, 'Whenever you're ready, come.' (Hostel manager)

The obligation to intervene in confrontations between residents was a second source of urgency. Within this account, as in others, can be seen an impressive presence of mind in attending to the immediate consequences of a crisis.

> Two residents were having a fight. So, they had a knife. They were going to stab each other. I decided to get in between. Yeah, it was a bit of a stupid thing, on reflection. But what I felt is that they're not going kill *me*, but they *would* have killed each *other*. What I didn't bargain for was that they were that *angry*. They didn't *care* who they were going to kill. The person who…actually had the knife and held it to my throat…said, 'I've *already* committed murder. I don't really *care* if I go back inside.' She had the knife to my throat. I thought, 'Oh, my *God*. My *daughter's* losing her mother.' I don't know what

happened to her, but then she just dropped the knife. I didn't shake or anything else, just took her upstairs and said, '*Pack*. You're *out* of here.' Really *angry*. Phoned up to try and get her somewhere else. Even though she just did this…we were looking to get her some-where else! Then, after it all finished, I started to shake. Cos I realised the *stupidity* of the whole thing…I was *crying*, like, 'God, my *daughter* could have lost her mother.' (Hostel manager)

The women's lifestyle, and their reluctance to relinquish it entirely, brought danger to the projects. A staff member recalled some black women who were racially abused in the street and gave 'as good as they got':

It was *nightmarish*…All the women had come back in. They were saying, 'Oh, *yeah*. We're *tough*.' They were all gassing and laugh-ing. The next thing, there was this *horrendous* noise in the front door: 'What the *fuck's* that?' We go and see. It's this *punk*…There were three guys. This big black woman, who they'd been racially abusing in the first place, was sitting with us and she goes, 'My *God*! It's *them*!' Suddenly, you see this *axe-head* coming through the door. They were *chopping the door down*…I was on the phone to the police. They ran off. We went downstairs and it was in *pieces*…There was *daylight* through the door…The police turned up and said they'd gone. So, I was hammering this wood back on the door. I just screamed at [the manager], 'My *God*! They've come *back*!' They'd come back again. This time they broke the *window*. We were cowering in the office. They were smashing window, throwing stones through the window. We cowered under the desk, cos glass was shattering around, and called the police *again*. They ran off *again*. I just said to [the manager], 'I *can't* have this.' I went chasing after them. Not to *stop* them. But just I wanted to *see* where they were going. To *show*, so the police would actually *get* them.

Women's propensity for self-harm also precipitated traumatic crises. An administrative officer recalled an occasion on which she was caught up in the aftermath of a serious incident at Special Care House.

The night before, one of the residents had really tried to finish herself off, *hugely*. She hadn't managed to cut her wrists quickly enough, so she jumped off the stairs. In the meantime, to make *absolutely* certain, she'd tied something around her neck and tried to hang herself. She tried just about everything and failed miserably. She signed herself out [of hospital] the next day. She walked in. *Oh, my God*. I *looked* at her. She looked like a British Rail map, with all the stitches. They were *everywhere*. She'd cut her *throat*, she'd cut her *wrists*, she'd cut her *arms*, she had a rope burn around her *neck*. I thought, 'My *God*, how can somebody be *alive?*'…She came in…with a blanket wrapped around her. She came straight into the main office, sat right beside me and wouldn't leave…I couldn't walk out, because she was sitting there holding my hand, even though her keyworker was on the other side of her. I was just getting slowly more *insane*. I could *not* deal with this at all. I couldn't *deal* with the *sight* of her. Yet, I wanted to give her a hug. I thought, 'Don't do that.' Then I thought, 'Well, maybe I *should*.' I did *not* know how to *deal* with her.

On occasions, the arrival of the emergency services served to prolong, rather than to terminate the stress of the event.

She had cut her throat…She came stumbling through one of the doors. There was blood everywhere. A staff member rang 999 and said that this woman had cut herself with a knife. Somehow, that got garbled up, so that the SWAT team—the emergency response unit— [came]…The *helicopter* came, several police cars, an ambulance. Because *they* understood that this woman was *threatening* people with a knife. I'm not sure—maybe I'm being paranoid here — whether the address came up as something that wasn't just [an ordinary] house. But they *all* turned up. Which was *awful* for the staff on duty. It was enough to deal with this *woman*, who was *bleeding* profusely, waiting for the ambulance to come, let alone the *police* piling in. (Hostel manager)

A tragic death at Stockdale House is graphically described in the case notes. After confiding many troubles to the staff member on duty, the resident withdrew to her room:

> Approximately 10 minutes later…I heard some terrific crashes from her room…She had smashed the glass [from the pub] and the light fitting and had walked all over the glass. The floor was covered in glass and her feet were full of big chunks of glass…She broke down and cried in my arms, saying, 'I just can't take anymore'… She regained control and let me clean her feet. She laughed when I suggested taking her to [hospital]…I went upstairs about 20 minutes later, but was unable to get into the room, as she had replaced the 'snip' on the lock…I went outside the front door as far as the gate about 4 times and looked up, to see if [she] was sitting in her window looking out, as she said she had on Sunday night…At half past 4 I heard the sound of someone trying to break into the hostel. I went to the door and found a policeman who asked me if we had a dummy hanging in the room on the first floor.

Some staff, recounting these experiences in interview, displayed symptoms of imprinted traumatic memories:

> I'll *never* forget it. I can *feel* myself starting to shake *now*…I was *still* shaking the next day. I was *desperately* upset. Because I'd heard things that I didn't want to know, but I *never* thought could have *happened*. I couldn't—I *never* thought a person could do that sort of thing to him/her/itself. It totally *threw* me…I remember *every single word* that was said from half past one till…quarter to six.

> Seeing a young Asian girl being sectioned, which was traumatic for her *and* for us who were *watching*. Because police come, social services come, the ambulance staff. She was *dragged, screaming* into the hospital van. I knew that those things *happened*. But to *see* it and *hear* the screams. I could *hear* her screams when she'd *gone*…I [heard] everyone talk about it for *days* afterwards, saying it was really *terrible*, the way she was taken away [in the ambulance] and she was *screaming*.

184

Perhaps more worrying, however, was evidence of the normalisation of trauma. Some staff appeared to have dissociated themselves from the human responses of shock, outrage, revulsion, and fear that such experiences usually inspire.

> Someone with mental health problems throwing everything around the office was a bit scary. Two residents having a fight in the hallway, which I just stood in the middle of, was a bit scary. Then somebody else running around with a knife was a bit scary. But at the time, you just *dealt* with them, do you know what I mean?…They were just…the things that happened that you dealt with. No, I don't think I really got scared. (Hostel manager)

> Afterwards, management said, 'You're shaking. Do you want to go for a walk?' Well, *no*…No, I just want to get back to *work*. Cos I see it as everyday stuff. (Staff member)

CONCLUSION

The emotional currents and behavioural excesses that characterised 'everyday life' in the projects were far removed from most conceptions of mundanity. This should not surprise us. While criminological studies of serious women offenders generally emphasise their relative scarcity in number (see, for example, Rumgay 1999; Steffensmeier and Streifel 1993), the Griffins Society collected them together under five roofs. Such concentrations of damaged and volatile women are rarely found in places other than the secure institutions of penal or psychiatric care.

In the less controlled environment of the community, the women's emotional and behavioural legacies of trauma, failure, and instability provided not only the backdrop to, but also the raw material for the rehabilitative enterprise. Much of the daily practice in the projects hinged upon direct engagement with these manifestations of personal turbulence, rather than the detached processes of clinical analysis and problem-solving therapy that rehabilitation is often assumed to comprise. Where critiques of rehabilitation have sometimes focussed on the tendency of professionals to *talk about* problems rather than to *act upon* them (e.g., Farrall 2002), staff

185

of the Griffins Society's residential projects had no option but to focus on immediate emotional and practical needs. While, as we have seen, these women had survived egregious experiences through applying problem-solving strategies learned in the least propitious circumstances, they were also intimidated by apparently simple conventional activities and social behaviours.

Understood in this context, daily practice within the project can be seen to be a continuing effort to infuse the tasks of everyday life with a normality that was sadly lacking in the residents' prior histories. In this sense, staff may be likened to Lofland's (1969) 'normal-smiths', those 'promiscuous imputers of pivotal normality' (p.213) who persistently communicate to the offender their perception of 'an essential core of normalcy that makes possible the living of a reasonably normal life' (p.215). Without this appreciation, much of the mundane activity within the projects is readily undervalued for its seeming focus on domestic and prac-tical issues, leisure pursuits, and informality between staff and residents.

Recognition of the women's plight, however, exposes the complex-ity and difficulty of each of these tasks within the rehabilitative framework. This, in turn, reveals the depth of stress on staff attempting to instil normal-ity in a confused emotional environment. This alone corroborates their claims to be 'strong women.' Their exposure to traumatic events, however, while admirable for presence of mind in coping with crises of a kind unimagined by most people, also provokes an uneasy awareness of the extent to which their own expectations of conventional normality—at least in their working lives—were altered by their experiences.

Chapter Seven

Desistance and Despair

*I'd never heard anything about a bail hostel before...I'd never even thought about it...So I thought...well it's better than being in prison. So I said, yeah alright, put it across. If I get it, I get it. If I don't, I don't. And I got it. And I really, I was just over the moon. It was like—I don't know, it was just like, my life had changed. I thought, yeah, I got a **chance**. (Former resident)*

We have seen that the groups of women who comprised the Council, staff, and residents of the Griffins Society projects were unusual. We have also tasted daily life within the projects, measured against a backdrop of 'truly' egregious events. But did it work? This chapter explores successful and unsuccessful outcomes of placements at the Griffins Society hostels.

Concepts of success and failure in this context of a turbulent environment inhabited by distressed and potentially dangerous women require careful consideration. Previous chapters, in illustrating the depth and chronicity of women's personal, social, and economic problems, beg questions about what degree and what longevity of change would constitute evidence of the rehabilitative success of temporary residence in supported care. Equally, a fixed criterion for success may be unrealistic, since, by virtue of differences in the intractability of their difficulties, for example due to their mental health status, women may vary in their capacity for change. In such a context, rehabilitation may be viewed as a *process*, rather than a specific outcome; its success may be assessed in terms of the extent to which an individual has been enabled to *progress towards* positive and lasting change (Farrall 2002). Moreover, the influences that promote positive, albeit limited, changes are of as much interest as the attribution of success or failure to a particular outcome.

All professional interviewees were invited to describe instances in their own experience of successful and failed placements at the Griffins Society projects. The criteria by which they judged a placement to have succeeded or failed were of their own choosing, in the light of their knowledge of the case. Professionals were also invited to explain how they would account for the success or failure of the placement. While this approach to evaluation appears to evade the conventional measurement of outcome against an inflexible, pre-determined criterion such as reconviction, in no case did a professional offer an attribution of success or failure that defied plausibility in the context of the case described. Professionals applied pragmatic appraisals of the potential for, and reality of change within the unique circumstances of specific attempts at rehabilitation.

HEAPING PROFESSIONAL ACCOLADES

> The particular client presents a complex variety of the most difficult and challenging behaviour patterns, and the progress she made whilst resident at the Hostel eclipsed that of her previous fifteen years of treatment in various care facilities…[A]ll the individual Hostel Staff members have provided a level of input that in our past and present experience we would normally expect to have to purchase at considerable financial cost, and would still, in many cases be of inferior quality…Apart from heaping professional accolades upon Stockdale House, we would like to emphasise how valuable a resource such facilities as the Griffins Society provide are, and we hope that you are able to maintain and expand your services. (Letter from Forensic Psychiatry Team 1989)

Such effusive praise from high-ranking professionals is not easily won. It speaks to an extraordinary accomplishment by relatively poorly trained staff in the volatile environment of a hostel, which, by virtue of its voluntary status, was the least generously funded of the Griffins Society's projects. Nor was this the only recorded successful graduation of a former Special Hospital patient from Stockdale House. Yet, we must look deeper than assertions of satisfaction with the outcomes of women's residence if we are to understand how the projects were able to produce such results.

Scrutiny of the accounts of success revealed six categories of influence considered by professionals to have contributed to their clients' success: organisational factors; programme structure; emotional support; qualities in the woman's decision making; changes in her lifestyle; and the manner of her departure from the hostel. These categories and their specific elements are summarised in Figure 2. Each bullet point in the Figure represents a factor that was cited by at least one professional as contributing to the success of the hostel placement. At a deeper theoretical level, we will also see that the success of the rehabilitative enterprise depended upon a change in women's preferred personal identities, from offenders to prosocial community participants.

A Safe Environment to Learn Things

> I have worked as a project worker in a hostel. If you don't have a good, supportive manager, when you have the likes of *my* client, then you have a problem...She *must* have been [good], because otherwise the staff *couldn't* have handled my client. She wasn't a pleasant person to work with, she wasn't at all...So the project workers *must* have had good support from the manager to have been able to manage her. (Probation officer)

As the previous chapter revealed, creating a rehabilitative environment that was supportive of change efforts was a feat of organisational mastery. The volatility of hostel life, and the vivid dramas that could unfold within it, were potentially capable of overwhelming therapeutic ambitions. Several interviewees drew attention to this necessary backcloth of organisational integrity to the more eye-catching activities of change production. Thus, some probation officers remarked upon the contribution of the hostel manager to their clients' success. In these accounts, effective managers were highly active and involved in the life of the project.

> She always seemed to me to be very efficient...She would phone me when there was going to be a meeting with the keyworker...The manager at the project seemed to have her finger on the pulse...She obviously took a great pride in the house. (Probation officer)

189

FIGURE 2: ACCOUNTING FOR SUCCESS

Organisational Factors	Programme Structure	Emotional Support	Decision Making	Lifestyle	Departure
• assertive manager	• full assessment	• encouragement and support	• impact of criminal justice system	• abstinence	• progression
• staff commitment	• preparation	• non-judgemental tolerance	• autonomy	• moderated involvement in risky lifestyle	• effective move-on arrangements
• staff supervision	• immediate action	• responded to staff	• perceived alternatives	• stabilised drug use/drinking	• after-care
• size of unit	• attention to special issues	• learned to accept support	• choice of direction	• detached from unhealthy relationship/s	
• created project as opportunity for change	• gender specific	• learned to manage emotions	• education/training	• established healthy relationship/s	
• created project as home	• goal setting	• developed empathy	• employment	• used positive family support	
	• planned change	• enabled to mature	• became active in treatment		
	• staff expectations	• developed sense of belonging	• changed identity		
	• boundaries	• altered self-image	• took responsibility in relationships		
	• consistency		• determination		
	• appropriate level of support		• learned to cope with disappointment		
	• engaged at project				
	• retained at project				
	• anchorage				
	• co-ordination with field supervisor				
	• practical help				
	• persistence				

We have seen that staff were exposed to repetitive challenging behaviour by residents. Effective managers assisted staff to understand and deal with women whose behaviour posed severe challenges to their tolerance. In this way staff were enabled, through the supervision they received, to moderate their perspectives and responses.

> Very careful managing of staff, allowing them to talk through how they felt, then looking at the issues underlying it. Not making decisions in the heat of the moment when everybody wants to *throttle* her…[This resident would] come down to the office *screaming* that somebody had used her shower. She was obsessive about cleanliness. Somebody had used her shower, she's not fucking staying here. She could be quite *intimidating* in her behaviour. It was quite aggressive. But then, looking at her behaviour at that point, she *wasn't* aggressive to anybody. She was just blowing up. Once the staff could see that she wasn't threatening anybody, she was behaving in a totally unpleasant way that would not be tolerated…then we could carry on working with that. So, we'd get her on an anger management course. It would have been easy for the staff to feel threatened and intimidated. But once we cooled things down, *examined* the behaviour, she actually wasn't threatening anybody. (Hostel manager)

Here, then, were practical examples of the manifestation of the qualities of strength and determination that were earlier said to characterise the staff group. Observers of their successful work never doubted staff commitment.

> They gave her committed staff. The women who worked at [the hostels] were partly motivated by concern for the needs of women. So, she probably had a genuine input in terms of concern. (Probation officer)

Within this framework of active management and staff commitment, the projects provided a base for rootless women to begin to progress towards desistance from crime. Certain qualities of the physical accommo-

191

dation and the supportive environment within it enhanced the opportunity for personal development: it was relatively small, it was safe and it provided an opportunity to focus on change without the distractions of survival in disadvantaged circumstances.

> She seems to feel it's a very *safe* environment to learn things. She's tested it. She hasn't been thrown out. She hasn't been rejected. She knows that, however much she screams that she hates it, it's the safest environment that she's *ever* been in. (Staff member)

> She went to college. So, it was successful in that. Because, if you haven't got a home to go to, if all your basics are provided for, then you can *concentrate* on your next step of studying, instead of thinking about mains and gas and kettles. That was all provided. [She] got a base to study from. (Probation officer)

These remarks identify the importance of a framework of stability and personal support within which the process of change can develop. Such a framework was the product of the physical environment, which the Griffins maintained, through their maternal approach, as a comfortable and homely place and the active concern of staff to infuse it with an ethos of safety and optimism. Thus, the provision of an 'opportunity for change' was no simple matter, reducible to bricks and mortar, but rather depended on the management of physical space and social milieu to engender the capacity to *recognise*, as well as to capitalise upon a chance to alter personal life trajectories (Rumgay 2004a). The importance of this setting will become clearer as we study the rehabilitative interactions taking place within it. It facilitated changes in women's emotional self-management, cognitive appraisal of the attractiveness of conventional life and occupancy of social roles that, ultimately, transformed their personal identities in fundamental and positive ways.

We Had To Work Very Hard

> Luckily, her referral was an excellent one that had got lots of background information—psychiatric reports, psychologists' reports,

pre-sentence reports, as well as previous convictions. It gave a very good overall picture. If you bothered to *read* that—which I don't think everyone always does—there is more to the behaviour. The behaviour *is* irritating and if not handled well it can be worse. But if you have an idea of how *she* perceives her situation and how *she* thinks about things, you see what's going on. (Staff member)

Despite the volatility of the hostel environment, accounts of successful outcomes identified elements within the programme that anchored the placement experience to a consistent push for change. In the staff member's remarks above, the ability to carry out a thorough assessment was seen as crucial to moderating ill-informed reactions to a woman's behaviour. Similarly, some interviewees pointed to extensive preparation for the intervention to follow. These accounts point to the complex detail of planning interventions for women with multiple needs.

> We'd already talked about rehabs, sorting herself out. We went to court. The judge said that if we could come back with a package, then he would consider it. So we got her into rehab—it was really *hard*...When we went to court with this package, the judge said that if we hadn't had [it], then she would have got seven *years*. (Hostel manager)

> She was ready. We took a long time getting to know the people that were referred to us...Part of the assessment was that we would spend time with them, going through what makes you sad, what makes you happy, what works, what doesn't work. We wouldn't go into what they were used to, in terms of 'Can you tell me about your offence?', 'When you were sexually abused, could you tell us more?' It was more *practical*. (Hostel manager)

Accounts suggested that active intervention in successful cases began immediately upon a woman's reception. The alacrity with which a woman could be engaged in reform efforts capitalised on the destabilising moment of transition, forestalling reassertion of her former lifestyle. This could be a crucial time: the reflective processes of scene-setting for success

193

in terms of organisational competence, assessment and planning gave way to pro-active rehabilitative effort. Successful practice exploited the disruption to entrenched behaviours that was provoked by entry into the unfamiliar hostel environment, creating an opportunity for change. A former resident graphically expressed the vulnerability of this transition and its implications for rapid intervention:

> The Bail Hostel helped me, because when I first come out I was tempted to start taking drugs again. It don't matter if they say they didn't, they *do*—*everyone* who was taking drugs before coming into prison, as *soon* as they come out, they got a bit of money in their hand, the *first* thing they go and do is go and get some…It's the same old circle. I didn't want that. So, I told them *straight away*, 'I need to go on a script, because I don't feel ready to be out on the street.'

In line with this pro-active approach in successful cases, issues specific to the individual woman's experience received prompt and careful attention.

> She was very high risk. She was attempted murder and other very high risk offences, again related to drugs. She'd been in Holloway for *seven years* and they hadn't known she was a heroin user! She came to us. [After a while] we realised she was using heroin. We managed to get her to disclose that and access some support. That was the beginning of her being able to address that. (Hostel manager)

In a similar vein, a probation officer pointed out the significance of a gender specific response to a woman's legacy of abuse:

> She was 18, sexually abused. She was mixed race, brought up adopted by middle-class white family in a rural area. Very confused about her race as a black person…She was sexually abused very young. She specifically wanted a female probation officer. (Probation officer)

194

Interviewees pointed to goal setting and planned change as significant motivators for stimulating and sustaining effort. Here, we can see the exploitation of women's personal ambitions to lever their participation in changes designed to align their lifestyles with conventional social norms.

> The child had been fostered. It was a big *incentive*. She *wanted* her child back. She knew that the *only* way that she could *get* her child back was to kick the drug habit. So, that was big enough incentive. That set her motivation going. (Probation officer)

In this example, we can see a direct appeal to a woman's identity as a mother, deployed as a tool for challenging her attachment to a conflicting identity as a drug addict. Of particular interest, is the emphasis that many interviewees placed on the demonstration by staff of their own *expectations* for positive change. Staff *demanded* effort from the women. Here we can see 'normal-smithing' (Lofland 1969) in action, as staff communicated their assumption that residents were capable of normative standards of behaviour with such clarity that it became increasingly difficult to refuse to conform.

> We gave her responsibility. As a drug user, and a very chaotic drug user with a very long history, she wasn't given any responsibility in life. *No one* would trust her. So *we* started to trust her, to give her some money to go and purchase items that the resident group had decided they wanted for their lounge…We'd say, 'OK, here's £15.00. I want you to go down to that shop where we've identified that we've seen a rug…and buy it for us'…At the very beginning, there were a couple of mishaps. But we kept *pursuing* it. (Hostel manager)

> We had to work very hard. She was into 'I can't do anything.' She was illiterate and she *wouldn't* do anything for herself. Well, she *said* she was. Actually, it turned out she wasn't illiterate! So, it was a bullying/enabling process with her. We *made* her do her stuff, because she *had* to do it…When she'd gone into her own accommodation, she would have floundered…It's the constant message, 'You

195

can do it.' Making sure that she *would* do it. They would help her. But they would gradually encourage her to do stuff by herself. So she got more confident, then was able to go and live on her own. (Probation officer)

These examples show the manipulation of self-identity in ways that provide women with a glimpse of a prosocial alternative to being an offender. As the primary audience for a woman's efforts at reform, staff provided explicit information as to the behaviour appropriate to a given situation and feedback on her performance. Thus, in successful cases, staff became important 'reference others' (Schlenker 1986), whose likely evaluation of the desirability of a woman's behaviour was salient to her construction of responses even in their absence. Such 'reference others' assume considerable significance in attempts to present oneself as a prosocial individual. Within social relationships, individuals glean important information about their personal identities and the extent to which their behaviour conforms both to the identity attributed to them by others and that to which they wish to lay claim (Tedeschi 1986). Validation by an audience plays a crucial role in the acquisition of social behaviour, since it encourages individuals to perceive their own actions as emanating from, and representative of a prosocial self (Schlenker 1986). Indeed, Maruna *et al* (2004) go so far as to suggest that declarations of achievement might be most powerful when they emanate from those, such as criminal justice personnel, whose evaluations are not moulded by personal loyalties, but represent authoritative recognition of merit.

This push to achieve greater self-sufficiency was constrained within a structured framework of clear boundaries and consistent treatment, which served to clarify expectations.

[She] respected boundaries. She needed to know how far she could go. Even though she hated it when she got the warning letter, she would then adapt her behaviour…It was like dealing with a *child* at times. She'd have tantrums and storm out: 'I'm leaving! I'm not coming back!' Then she would be back in time for curfew. (Hostel manager)

196

Nevertheless, within this clear framework, many interviewees identified the adaptation of the rehabilitative effort to accommodate individual capacity. This entailed respecting pre-existing competence as well as enhancing support for the more needy. Field staff also adapted their pace to complement accomplishments at the project. These accounts show how a wide range of different aptitudes were sensitively managed.

> [Halfway House was] suitable for my client, given how independent she was in herself. It's no curfew…a less supportive [project]. [The manager's] assessment of my client was the same as mine. She told her where the Job Centre was, told her the local stuff that was around, was letting her get on with it, wasn't pushing her into anything or holding her hand through it. She knew that she was fine. (Probation officer)

> Her attendance with *me* never improved. But I took the view that there was effective monitoring and supervision. So as far as probation was concerned, that to me was quite satisfactory…Probably it's arguable that I *should* have breached her at the very beginning. But, in retrospect, it was a *good* decision not to breach her because she got a lot of valuable input at the Bail Hostel. (Probation officer)

> One thing that was very well managed was that she was moved up to the cluster flat…She couldn't handle it. So, it was making her move back to the hostel in a *positive* way, so that it didn't feel like punishment, but, *at the moment*, you're not *ready* for this. So it was case management, not us giving up at the first hurdle…So we moved her back to the hostel for everybody's benefit. Then she worked very well. (Hostel manager)

A key to success appeared to be staff's ability to engage a woman at the project and to retain her there, sometimes against the odds. Similarly, some interviewees referred to the anchorage that the project provided as a point of stability in an otherwise chaotic existence.

[She] was all over the place. She *worked* with us, she *stabilised*. We got her re-housed eventually…She was very, very chaotic when she arrived. Her thinking process was so *irrational*. You knew you had to *try*. It was like she was on drugs. I don't think she was. She was so angry and emotional, very distressed. (Staff member)

Because she tended to leave prison and drift off, it was important for someone to be *hanging onto* her. Because there was a condition of the order, she had to *stick* with it, say, 'I'm here for the next few months. I *have* to stay and get on with it.' (Probation officer)

Several of the foregoing accounts have implied the significance of co-ordinating the efforts of project staff with field workers and others involved in the rehabilitation effort. Sometimes this was cited as a key element in success.

We had regular three-way meetings…She had a *lot* of support…She had a *lot* of support, because she was having regular supervision with *me* at this office. She was having regular supervision with the *keyworker* at the Bail Hostel. (Probation officer)

There seemed to be a good level of communication, in that I used to *frequently* speak to staff about this particular woman. So, that was the most significant aspect…I did *regularly* communicate with this woman's keyworker…So, that was *good*. There was *continuity*. (Probation officer)

At a fundamental level, the projects were adept at providing practical help: 'They were pretty well geared to give her full information about her entitlement to the variety of benefits and statutory resources. They took an interest in her' (Probation officer). Finally, the sheer persistence of staff in their efforts to help women succeed, which was earlier noted as a strong feature of everyday practice in the face of constant challenge, was acknowledged in several cases.

She'd even been to the Bail Hostel and wandered off at some point. They took her back after some months. She did well there, because they *hung on* and *stuck* with her. (Probation officer)

Are you aware of the Henderson Hospital? It's a hospital that takes people who have personality disorder, psychopathic behaviour and deals with them in a therapeutic way...She lasted there about two *weeks*. She came back to us. Eventually she got a job on the Big Issue. She got re-housed...I remember she decorated her room over Christmas with flour. She damaged her room. We *did* have her breached for that. She went into custody, but then we took her back. (Hostel manager)

Such persistence provided opportunities for repeated practice in unfamiliar behaviours. The learning of new behavioural 'scripts' appropriate to particular social situations takes time and repetition, particularly when they contradict more well-established responses (Rumgay 2004a). Moreover, social behaviours that are repeated frequently are more likely to become integrated into an individual's sense of self (Schlenker 1986). Those that have been deployed most recently are likely to have more relevance to an individual's current self-identity (Schlenker 1986). Thus, for offenders, repeated practice enhances the incorporation of new pro-social behaviours into personal identity, while weakening the salience of earlier patterns of response.

Thus, structure, planning, consistency, adaptation to individual needs and persistence featured in successful placements with a clarity that overrode potential distractions, claimed the woman's attention, and fostered positive efforts at personal change.

We Treated Her Normally

I *do* think that the *support* system there was good. At that time, they had...a liaison probation officer. They had a warden...who was warm, sympathetic, responded to them. They had staff members like Miss O-...So, [the women] were getting a *lot* of support. They were making *relationships*. (Liaison probation officer)

Many comments referred to the quality of emotional support that was provided to successful women at the projects. The comments above and below illustrate the perception of staff as a resource for encouragement, reassurance, and relational development.

> She felt that there were usually people around that she could *turn* to. She was somebody who would *do* that, because she would get quite *anxious* about things. She was slightly paranoid at times. She would imagine that a particular resident would have it in for her or that there was a problem. So, she would *go* to staff in that situation. (Probation officer)

Perhaps paradoxically, despite their explicit ambitions for improvement, staff were frequently praised for being non-judgemental. This, again, might be viewed as 'normal-smithing' in practice. Staff worked on the assumption that women were capable of socially responsible behaviour, looking for explanations of any lapse from grace, rather than treating conformity as a surprising exception to the general rule of deviance.

> The main thing was treating them like a *normal* human being, *talking* to them. We're not going to *judge* you for what you did. Let's deal with *why* you did it. I'm not going to bash you on the head *because* you did it…Let's see if next time you can choose another path…We treated her *normally*. We didn't treat her different because of what she'd done. (Staff member)

In this context, many comments referred to the tolerance with which women were treated. Tolerance was the emotional quality accompanying active persistence in seeking change efforts.

> When she first got there it was fine, because she had waited so long. Then she started to feel her feet and push her weight around and test it out: 'What do *they* know? *They* haven't lived on the streets. *They've* never imported four and a half kilograms of cocaine…*Tossers*, they don't know *anything*.' (Probation officer)

> She would have been made to *leave* an average probation
> hostel…Because there would have been less *tolerance* of how she
> was…A conventional probation hostel, in *my* view, wouldn't have
> been as tolerant as I assume Stockdale House to have been. So, I
> think that they bent over *backwards*…She was very *angry*. She
> might have been very *testing* at times. (Probation officer)

Tolerance, in this context, was not equivalent to *laissez faire*. One
manager reflected on the balance of risks and opportunities that must be
actively managed in offering a tolerant environment:

> The balance between they're messing up, but they're keeping the
> house *safe*, the rent's coming in and the women are in one piece.
> That balance is *hard*. But we could *do* it in Stockdale House,
> because of the staffing level…There was somebody there 24-7. You
> could take some risks because of that. (Hostel manager)

Within this relational framework, successful women showed a
strong positive response to project staff, albeit that, as the remarks above
indicate, this might have taken some time to emerge in ambivalent, distrust-
ful individuals steeped in offending lifestyles.

> [She] *did* end up re-offending. But always *responded* very well to
> the Griffins, *knew* that she was getting support there, *wanted* to
> address the issues. They, by degrees, were becoming less serious.
> The risk was less high. (Hostel manager)

Within this environment, successful women learned to accept
support: 'She did *stay* for getting on two years…fighting against it, but then
using it' (Probation officer). They also learned to manage emotions that
were experienced as beyond their control: '[She] started anger management, has made *huge* attempts. She's not perfect by any means, but she has
made some real *attempts*. Her risk to the public has gone down dramati-
cally' (Staff member). Successful women also began to appreciate the
feelings of others.

201

She could *not* converse with you. She would *scream* at you, *shout* at you, and use *obscenities*. She didn't *know* how to have a conversation, she didn't *know* how to argue or put her point across, she was always on the *defence*…A lot of staff found it very difficult to manage. By the time she was resettled…she was a completely different person…She would *listen* when you said, 'I'm *not* going to work with you if you *scream* at me, because it *upsets* me. I don't like it.' This was *amazing*. (Hostel manager)

There's a bit of her now that starts to recognise that she makes others feel [bad]. Therefore, there's more recognition of the effect her offending had on people as well. She couldn't even *begin* to acknowledge how others felt…It was like a way of protecting herself, as if she's the only one…rejected, let down, hurt. (Staff member)

Thus, professionals described a maturational process as women acquired the emotional skills to negotiate events and relationships in appropriately adult ways. Giordano, Rossol, and Cernkovich (2002) suggest that increasing skill in emotional self-management is accompanied by an enhanced sense of personal agency, strengthening belief in control and self-determination. Thus, emotional maturation is a crucial element in the process of withdrawal from a criminal career, raising optimism as to the likely success of the enterprise.

She caught up with her real age. Women in prison tend to get *stuck* into their early 20s…They never move on to the other *milestones*. Our lives tend to be marked by acquiring possessions, being promoted in work, having children. She'd done *none* of those things. She got *stuck* in her late teenage years. But she moved on. (Probation officer)

Allowing her to mature. The offence that she got involved in was a very serious offence, with some other young people, of kidnapping to torture…She was able to develop and look back on that. (Probation officer)

In this context, women developed a sense of belonging in and responsibility to the project. This can be understood as a significant shift in perspective, in which the physical environment becomes embued with personal meaning. The development of attachment to the place where one lives represents its importance both as a concrete testimony to settlement and as a symbol of the value now attached to the hallmarks of conventional lifestyles (Mercier and Alarie 2002).

> When she settled to it, there was a period of calm when she was waiting for her council nomination to come up. She treated it like her *home*. She used to get *annoyed* with other residents who came in and disrupted it—'*created*', as she put it. (Probation officer)

These emotional advances could result in a transformation of self-image, revealed in significant alterations in the quality of self-care, which may be understood as a 'discovery of self' (Mercier and Alarie 2002:236), reflecting a new appreciation of personal potential.

> She was also able to develop in self-confidence, which largely assisted her to overcome a depressive mental health condition, which was probably triggered by her experiences of custody and feeling of failure. (Senior probation officer)

> She wouldn't even share with us when she *cut* herself. She would do the stitches herself. Now, each time she cuts, she comes. We go to hospital together. She shares her feelings why she did it. Before, it was so *secretive*. So I can see she's getting out from where she started. (Staff member)

She Got A Grip Somehow

> If I wouldn't have gone there, I would still have been either roughing it at friends' houses, still on drugs, or back and forth at my mom and dad's house. I just didn't want to. When I was 26, I said to myself, 'There's no *way* I'll still be taking drugs by the time I'm 30.' I stopped when I was 27. So, yeah, they did help me a lot. (Former resident)

Interviewees frequently recounted significant changes in the qualities of the decisions that successful women took concerning their futures. A striking aspect of these alterations was the assertion of autonomy in decisions and behaviour, even while temptations and distractions continued to proliferate in the environment. Maruna (2001) remarks on the significance of this shift from helplessness and passivity to self-regulation and mastery over personal destiny in the process of desistance from crime.

For some women, the criminal justice system itself appeared to have an impact on their aspirations, not least through the delivery of aversive experiences, which spurred them to capitalise upon the opportunity for change presented by the hostel placement. Here, women appeared to reassess their valuation of the costs and benefits of the criminal lifestyle (Shover 1996; Sommers, Baskin, and Fagan 1994).

> We were saying to her, '*Listen*. Crime don't *pay*. You've got caught three times. You have *nothing* to show for it. Absolutely *nothing*. You need to change your life around.' I met her in Peckham…She gave me a big hug, said, 'I'm glad that I *learned* from that custodial sentence. It took that one to make me *realise* what people were saying to me all the time—that I need to *do* something for *myself*.' (Hostel manager)

Witnesses to this process were clearly impressed by women's shift to taking control of their destinies, asserting their autonomy often in challenging circumstances.

> She was a young woman in an environment where there's a lot of drugs around…She managed to *contain* herself within that environment without getting involved. Managed to stay on her *own*, not being drawn into peer pressure…She was spending the day with other women,…they were committing offences, stealing from someone's handbag…She realised that she didn't *want* to get caught up in all that. She didn't *want* to go back to court. She *wanted* to sort herself out. (Probation officer)

Discovery of personal agency was accompanied by recognition of alternative ways of managing their lives. The futurelessness observed in the previous chapter dissipated.

> By the end of the time, you could see a real *shift*. She was coming *out* of it. She was thinking about her *future*. Before, she didn't even think she *had* a future. It was like a *brick wall* when she looked into the future. But she was thinking about what *career* she wanted to go into. She saw there was a world *outside* of heroin. (Probation officer)

> She...decided she wanted to *grow up*. She *surprised* me. She really made a *fundamental* change from being a wayward person...She got a *grip* somehow. (Probation officer)

Active choices of direction followed such awakenings. Giordano, Rossol and Cernkovich (2002) argue that, for the desisting offender, optimism as to the possibility for change is derived from transformations in the areas of an individual's emotions, cognitions, and social roles. Thus, emotional maturation and alterations in the perceptions of the relative attractiveness of conventional and deviant lifestyles assumed practical reality in the acquisition of new roles. Notably, these deliberate choices to move in positive directions would previously have presented overwhelming challenges to the confidence of these women.

> She did very well. Got involved with Clean Break and ended up in a good position. She made a very good turn around...She sticks in my mind, because I ended up meeting her again through work. She ended up working with offenders herself. (Probation officer)

Education, training and employment now became real possibilities in the women's lives.

> She started work training at college. Then she got a job with this company that hires clothes to the opera, to the film sets. (Staff member)

> She's working in a high street shop as a manager. I met her last year—went into the shop, she says, 'Hi'! I was chuffed with how she was doing. (Staff member)

Women whose mental health difficulties precluded such striking advancement were also capable of greater independence and activity.

> She now spends more time *outside* of this project. She's working full-time in a charity shop. Whereas all *day* it would be so *difficult* to get her *out* of here. (Staff member)

A notable aspect of this new energy for positive change was that women became active in their rehabilitative treatment, rather than passive or resistant.

> She was *totally* abstinent for the whole of that time. She used to go to AA meetings on a daily basis. That kept her sober. (Staff member)

> Her son was on the 'at risk' register. Social Services would *not* help her until she *admitted* that she was a risk to her son because of her drug use. So, she had to do that. That was hard for her. Then she brought herself up, *decided* this was what she was going to do. She went off to rehab. (Staff member)

Successful women, therefore, took active steps to claim an alternative, prosocial identity while relinquishing their attachment to the criminal lifestyle. Desired roles such as parent, employee, or community participant thus represented both the incentive and the means to stake a claim in conventional social life (Rumgay 2004a). Some women went so far as to change their legal identity as a mark of their altered self-image.

> I was told by staff at Halfway House that she had changed her name by deed poll. They also explained that she would not want to be contacted about [the research] as she felt that she had left that part of her life behind her and moved on. Her name change was part of this. (Observation notes)

In this context of an increasing sense of personal agency and active decision making a number of women were seen to take new responsibility in their personal relationships.

> A young woman who, in an emotional state, threw her infant baby out of a window. It was one floor up, hitting the concrete floor. The baby was OK, but there were concerns about her mental health. She was initially in Holloway, then released for mental health treatment...We *did* take that girl in...Once the mental health service felt that she was much more stable, a decision was made that Social Services felt that they could give her child back. So we then wrote to the judge, who released that clause from the probation order. She was able to go back and carry on. (Liaison probation officer)

In line with Maruna's (2001) observation of the desisting offender's discovery of a pro-active self, women's actions during these times were characterised by positive determination.

> We were worried...that she was just going back to a life of crime. Because if you've got all your family within the criminal justice system and they're all petty thieves, it's easy for you to get back into that. She was *determined* not to. (Hostel manager)

> She was very focused. She saw it as, 'OK, I've gone through the system. I *still* have my life to live. I *need* to do that. I *need* to get back. I *need* to.' (Staff member)

It did not follow from a change in personal perspective that the path was entirely smooth. Yet, successful women coped with the unpredicted contingencies and disappointments that occur in conventional as well as in deviant lifestyles. This was a further indication of the emotional maturity that, as we have seen, they were believed to have gained.

> She moved into her own flat with her boyfriend, which has since broken down. Before, that would have been a *mega*-devastation in Sarah's life. She was *still* carrying on with her course...So she was

207

able to deal with breakdown in relationships better. (Hostel manager)

She got pregnant, had the baby and was really *happy*. She'd looked at wanting to go to work, be a Traffic Warden. She'd found out about the qualifications. She was doing all the things that, ideally, get [you] into training and education. Having a baby kind of blew that bit. (Staff member)

Narratives of successful placements repeatedly emphasised a significant shift in perspective from futurelessness and passivity to optimism and agency characterising the women. From this viewpoint, the vicissitudes of everyday life appeared no longer to be dramatic evidence of irretrievable personal failure, but as obstacles to be navigated on the pathway to—and through—a conventional existence. In much the same way, Maruna (2004) describes the desisting offender's shift in perspective from a depressive thinking style, in which negative events are experienced as emanating from a fatally flawed personality and representing an unchangeable reality, to an optimistic perspective, contextualising disappointments within the normative transitions of ordinary life.

Filling Her Life Up With Other Things

She'd come out of prison. She'd stopped drinking. She had a drink problem. She *stopped drinking*. (Probation officer)

As many of the foregoing comments suggest, altered perspectives, decisions, and associated behaviours were accompanied by changes in damaging lifestyles. As in the above recollection, a move to abstinence by previously entrenched drinkers and drug users was a striking advance. While not all successful women achieved this, they nevertheless moderated their involvement in risky lifestyles to the extent that they were able to expand and enrich their experience of positive influences while reducing exposure to negative ones.

It wasn't an *overnight* success. She still did have contact with people in the heroin world, but not as much. She found things to do. Before, she was out with her friends, *stuck* inside taking heroin…Heroin had been a *huge* part of her identity. But now it was *peripheral*. She was filling her life up with other things. So, I think that was a *great* success. (Probation officer)

Some women were able to detach themselves from damaging relationships.

She was dangerous in the sense of someone who was a young woman…very much under the influence of a very seriously disturbed older man. Once that was *gone*, you could begin to sort things out for her…She *was* very much into it…But somehow, *without* him, maybe the leadership wasn't there. (Liaison probation officer)

Some established healthy intimate relationships, perhaps for the first time.

She then became a much more overt lesbian and developed a good relationship. They got a flat together. The last *I* knew, there was no more armed robbery. (Liaison probation officer)

Some women were able to draw on positive family support.

She had an older son…[who] got a place to go to university, but took a year out so that he could stay at home with the younger child…while mom was in custody and then at the Bail Hostel. (Hostel manager)

She was very unhappy. I think there was physical violence there…There is a lot of family involved now. Funnily enough, the husband had been extremely supportive. He didn't *realise* how she *felt*. He's been extremely supportive towards her. (Staff member)

This last example illustrates a growing ability to capitalise on the positive aspects of close relationships while detaching from their more

destructive features. Such competence in drawing selectively on the benefits of close relationships, particularly given the paucity of support
networks in emotionally impoverished lives in the context of multiple
disadvantages, has been found to characterise resilient individuals who
successfully navigate high risk childhoods (Werner and Smith 1992).
Giordano, Rossol and Cernkovich (2002) also point to competence in
moderating the intensity of damaging close relationships as a significant
change among desisting offenders.

Thus, successful women altered damaging and self-defeating
lifestyles in ways that promoted health, independence and pro-social relationships. In that sense, they sought out the company of 'normal-smiths' in
everyday interactions, increasing their contact with conventional life
through employment, leisure activities, and intimate relationships and thus
reducing the salience of the temptations of the criminal lifestyle (Lofland
1969; Rumgay 2004a).

A Big Step Forward

> She came out of a young offender's institution, into the Bail Hostel.
> She went from [there] to Stockdale House…I met her about five or
> six years later. She was in independent accommodation, doing very
> well…That's a snapshot of somebody that…benefited from it…And
> *she* was a very *damaged* young woman. (Probation officer)

A notable feature of these success stories was the positive mode of departure from the hostel, usually into independent accommodation. Departure
from residential care represented a positive progression in the rehabilitation
effort. In several cases, this was facilitated by gradual steps towards independence through the different projects.

> She did in fact telephone me about a year after her order expired.
> She had been re-housed…So, she'd stayed the course, going from
> Stockdale House through to a less supportive [Halfway House], into
> an independent place. That was a *big* step forward for this woman,
> because she was very *vulnerable*. (Senior probation officer)

210

A number of interviewees commented on the benefits of the Griffins Society's effective links with housing providers.

> I remember thinking what a *luxury* that was. If a resident did well, they probably would get re-housed in six months, which, even in those days, was *astonishingly* quick – which was a great *incentive*. I don't think that should be underplayed. (Senior probation officer)

Women were able to acknowledge and take steps to meet their continuing support needs.

> Back to having care of the child. She moved away from the hostel, back to her mother and father's home. Because she was a very *young* mother as well. So, she…moved out properly. (Probation officer)

Finally, women were provided after-care through the Griffins Society itself to support them in the transition to independence.

> There's a good follow-up. They didn't let people move out and not follow them up. Because they'd got used to the company and support. So, that was *good*. They didn't get cut off. They would go round, visit them in their new flat, make the links. That was *helpful*. (Probation officer)

The transition from a supported environment to independent living is, indeed, a big step forward, and potentially hazardous for vulnerable women. Successful women, however, left the Griffins Society projects in optimistic circumstances. Departure was planned, prepared, and supported. In total, these accounts of successful women can be seen to show a remarkable affinity with the findings of research on processes of natural desistance from crime. Accommodated within a safe, structured, and consistent environment, in which they were treated as conventionally competent individuals, women recognised an opportunity for personal change that appeared hitherto to have eluded them (Rumgay 2004a; Giordano, Cernkovitch, and Rudolph 2002). From this vantage point, they were able to capitalise on practical and emotional support, to take a grasp of the direction of their lives and to move towards independence.

SO MUCH LOVE CANNOT FIX PROBLEMS

> One woman haunts me *still*. If I cry, bear with me. (Probation officer)

Accounts of unsuccessful placements enable us to appreciate even more clearly the contingencies that may negate this process of transition towards desistance from crime and embracement of conventional life. These accounts could be grouped into similar categories, summarised in Figure 3, of organisational factors, programme structure, emotional support, decision making, lifestyle, and departure. In these instances, however, the narratives reveal the vulnerability of women to negative environments and ineffective support. In so doing, they demonstrate again the challenge of creating and sustaining a positive rehabilitative experience for a group of damaged women collected under one roof.

Backed Up Into A Corner

> A long-term heroin user, who had done very little about her heroin use in custody, with a history of supporting her addiction through prostitution, was accepted by Halfway House. *Very* quickly relapsed and began to use the hostel as a centre for prostitution, which, understandably, didn't amuse the *neighbours* at all…Looking back, if [the manager] was to be given the decision on accepting new residents, she should have been given a lot more input on *how* to do that. This woman *obviously* was not suitable for comparatively low level support at that time in her offending career…I was *very* surprised that [Halfway House] accepted her. Looking back on it, there may well have been issues around [the manager] wanting to please *me*, wanting to keep a good relationship with the liaison probation officer. (Liaison probation officer)

This recollection marks a number of organisational criticisms arising in relation to failed placements. It identifies lack of adequate training,

FIGURE 3: ACCOUNTING FOR FAILURE

Organisational Factors	Programme Structure	Emotional Support	Decision Making	Lifestyle	Departure
• weak manager • poor staff supervision • lack of training	• poor risk assessment • poor planning • support needs too high • unable to engage • need rejected • selective responsivity • failed to push for achievement • poor relapse management • inconsistency • rigidity • staff divided over treatment plans • poor coordination	• anger/violence not controlled • "contagion" • intense relationships • impact of persona on staff • impact of persona on residents • feeling of impunity • emotional problems unresolved • inappropriate 'task' focus • ostracised • good intentions not enough	• inappropriate ambition • go home • rigidity • prioritised self-interest	• drinking • drug use • self-harm • 'stuck' • relationship with male • endangered other residents • unresolved or irresolvable relationship problems	• breached • evicted • imprisoned • absconded • deliberate • nothing planned • rapid • accidental death • suicide

213

poor judgement, and an attempt to serve inappropriate goals through accepting an unsuitable referral. Notably, in this instance, most of these weaknesses were attributed to the project manager, whose primary importance persuaded even this cautious probation officer to be a silent witness to her misjudgement. At other times, weak management bowed to staff pressure, leading to decisions taken with poor justification.

> Management felt *pressured* into keeping her there, because the *staff* weren't keen to get rid of her. So, they argued her case…Then, they'd be backed up into a corner, which isn't *right*. If she has to go, she has to *go*, regardless of how cute and popular she is. (Staff member)

Thus, unsuccessful placements were often rooted in periods of organisational weakness, which provided a spawning ground for poor quality practice. As we shall see, organisational impediments introduced a level of 'noise' into the rehabilitative environment that impeded women's capacity to recognise and capitalise upon opportunities for change. In particular, failing women were unable in this environment to accomplish the transitions in emotions, cognitions, and social roles (Giordano, Rossol, and Cernkovich 2002) that were integral to the transformation of personal identity among the successful.

Why Are You Accepting This Woman?

> There was this feeling amongst [staff], 'We *can* have Joleen. We can *help* her.' We used to have a registrar from Broadmoor, who gave us training sessions…So, we discussed Joleen with him. He was *alarmed*. He said, '*Why* are you accepting this woman?…If you feel that you give me a *reason*, you need to document it; *why; what* sort of work you're going to do with her; *how* you're going to do it with her. Because this woman is *very* damaged.' (Staff member)

Within the programme structure, poor risk assessment played a key role in the failure of many placements. At times, as these narratives acknowledge, good intentions outweighed the better judgement of staff on their ability to care adequately for high-risk women.

We had put an *investment* in her. We didn't *want* to breach her. So, I asked another hostel to take her on…as a respite, to give everybody a breathing space. She set fire to the other hostel *that night*. I felt uncomfortable about that, because it was obviously poor assessment on my part about the risk that she posed. (Hostel manager)

More broadly, inadequate planning for the placement was cited by other professionals as significant in its breakdown.

I inherited her with the condition that she lived at the Bail Hostel and…went to a day centre about her drugs…She was like other people that I've had there who haven't worked very well…They come to the Bail Hostel without it being very *clearly* negotiated *how* they're going to work or *what* they're going to do…We end up with the order…There's no hand over. Often the issue's just *dumped* on us. (Probation officer)

She had conditions in her licence that weren't agreed with *anybody*. The prison just put them in. Like, she must meet with a psychiatrist. She stopped taking the *medication*, she started using illegal *drugs*, she started carrying a *knife* around. She was starting to worry everybody. (Probation officer)

Willingness to attempt to accommodate high-risk women, to the point of obscuring full assessment and planning, resulted in an accumulation of support needs that could not be met within the capacity of staff.

The *first* time she attempted suicide, she was taken to [general hospital]. The *second* time, they suggested she [go] to [psychiatric hospital]. We spoke at length. She felt that I was being *hard* in saying that she couldn't come back to Stockdale House. But *I* was saying, it was a cry for help, but it was a cry for help that *we* couldn't assist with. (Hostel manager)

Staff were generally unable to engage women who ultimately failed in the rehabilitative attempt. However, in hindsight, it was not always easy

215

to attribute responsibility for this lack of response. Professionals were at times uneasily aware of their own reluctance to reach out to challenging women.

> No matter *what* the staff could have done, she would have ended up in the same position. She had a bad crack problem…She had this *siege* mentality…*Everybody* was her enemy. That contributed towards her aggression. (Probation officer)

> I couldn't *relate* to her. She was very devious, *unlike* other women. They could *all* be devious. But there was something about her that I *couldn't* relate to. That was a failing on *my* part, I think. Everybody else had a problem with her, too. (Staff member)

In these examples, it might be hypothesised that staff, for whatever reason, began to participate in the woman's negative self-image, in which antisocial, unco-operative behaviours were attributed to deeper, characterological failings. Certainly, in the last example, a staff member appears to acknowledge an inability to avoid such an equation of behaviour with personality. The focus on characterological deficiency, however, implies an impact on behaviour that is enduring and pervasive (Tangney 2002). Thus, staff reinforced, rather than challenged, failing women's pessimism as to their chances of change. At times, indeed, there was a clear admission that staff had rejected a woman's need for help, when they privileged their assumptions about personal motivations over the evidence of visible behaviour.

> *Twice* she called me up at the hostel, said, 'Would you help me commit suicide?'…But I thought she was *joking*…I didn't take it as *seriously* as I *should* have done. Then one day, police knocked on the door, said that she'd jumped. Oh, *gosh*. This is somebody who'd been *talking* to you and *saying*, 'This *is* how I'm *feeling*.' (Hostel manager)

> Whilst she was at the Bail Hostel, she alleged that she was raped. I wasn't in a position to say whether or not it was *true*, but the [staff]

216

responded by saying that they didn't *believe* her. They said that if it was true, she would be prepared to go to the police. Well, that's *nonsense*. Given her history, it's not *surprising* that she had concerns about involving the police. The project staff didn't serve her needs very well at all. (Probation officer)

These attributions to perceived personality obscured the direct relationship between women's behaviour and staff responses, which, as we have seen, helped to persuade successful women to persist in attempts at change. In some cases, it appeared that staff were selective in their preferences for certain women, to the detriment of both the favoured and the less popular.

In my opinion, she was given *preferential* treatment over everyone else...She used heroin to the point where all her teeth were rotten. They had to take them out...She was going to the Drug Dependency Unit. She was *trying*. All the workers were *behind* her. That's why she became—how can I say it—the *special* one. (Staff member)

Personal issues got too much in the way for staff working with the residents. For some women, there would be *incredible* empathy. For others—like *this* case—there wouldn't. (Probation officer)

Similarly, unsuccessful women were not pushed to try to achieve progress. Here, we can see the failure of the normal-smith's message that change is within the capacity of the struggling deviant.

She *tried*. But I don't think there was enough determination *behind* her. I don't think there was enough from the staff. I don't think they were *pushing* her enough. They could have done a *lot* more. (Staff member)

Such a failure to sustain the message that change was possible lay at the heart of poor relapse management in one case.

She had a *pattern*. You could *tell* when she was going to back into drink and drugs...That's when they should have *been* there, to *catch*

217

her at that point, say, 'Come on. You've got to go back in [treatment].' *Encouragement*. (Staff member)

The absence of persistent encouragement to women to practice new, prosocial behaviours increased the likelihood that the weak initial attempts of individuals with low expectations of success inculcated by long histories of failure would be relinquished in the face of even minor challenges (Schlenker 1986). Instead, women received inconsistent messages as to the standards of permissible behaviour, both in individual cases, when lapses were variously tolerated and punished, and between different parties, when disparities in their treatment became visible. As the previous chapter revealed, these vulnerable women frequently sought confirmation of their pessimistic self-images, to the extent of attempting to refute staff's offers of positive appraisals. In failing cases, staff responses to women's efforts 'to verify negative conceptions of self' (Arkin and Baumgardner 1986:85) tended to reinforce their existing self-views.

> She would do things that warranted to be *breached…Other* people would be breached on it…If *she* did it, it was OK. Someone *else* came in drunk like that, they be *bang* on them. (Staff member)

Equally, one manager recalled a salutary lesson in enforcing inappropriately rigid rules. This account clearly illustrates a woman's exploitation of a golden opportunity to confirm her own self-doubt.

> It was a decision that a member of the care team took…that she should *abstain* from alcohol, otherwise, it's *not* going to work, she needs to come back into *hospital*. Once that decision was given back to her, it was *obvious*: 'All *right*. All I need to do is go out, have a couple of drinks, I will be taken back to hospital.' So, the *first* time she hit a stressful period, *that's* what she did. It escalated from there. We've learned that we're *never* going to say to anybody, 'If you do this, you'll be *out*', apart from issues that impact on other people, such as violence. (Hostel manager)

Thus, the clarity of requests for prosocial behaviours and challenges to negative personal identities, so beneficial to successful women, was drowned in the noise and confusion of characterological attributions, contradictory reinforcements for effort and confirmation of women's pessimism. Staff divisions over the appropriate course of action could exacerbate these problems of inconsistency.

> We went through the process of discussing Joleen, agreeing whether to assess her or not. The staff team was so *divided* on her…I was one who felt that [we shouldn't], but I was new in the project. (Staff member)

> I had to put my feelings on the line, speak up against people in the team who felt that we should give that person a chance…She was pro, I was anti. So, we had a split there. (Staff member)

Similarly, failure of different agencies to agree upon strategy almost inevitably produced negative outcomes.

> She was a very, *very* difficult woman to work with. She probably should have gone into psychiatric care rather than the criminal justice system. She got six years. There were very strong feelings around the time of sentence that it was *economics* that prevented her from getting a bed in a special hospital, rather then *need*. She was the sort of woman who fell between two stools. Was she a *psychiatric* case? Was she a *criminal* case? …What *we* wanted was to get her sectioned. But the psychiatrist said there wasn't room for her. The probation service had to have her recalled. (Staff member)

> We breached them. Took them back to court. The magistrate threw the breach out, promptly re-bailed them *back* to the hostel…That I found very, *very* difficult to manage, because I didn't *want* them in the hostel. Yet, we had the court saying they *had* to be there. (Hostel manager)

Here, then, we can see the fruits of the failure of 'normal-smithing' in staff practice, its place being overtaken by personal and situational preferences and vulnerability to the pressures of staff divisions. Failure to convey to women the assumption of social competency was not simply neutral in its effect, but yielded ground to stronger messages that nonconformity to socially acceptable norms was expected, intermittently sanctioned, and frequently condoned.

We All Wanted To Beat the Shit Out Of Her

> This woman was *screaming*. She was *frenzied*. She *chucked* my arm off her, *lashed* out at me—this all happened so *quickly*—*kicked* me in the groin. I was *stunned*. She did eventually apologise…Then it built up…She went more and more *shit* stirring. Then she went *ballistic*, went for the big black woman…with a carving knife…She was going *bananas*. Three of the residents had her restrained. The black woman wanted to beat the *shit* out of her. But we *all* wanted to beat the shit out of her! She was *very* aggravating. It was a time when it was difficult in the house. She played on [that]. (Staff member)

Positive emotional support was notably lacking in these accounts. Indeed, some, such as the above narrative, evoked a sense of uncontrolled disorder within the hostel environment. Disturbed women both fuelled and were fuelled by staff's inability to calm them: 'It was behaviour they had no *control* over. They couldn't *cope* with it. So that was that' (Probation officer). Such incipient violence was contagious within the close confines of the projects: 'They decided to get their [revenge]…They made some phone calls…They were going out for trouble' (Staff member). Relationships between residents could be intense, leading to a propensity for disruption affecting the entire project: 'She decided her girlfriend dumped her for somebody much nicer and better looking…She started creating *mayhem*, shit stirring, because her girlfriend was still living in the hostel' (Staff member). As we saw in the previous chapter, a resident's personality could adversely affect her treatment by staff and residents.

She *had* to leave. I don't think she lasted even three *months*. She was so *chaotic* when she was here. The *influence*. Everyone in the house became just *like* her—the residents, the staff. She had such an *effect* on staff members. (Staff member).

In such situations, as staff withdrew from engagement through intimidation, anger or weariness, women came to believe in their own impunity. Women's negative personal identities triumphed and could be enacted in blatantly provocative ways. The relationship between the deeply pessimistic self-images which, as we have seen, had been inculcated in many of these women throughout their lives, and the persistence of anti-social behaviour (Tangney 1986) was nakedly exposed in this context. Indeed, the environment served to perpetuate well-established hostility in outlook and behaviour which, in turn, militated against any change effort (Giordano, Rossol, and Cernkovich 2002).

She was left to her own devices. She used to sit on the stairs, drink outside…You'd say, 'You know you're *not* supposed to drink.' She'd tell you to fuck off. (Staff member).

There was also the cockiness from them: 'Well, there's nothing you can do, because the courts will just bail us back.' (Hostel manager)

Failing women's emotional problems remained unresolved during their placement, through staff's inability to grapple with troubling issues. One manager connected this to an inappropriate focus on tasks and behavioural issues, rather than looking deeper for the source of women's psychological difficulties:

A young woman who lost *two* of her children. Both had *died* because they were born with multiple illnesses…Then she was sterilised whilst in prison. She came out wanting a child really badly, getting into inappropriate relationships. *Nobody* worked with her around the issues of her *children*. So, she drank. When she was drinking, she was a danger, not only to herself, but to everybody else in the house, because [she was an arsonist]. I see that as a real *failure*, because, on reflection, there was so much more we could have done…We concentrated on the *alcohol*. What we *should* have concentrated on were the issues that *led* her to use alcohol. (Hostel manager)

Giordano, Rossol, and Cernkovich (2002) comment on the destructive intensity acquired by personal relationships where alternative foci for attention and emotional energy are lacking. Indeed, we have already observed the emotional intensity of hostel life, as well as the inactivity enforced by unemployment and scarce resources. The poorly controlled behaviour of some women resulted in ostracism by other residents. However understandable that response might be, it was a recipe for disaster.

It was *never* going to work, because of the *hostility* towards these women, that they could have *done* something like that. Left another woman to *die*. (Hostel manager)

A staff member, reflecting on one woman's failure, concluded ruefully:

We realised that so much *love* cannot fix *problems*: 'Oh, she'll come, we'll give her all our *time*, we'll give her *love*. She'll be *fine*.' And Joleen left. So, maybe not. (Staff member)

Putting Themselves First

Insights into failing women's decision making shared a common theme: the inappropriate prioritisation of immediate personal interests over broader concerns for practicality, the longer term and other people. One woman, for example, developed a highly inappropriate ambition:

She decided that she was going to have a *baby*, because then she could *control* it. She was only 17 herself! She got pregnant. She was getting more and more mad…She thought having a baby was the *one* thing that she could do *right*. *Nobody* could take it away from her. I'm not so sure. They probably did in the end. (Staff member)

Another appears to have given in to homesickness.

> She came from Yorkshire. She wanted to be with friends back where she was born and brought up. Coming to London, to a new culture and environment, perhaps she found it very difficult to adjust in London. She absconded…Couldn't say where she's gone. (Probation officer)

One woman's progress appeared to stall, due to her inflexibility.

> She seems to benefit the *least* from being here, because she's so *rigidly* set in her views. Even when she *does* come for support, how much does she get from [it]? Because she goes away with the *same* views…But she's been here for [some time]. Perhaps she did an enormous amount of work initially. It's tailed off. She's reached a plateau. That's *it*. That's her level. (Staff member)

One account summed up the quality of these poor decisions:

> They were putting themselves *first*. They were using on the premises. They didn't want to be [implicated] in any way, for it to be in their room. So: 'We'll remove the woman'—the poor woman who'd *overdosed*. I should imagine it was fear, but that's *not* what you do. That's *totally* unacceptable. (Hostel manager)

Schlenker (1986) argues that a weak self-image impedes the ability to resist the challenge to confidence presented by external events and interpersonal exchanges that appear to refute claims to a reformed, prosocial identity. Moreover, low expectations of successful change may encourage pre-occupation with a negative self-view. Leary (2002) further suggests that such self-absorption reduces the cognitive capacity for recognising and empathising with the plight of others and for problem-solving. Unsuccessful women thus yielded to their persistent expectations of failure and resorted to well-established repertoires of anti-social and self-defeating behaviours. They failed to attain the autonomy and mastery of their ultimate destiny that characterised the transformation of successful residents.

Instead, they prioritised according to immediate situational pressures, making decisions that only served ultimately to deepen their plight.

I Can't Imagine That She's Alive

> The men would *queue* for her at the front door. They were taking *turns*. I *asked* one, 'What are you *doing* here?' He said, 'I'm waiting for my turn.' She was selling herself. (Staff member)

Far from abandoning or moderating their destructive behaviours, failing women often imported their lifestyles into the hostel environment. Where successful women became active in treatment, failing drinkers and drug users continued high levels of substance abuse.

> She was *killing* herself. It was very obvious *self-destruct*—self-injury, suicide attempts. As though she felt as if she was falling to pieces. Whereas, when not drinking, we were able to set targets, goals, care planning to try and support her, when drinking, we couldn't. So, the whole issue would escalate. (Hostel manager)

> This alcoholic lady, who *must* be dead by now. She took her liver to the dry-cleaner every week. She probably wouldn't *have* a liver any more. She had a *mega* drink problem. I can't *imagine* that she's alive. (Liaison probation officer)

For some, a habit of self-harm continued or worsened.

> Most of the women there used to self-harm. But *this* was self-harming that was *beyond* what the project could cope with. If you've got *one* person at that *extreme*, it has a knock-on effect on *everyone*, including staff and residents. (Staff member)

The persistence of women's negative self-views and pessimism entailed the perpetuation of well-established behaviours. Women appeared to be stuck within a damaging lifestyle, either seeing or wanting no possibility of relief.

It was as if she was *stuck* at that point. She couldn't *see* any way out. Or she didn't *want* to see any way out. (Probation officer)

The woman we have had here three or four *times*. For her, this is a *doss* house. She's just here because the judge *sent* her here. She will run away after a few days. There's *nothing* we can do about it. She's a drug user. She doesn't *want* to deal with the drug issue. She *enjoys* using drugs. You *can't* do any work with her. She's not prepared to. She doesn't *want* to do any work on it. She *enjoys* working on the street, getting out of her face. There is *nothing* we can do about it. (Staff member)

Similarly, some women perpetuated damaging relationships with men. In a social environment in which partners capable of supporting change were relatively scarce (Giordano, Rossol and Cernkovich 2002), they persisted in relationships that militated against improvement in self-view and behaviour.

A very confused young woman. She was having problems with a boyfriend. She was breaking the rules by having boyfriends sleeping overnight at the hostel. She was only 18 at the time. She must have absconded, run off with some boyfriend…It was about relationship…[She was] making inappropriate decisions about who to take as a boyfriend. It was anyone who came along. (Probation officer)

These damaging behaviours had wider implications than a woman's personal chances of reform. A consequence of the importation of destructive lifestyles into the projects was to endanger other residents.

They were in a room with another woman who overdosed. They *dragged* her into the hall. *Left* her there. She was only found because another woman panicked…The woman could have been in the hall and *died*. These two women dragged her out of her room because they didn't want to be implicated. (Hostel manager)

Thus, the futurelessness observed earlier was manifested in perpetually self-defeating behaviours. Unsuccessful women effectively imported their damaging lifestyles into the hostel itself, destroying any potentially positive influences towards change.

We Booted Her Out Christmas Day

> She kicked in the office door and went for [the manager]. *She* wasn't having it. She was having her *out*. [She] *wanted* her out, anyway, because she *knew* that she'd done things in the past that warranted her to be breached. (Staff member)

The departures of these failing women were, without exception, of poor quality. Many were breached, as in the account above, for evading their responsibilities within the project.

> She got recalled to prison at *my* instigation. Because relapse into drug use is *one* thing, but not being prepared to *do* anything about it is another. (Probation officer)

Despite, as observed previously, attempts by staff to limit the damage of evictions, in these cases, they often occurred at the worst possible times.

> We were getting ready for Christmas Eve. We said, 'You *can't* stay here, because we can't *protect* you.' All the residents wanted to *kill* her. We thought it was in her *interests* that she went…So, it was very much for her *protection* that we booted her out Christmas Day. But everyone [thought] it's *terrible*, it's *terrible*. (Staff member)

Some women's behaviour ensured that they left the projects for custody.

> There was scaffolding outside of the art gallery in the Strand…She climbed it one night. Ended up in custody again…She was threatening, that's what the police acted on. She was so intoxicated, climbed all that, threatened to kill herself, threatened to damage…They

would have looked at her past history of arson. You can't take the *chance*. (Hostel manager)

Others voted with their feet: 'She went missing, wasn't picked up again for months' (Probation officer). Several seemed deliberately to accomplish their exclusion from the project.

Before Simone went into the office and assaulted [a staff member], she had said, '*Anywhere* would be better than *this* place.' [A staff member] suggested that Simone might have been fully aware that she would go to prison. She decided that this was preferable to life at Special Care House…[A]lso…she had volunteered her original surname, which she doesn't use any more. She has a very long list of convictions under her original name, but no offences recorded under her current surname. That she volunteered this information to the police was seen by staff as Simone making sure that she was charged and evicted. (Observation notes)

Failing women left the project without plans for their future: 'She found it too hard to be in the hostel, so she moved to Luton…I found out later that she got herself into another violent relationship and had a child' (Probation officer). For a few, the result was tragic.

Two women who died. We *couldn't* keep them, because their illegal drug use was too much…It was also the *dealing*, the *behaviour* they were bringing to the hostel…We evicted them. They went to bed and breakfast and *died*. OD'ed together. Dead, in the same room…They had an accident. Yeah. That was *hard*. Really *hard*. (Hostel manager)

The young woman who committed suicide within the house. Because she'd been physically, sexually abused by her father. He was *calling* her from *prison*. (Hostel manager)

In all cases of failed placements, women departed the hostel amid deeply negative circumstances, with little or no hope of improving their

quality of life or even of retrieving the damage caused during their residence. Rather, they were further mired in the harmfulness and pessimism of
their criminal lifestyles. For a small number, it marked the final—and
fatal—twist of a seemingly inexorable downward spiral into degradation.

CONCLUSION

While failing women appeared to be—and, importantly, to *believe* themselves to be—'doomed to deviance' (Maruna 2001), successful women
emerged from their experience at the Griffins Society projects with a sense
of personal mastery over their destinies and faith in the possibility of
advancement in conventional lifestyles. The barriers to this transformation
in personal outlook can be found both in women's psychological condition
and in the quality of the therapeutic environment of the hostels. Clearly,
there are so many hazards along the path towards rehabilitation that the
accomplishment of successful outcomes testifies both to the abilities of
staff to nurture change efforts amid the volatility of hostel life and to the
determination of women to seize the opportunity that it presented.

Successful women surmounted the profound psychological obstacle
of despair which, given the extent of their criminality, the severity of their
personal problems, and their previous failures in rehabilitation was not an
unreasonable estimation of their chances of achieving change (see Farrall
2002). The role of hope in promoting successful rehabilitation appears to be
important but is poorly understood. On the one hand, pessimism is related
to failure and hope (or optimism) is related to success (Burnett and Maruna
2004; Farrall 2002; Jackson, Wernicke, and Haaga 2003). On the other, a
high level of hope may lead to unrealistic self-confidence, resulting in
reluctance to accept external assistance (Jackson, Wernicke, and Haaga
2003). Women at the Griffins Society hostels, however, did not appear to
suffer from an excess of optimism. Indeed, the ambivalence of women as to
their hostel placement may well have been related to their pessimism about
the likelihood of success. Nevertheless, the outlook of successful women
altered in ways that not only promoted change during their residence but
also sustained their efforts at reform following their departure.

Research on emotional changes occurring during residential drug
rehabilitation has shown increasing positivity alongside reduced feelings of

powerlessness and fatalism (Ravenna *et al* 2002). These shifts may reflect an evolving sense of independence from immediate situational influences as behaviour becomes increasingly agentic. Certainly, movement towards autonomy was a powerful indicator of the personal development of successful women. As we have seen, daily practice within the hostels emphasised the practice of autonomy within a supportive environment. This approach, rather than the imposition of change through external control, is thought to encourage the assimilation and integration of new behaviours into the individual's sense of self, increasing the potential for sustained improvement outside the rehabilitative setting (Schlenker 1986; Simoneau and Bergeron 2003).

Successful women's increased confidence in their capacity to function as autonomous agents was exemplified in their independence from damaging relationships. Notably, this was not only reflected in total separation, but, in several cases, in a discriminative detachment from harmful aspects of relational involvement while drawing on the strength of positive elements. In this, successful women may be seen to have acquired some of the skills that have been observed to characterise resilient individuals who emerge successfully from harmful familial backgrounds (Werner and Smith 1992). In this way, women were enabled to maximise their opportunities for support while, often, continuing to live in environments in which adverse influences flourished (Falkin and Strauss 2003). This ability, again, has been observed to characterise women who successfully negotiate social and personal disadvantage (Brodsky 1999; Wandersman and Nation 1998).

Thus, as we have seen, successful women became 'active participants in the decision to give up crime' (Laub and Sampson 2003:146). Their hostel experience did not impose upon them the enduring changes in perspective and behaviour that marked their progress, but encouraged the development of new coping abilities that spawned hope for a better future as women began to perceive them as part of their personal repertoire of survival skills, often against the odds (Rumgay 2004a). These narratives of hope and despair, however, reveal the close connections between and mutual influence of women's personal characteristics and qualities of the therapeutic environment of the hostels.

A crucial aspect of this interaction appears to be the interruption of entrenched routines of anti-social and damaging behaviours, coupled with their replacement by strong expectations for, and engagement in conventional activities (Maruna *et al* 2004). This disruption was provoked both abruptly by the transition from street to hostel life and, over time, by the persistence of the 'normal-smith's' message of competence in normality. Thus, in successful placements, staff achieved primacy as the audience for and evaluator of women's attempts at reform, conveying a powerful message as to the possibilities for change that came to be preferred over previously well-established negative appraisals by self and others.

Chapter Eight

The Philanthropic Ideal

Although I'm saying there was no sense of direction, they didn't know where they wanted to go, but they knew what they wanted it to feel like. (Hostel manager)

C an the example of the Griffins Society provide an answer to the challenges to contemporary philanthropic volunteering in offender rehabilitation: that it is inadequate in its response to modern-day risks; that its motivation is suspect and inappropriately driven by self-seeking and sentimentalism; and that it has a limited, bureaucratically constrained role in today's corporate structures for the delivery of human services?

Since the early 1990s, we have witnessed a hardening of political and public attitudes towards offenders, a rising fear of crime even while crime itself has reduced, and a concentration of policy activity on the pursuit of community safety. Our intolerance of risk has shaped the criminal justice agenda, not least in its impact on those organisations traditionally charged with care and rehabilitation of offenders. Women have fared poorly in this punitive climate, with the average female prison population rising from 1,577 in 1992 to 4,299 in 2002, an increase of 173 percent (Home Office 2003), without a corresponding increase in the seriousness of their offending. What can we learn from an organisation, which concluded that its efforts were unsustainable as this groundswell of hostility towards offenders began to take effect, that can illuminate our contemporary predicament of high levels of imprisonment, hypersensitivity to crime and heightened expectation for its elimination through incapacitation and exclusion? In an attempt to answer this question, this chapter will explore the tensions between the Griffins Society's approach to offender rehabilitation and contemporary preoccupations with risk, the motivation of Council members for their philanthropic enterprise and the continuing significance of such activity in contemporary society.

I DON'T BELIEVE THAT PEOPLE ARE EVIL

> I never *ever* heard a critical comment on the actual running of those hostels. I know there were problems, people knew there were problems. But I've only *ever* heard complimentary comments, which has staggered me. (Council member)

To contemporary eyes, early practice in the Griffins Society's projects might appear, at first glance, to reflect either an irretrievable age of innocence in which female offenders were simply harmless rough diamonds, or an alarming ignorance of the personal risks involved in close contact with deeply damaged individuals. Neither of these suppositions do justice to the Society's achievement.

The first assumption presumes a deterioration in women's offending patterns, reflecting a new population of high-risk, violent females, the rise of which is often attributed to loosened social controls on their behaviour in the wake of greater social equality (see, for example, Adler 1975). There is, however, little convincing evidence that female crime has increased in seriousness, but rather it continues primarily to reflect, as it has over many years, the economic hardships of marginalised women (Hedderman 2004). Nevertheless, as we have seen, despite the ready availability of a non-violent, low-risk target group, the Griffins Society broke new ground from its early days in accommodating women whose offences and personal disturbance would have ensured their exclusion from most other hostels. Moreover, while tragedy was not unknown in the projects and while daily life was frequently turbulent, it succeeded in housing a concentration of volatile, often violent women, while earning the admiration of most who became familiar with its enterprise. Such plaudits are not easily won from a discriminating audience comprised of probation officers and high-ranking civil servants with plenty of experience in the risks attached to community treatment of offenders in terms of both personal safety and public credibility. Indeed, we have seen that the rehabilitative results of the organisation's enterprise were remarkably positive; that success was not an invariable outcome is not surprising, given the depth of personal disturbance with which it was confronted daily. Thus, the second supposition that the Griffins Society was characterised by ignorance of the hard realities of offender-based risk, which was fuelled by class-based perceptions of Council members as naïvely well-meaning, sheltered ladies, does not withstand close scrutiny.

Models of offender rehabilitation reflect the preoccupations and conceptualisations of their time (Hough 200). Thus, the Griffins pursued a model of family life within their early hostels that did not simply reflect their personal expectations as women privileged with stable lifestyles, nor, more broadly, their instinctive maternalism as 'women looking after women,' as one Council member put it. This model chimed with prevailing views on offenders' rehabilitative needs and appropriate strategies for meeting them. For example, a Home Office (1966) report on residential provision for offenders, published coincidentally with the first year of operation at Stockdale House, described a common approach of employing married couples sharing complementary roles as wardens, the popularity of 'motherly' housekeepers and the potential for a hostel to become a focal point for activities designed to reduce social isolation. All of these features characterised Stockdale House. Notably, this report went so far as to assert that 'since the problems of women and girls are substantially different from those of male offenders, they will not be solved by the same methods' (p.14). In an eerily accurate forecast of Halfway House, it continued:

> [I]n general, women demand a much larger degree of independence than men, even though basically their greatest handicap may be loneliness and their greatest need companionship. For this reason some form of bed-sitter accommodation is likely to be more acceptable to them than the communal...type of hostel. Small units, containing not more than six bed-sitters, with a capable housemother or landlady to provide support and help when needed, might be suitable for most types of women offenders. (Home Office 1966)

The Griffins do not seem to have spent their time perusing this document. At least, at no time in this research did any Council member mention that official Home Office guidance was a formative influence on their innovations. The alternative possibility, that one or more of the Griffins had the ear of the working party that compiled the report, is not to be discounted, but again, no Council member mentioned this. The important point, however, is that this model of rehabilitation, appealing to the metaphor of family, and particularly parental relationships, was not regarded as contentious in their time (see also Sinclair 1975). The boldness of the Griffins' enterprise lay in their enthusiastic application of that model to the most challenging offenders. And while their family model was modified over time as the projects expanded, the Griffins' brand of maternalism ensured the continuation of a homely, rather than institutional environment. Interviewees repeatedly remarked upon the high quality of life within the hostels. For example, a probation officer enthused: 'The house, the way it was presented and cared for sent out such a strong message as you walked through the door that you *deserve* this. You're someone who *needs* to be treated well.' Another probation officer remarked, without a trace of irony: 'I went to my client's room and I looked around and I thought, gosh I couldn't afford to furnish *my* bedroom like this!' A Council member reflected:

> It had a personal touch, the like of which probably won't happen again. It couldn't be constituted like that again. It's just gone…We had a pretty high moral code and we treated the residents with respect. (Council member)

Moreover, in a subsequent report, the Home Office advocated the contribution of volunteers to the care of mentally disordered offenders in terms that echo Lofland's (1969) account of normal-smithing:

> We were impressed by the argument that, in after-care, trained personnel—probation officers, prison welfare officers, psychiatrists and nurses—necessarily view the patient in terms of his pathology and deviance; the volunteer should be encouraged to retain his view of the individual not as an ex-patient or prisoner or as a social deviant but as a member, albeit it disabled, of the society to which he too belongs. We think that after-care has two stages; the first should be the offender's preparation by professionals who under-

stand his difficulties and who use their knowledge of his psychopathology to help him and his family to adjust, while the second is the reassimilation of the individual into society by its own members who act as a model of normality for him. (Home Office 1967:25)

The Griffins Society's projects, as we have seen, were infused with this approach, which appears to account for much of their success. Again, the concept was not unfamiliar, but the steadfast pursuit of 'normal-smithing' in the face of the challenges posed by severe personal deviance and wide class division was revolutionary. The organisation, at its most successful, managed risk through persistent appeal to the standards and expectations of everyday life in conventional society, both in terms of the behaviours demanded of its miscreant charges and, importantly, in terms of the treatment that was due to those women. In the context of contemporary expectations that Home Office funded hostels will provide containment for the most serious and socially excluded offenders, such an approach might have a particular relevance. Reinforcement of deviant status cannot provide offenders with a rationale for change in the direction of conventionality. While a sufficient level of control might restrict the expression of anti-social behaviour, such behavioural change is likely to be maintained only until the removal of external constraints (Cahill *et al* 2003). Conversely, persistent confrontation with expectations for prosocial behaviour, embedded in the assumption that the offender is one to whom such expectations apply no less than any other, contains, as we have seen, the potential for a change in self-identity to embrace conventionality rather than deviance. One Council member expressed this view in non-professional language with the assertion, 'I don't believe that people are evil.'

The continuing progress of the surviving hostels also cautions us that to assume that their model of rehabilitation outlived its usefulness as societal conditions changed may reflect an overly simplistic account of historical shifts. Our contemporarily heightened consciousness of risk does not necessarily demonstrate that risk itself has increased substantially. While violence and tragedy occurred within the hostels, it is not clear that it happened at a level above that which might be expected among a concentration of damaged and volatile women, who were excluded, not only from other hostels, but in some cases from more formal institutions such as psychiatric facilities. It is true that Stockdale and Second-Stage Houses closed when the Griffins were forced to acknowledge that they no longer offered safe rehabilitative environments and saw little hope of re-establishing them as such. Nevertheless, this occurred in a context of declining support for these projects and a consequent impoverishment of resources, in which appropriate staffing could not be sustained, that was not inflicted on the Bail Hostel or Special Care House.

During the 1980s and 1990s, there was a marked loss of policy interest in voluntary after-care, as varieties of compulsory post-release and intensive probation supervision proliferated. This declining concern coincided with rising interest in closer surveillance of high-risk offenders. Its legacy culminated, after the Criminal Justice Act of 1991, in the withdrawal of centrally supported after-care provision for all prisoners released from sentences shorter than 12 months. Since this accounted for the majority of prisoners, it amounted to massive neglect of their resettlement difficulties and associated risks of reoffending, predicated on a crude equation of future risk with length of previous sentence. This policy focus contributed to the starvation of resources for the Society's voluntary projects, which combined with the intensity of the women's problems to create heightened risk in the hostel environment. Thus, Stockdale and Second-stage Houses were at least as much the victims of a poorly developed central policy for identifying and managing risk as of an inadequate model of care.

Clearly, the Society's approach to risk management should not be assessed in isolation from its context in policy and general practice at any point in time. This point is reinforced by the example of the dispute between the National Association of Probation Officers (NAPO) and the Home Office over hostel staffing levels at night and weekends. A year of industrial action began in March 1992 after attempts, dating back to 1985, by NAPO to convince the Home Office of the need for double cover were deemed to have failed (Adams 1992). In NAPO's newsletter, it was alleged:

> [T]he Home Office made it clear that they have no intention of providing a minimum of double staffing cover in all Probation and Bail Hostels. This is an understatement. From 112 such hostels, the Home Office only provides routine double cover in four hostels,

236

with cover in two further hostels provided by extra funds from local Probation Committees. This leaves 106 hostels operating without full double cover, usually during evenings, overnight and at weekends when incidents more frequently occur. (Adams 1992:1)

It is to be remembered that this dispute concerned probation and bail hostels, which were fully funded by the Home Office and which were generally assumed to accommodate the more serious offenders (although, as we have seen, the Griffins Society did not differentiate between the populations at their projects according to their funding status). That provision of double cover could, allegedly, be described by civil servants as 'paying staff to do nothing' (Adams 1992:1), and that single cover was routinely assumed to represent the practice norm as recently as 1992, reveals much about context in which the Griffins fought for the security of their hostels. Calling for industrial action, NAPO reported that 'there were around 2,500 serious incidents last year in the 112 hostels in England and Wales. NAPO believes that as many as one in three staff members are involved in an assault each year and virtually all experience threatening behaviour or abuse' (Fletcher 1992:2). Accurately perceived within this wider context of a 'normality of risk', what might otherwise be construed as wilful or naïve neglect on the part of the Griffins is recast as tenacious efforts to sustain stability. Staff, indeed, repeatedly volunteered, unprompted, their view that they enjoyed working conditions and Council support superior to standards in other hostels. The willingness of the Griffins to take their fight to the heart of the Home Office suggests that, far from lagging behind the van of progress, they were ahead of most of their peers in recognising personal vulnerability in the hostel environment.

The Griffins were not careless in their approach to risk. Yet, they were continually pioneering new pathways in residential rehabilitation. They and their staff learned their lessons, perforce, through experience rather than the example of others who walked the path before them. Unique innovation, by its very nature, lacks established practice models. To today's observer, versed in contemporary methods of bureaucratic quality control, the Griffins' management style might appear to neglect the necessary mechanisms for assuring accountability; rather they might seem more interested in their enjoyment of social contact with staff and residents. Yet, this perspective is once again coloured by class-based prejudice. Closer inspection reveals that the Griffins' 'hands on' style of management *was* their quality assurance mechanism. Interviews with both Council members and hostel managers left no doubt that the Griffins were astutely aware of much of the minutiae of life in the projects and were at pains to involve themselves in it and to take responsibility for its regulation. They erred, not in neglecting the welfare and safety of staff and residents, but in trusting, sometimes erroneously, that staff unanimously shared their commitment to their mission.

It may be, therefore, that the durability of the Griffins Society's model of care should be tested against the survival of three adequately funded projects, rather than the demise of two impoverished ones. It is not argued here, however, that a model of family life is the 'correct' basis for successful rehabilitative practice. Rather, the point at issue is that this model provided a vehicle through which certain fundamental values and their associated behaviours could be successfully communicated to women whose histories rendered them relative strangers to the incentives for pro-social conventionality. Indeed, as we saw, the fatal blow to the Griffins was not a proven failure of their care strategy, but the psychological wounds inflicted by the loss of their flagship project, combined with their growing belief that they *themselves* had become an outdated resource in the voluntary sector.

WE JUST DID IT

> We were, maybe a bit tragically, doing what our parents had done…When I look around all of us, it was either expected or drummed into us. One put back in to society. So we were only doing what, not came naturally, but what was *expected* of us. We just *did* it. We just fell into it and carried on doing it. (Council member)

Philanthropy thrived in the upper-middle class social networks in which the Griffins moved. Although they were aware of the unusual nature of the recipients of their attentions, volunteering itself was ordinary activity for these women. They did not puzzle over it. Thus, the Griffins' idiosyncratic philanthropy is problematic primarily for the observer. Making philosophical or psychological sense of it is not easy, since the Griffins did not consider that it required such explanation. They themselves did not reflect deeply on its philosophy or ideology, nor did they regard their behaviour as unusual. We appear to lack, therefore, a direct lead by the Griffins themselves in any attempt to understand their enterprise at a theoretical level. They, and philanthropists like them, constantly puzzle us.

> Well, they must have had *something* which drove them, because they were so single-minded in their pursuit of what they were doing. What drove them? I don't know. (Assistant Chief Probation Officer)

Yet, perhaps the very absence of deep reflection itself provides a clue to understanding. Their lack of ideology does not imply thoughtlessness. Nor does their frequent and, at first glance, bewildering assertion that they were simply 'having fun' imply a lack of sincerity. Indeed, we have had many opportunities in the preceding pages to observe their deeply held commitment to their project and the unstinting energy that they applied to it. Several described this commitment as 'love.' Perhaps, then, we should take the Griffins at their word. Perhaps we should explore the nature of this philanthropic love by examining their straightforward, uncomplicated view, rather than seeking opaque motives for behaviour that contradicts our instinctive presumptions about Lady Bountiful's character just because, as academics and professionals, we are habitually drawn to the inaccessible in preference to the obvious.

The ordinary, uncomplicated language in which the Griffins described their philanthropy is not unusual. Studying volunteers' accounts of their motives, Wuthnow (1995) remarked that their explanations 'make their behaviour seem routine or unexceptional' (p.79). By offering concrete narratives of specific acts of caring, rather than arguments based upon conceptual ideology, Wuthnow's volunteers represented their activities, not as deriving from their own compassionate personalities, but as embedded and arising naturally within situations and events to which they were exposed. Even acts of extreme altruism that threaten the lives of the actors themselves, such as the rescue of Jews by Gentiles during the Holocaust or of victims of the 2001 attack on the New York World Trade Centre, and that are regarded by observers as outstanding heroism, are commonly described by the actors as unexceptional acts of kindness. Rather than seeing their behaviour as egregious, as it appears to the onlooker, altruists tend to assert that they merely did what anyone would do in a similar situation; they simply gave their help to people who were clearly in need of it (Oliner 2003; Oliner and Oliner 1988). It is not claimed here that the Griffins offered more than 'conventional altruism' (Oliner 2003), but rather that certain commonalities can be found in the qualities of philanthropy notwithstanding differences in the degree of self-sacrifice volunteered by the giver (Allen and Rushton 1983; Oliner 2003). Moreover, '[f]rom day to day, the activities of most of the rescuers were more mundane than glamorously heroic. For each dramatic act of rescuing a Jew from incarceration there were months and years of ongoing activities to feed, shelter, and clothe him or her' (Oliner and Oliner 1988:49). Thus, the most extreme altruism may be recalled in terms of small everyday behaviours.

The Griffins did not meet with offenders during the normal course of their lives. Even Council members who were magistrates were not required to engage in direct interaction with those who passed before them in the courts. Their introduction to such close encounters arose through their involvement in the Griffins Society, which, as we have seen, was prompted by their membership of a particular social network rather than by ideology. Yet, once introduced, the Griffins extended compassion and generosity to the women in their care with both naturalness and vigour that surprised many witnesses. This does not of itself mark them out as unusual individuals: 'the moral life is not something that emerges suddenly in the context of traumas; rather, it arises piecemeal in the routine business of living' (Oliner 2003:207). In this view, exposure to human suffering *commonly*, though not unfailingly, brings a direct, situation specific response to need through its immediate empathic impact. The Griffins, through participation in their social network, consented to be thrust into a set of circumstances in which their philanthropy was encouraged to flourish. It emerged, consequently, as a practical, sympathetic response to the human need they encountered within the projects.

Nevertheless, as we have seen, the Griffins' motivation for their philanthropic enterprise was often regarded with suspicion by witnesses informed more by class-based assumptions than real acquaintance. Indeed, any discussion of philanthropy is fraught with the difficulties of striking a balance between attributions of abnormal compassion on the one hand and calculating instrumentality on the other (Wuthnow 1991). It has been argued here, however, that the Griffins did not suffer from abnormal compassion, but rather that they voluntarily placed themselves in an environment in which normal compassion would naturally find expression.

The alternative charge of instrumentality was most commonly to be seen in suspicions that Council members exploited their residents' disadvantage for the personal satisfaction of appearing to help. According to this view, they were primarily interested in their own self-gratification rather than in the women's welfare. This suspicion reflects the deep scepticism as to the human potential for truly unselfish altruism that has long been debated among philosophers and psychologists (Galston 1993). The charge that no act of compassion can be truly selfless has persisted in the face of altruistic behaviours, such as those exemplified earlier, that are, to say the least, not easily accommodated in accounts of self-interest. The Griffins were easy targets for such derogations of their philanthropic activities by virtue both of their class and of the cheerful candour with which they themselves announced that they were 'having fun.' Despite their awareness of class-based perceptions of 'ladies of leisure', they were quite without embarrassment in this claim, appearing to suppose that 'having fun' was self-evidently reconcilable with genuine generosity of spirit. Indeed, at a common sense level, the implication that philanthropy should be enacted *without* intrinsic pleasure presents us with an absurdity of grudging compassion. Moreover, seen in this light, we might support the claim that 'self-interest is too powerful a motive *not* to be harnessed for moral ends' (Martin 1994:127, emphasis added).Volunteers commonly explain their motivation, at least in part, in terms of the pleasure they derive from their acts of caring; such motivation is, however, expressed as a multi-faceted phenomenon, comprising elements of humanitarianism, reciprocity and personal growth as well as the pursuit of happiness (Wuthnow 1995; Martin 1994).

In part, the Griffins were perhaps vulnerable to imputations of self-gratification by virtue of the absence of any tangible gain accruing from their activity. Again, such attributions could be fuelled by class prejudice. Part of the problem, however, derives from the tendency to define altruism in negative terms that identify only what it is not. For example, Page (1996), acknowledging that most compassionate acts are likely to be accompanied by 'at least a modicum of self-satisfaction', suggests that 'an action merits the ascription altruistic provided that no material gain is sought and that any intangible rewards are not the "primary intent of the behaviour"' (p.6). From this, however, it follows that, while we may be able to identify 'fake' altruism by the selfish motivation for material or psychological rewards, we lack the hallmarks of genuinely altruistic behaviour. Thus, we continue to lack the means to recognise philanthropy on the basis of its inherent positive qualities.

Here, perhaps, we are misled by the presumption that the psychological reward of pleasure accruing from compassionate behaviour is derived solely from the self-regard of the actor. This perspective ignores the presence of the recipient in the 'social relation' of philanthropy (Ostrander and Schervish 1990). It does not follow from the presence of a positive psychological reward that it is entirely self-generated by the actor in the performance of the helping act. Many studies of philanthropists and volunteers, both wealthy and otherwise, confirm the importance of a personal connection between the donor of time and/or money and the recipient (Ostrander and Schervish 1990; Ostrower 1995; Payton 1988). Martin (1994) remarks that 'philanthropy tends to work best when it is a two-way interaction between donors and recipients who regard each other as moral equals, rather than a one-way abandoning of resources from the rich to the poor' (p. 16).

Moreover, the derogation of dependency in a culture that emphasises self-reliance indicates the crucial importance, to the beneficiary of help, of sustaining reciprocity in the relationship with the benefactor (Martin 1994; Payton 1988). The giving of pleasure to the benefactor may thus be viewed as reciprocation on the part of the recipient for help given (Wuthnow 1991). Indeed, Wuthnow (1991) observes that volunteers, narrating their experiences of helping, do not end their stories at the point of giving, thus portraying it as altruism in its absence of reward, but conclude by completing 'the transaction, by claiming to have enjoyed it. Thus we run no risk of concluding that the gift was given grudgingly or for an ulterior motive; the giving was made worthy by the receiving' (Wuthnow 1991:94). This argument does not claim that the recipient must show abject gratitude for the gift of help, for that would sustain the imbalance of the relationship.

Rather, it is the intrinsic pleasure of a kindness appropriately given, made visible by the presence of the recipient, that provides the benefactor's reward.

Notably, the Griffins were already involved in a reciprocal transaction by virtue of their recognition of *noblesse oblige*: they were returning some of their privilege to the common good. Yet, they also accrued a further benefit from their philanthropic activity in the form of fun and pleasure. These feelings may be interpreted as a form of reciprocal exchange for their help rather than as an aspersion on the selflessness of the Griffins. It has been suggested that while such satisfaction is intrinsic to the act of compassion, rather than dependent on a specific response from the beneficiary, this does not mean that the recipient's presence is superfluous. Crucially, although the Griffins' style of 'hands on' management brought them into physical proximity with a group of women who somewhat rarely displayed overt appreciation of their efforts, it was that very proximity that enabled them to experience the intrinsic pleasure of giving (Payton 1988; Wuthnow 1991).

TIME TO HANG UP OUR BOOTS

> I think I probably felt rather a failure, because it seemed to me that we should have been able to carry on…Well, I suppose one wasn't *used* to closing things down, really. One wasn't *used* to things not working. (Council member)

The Griffins inhabited a world in which voluntary activity by privileged women had a long history that has powerfully shaped social provision for the disadvantaged. The interview extract above speaks poignantly both to the accomplishments and the demise of their enterprise. At times, during this study, it seemed as though this particular group of volunteers had leaped fully formed from the pages of a text on nineteenth century female philanthropy and simply taken up in the mid-twentieth century where they had left off in the previous one without noticing the lapse of time. They appear to have had no sense of, or, perhaps more accurately, to have been quite unconcerned by the anachronistic nature of their activity until they realised the impossibility of replacing themselves. Nevertheless, by the

243

time of their withdrawal, they had concluded that their idiosyncratic style of philanthropy was superfluous to, and unwanted in, the contemporary welfare landscape. As one Council member remarked in a letter to a former chair, explaining the decision to withdraw: 'We're dinosaurs…It's time to hang up our boots.'

While the Griffins were realists in their acceptance of the modern, professionalised territory of social welfare, and applauded its merits, they were also deeply hurt by its impact. Since, as we have seen, their enterprise represented a personal investment, not only materially in terms of time, energy and physical resources, but also emotionally in terms of their philanthropic 'love', so their withdrawal was flavoured both by practical release from an increasingly intolerable burden and by feelings of loss and rejection. This process found its most obvious expression in their disappointment in, and resistance to the growing pressure to adopt a 'hands off' management style, in which they would oversee fundraising and bureaucratic accountability, but refrain from engagement in the everyday life of the projects. We should, however, ask whether the loss has been born solely by the Griffins.

The negotiation of transfer of the management of their surviving hostels to a larger organisation included an agreement that some Council members would sit on its management committee. This arrangement did not last. Having secured the future of their projects—a loyalty that included their continuing financial support of Special Care House until it achieved viability—the Griffins withdrew. Undoubtedly, their potentially considerable, and largely lucrative value to the organisation was comprised in large part of their social influence. Yet, under the new terms of their participation as committee members, they were no longer 'having fun': 'I knew I wouldn't want to stay on, because I really had no interest in just turning up with a lot of people who I didn't know, one evening a month. It seemed so anonymous and pointless and uninteresting' (Council member).

While their withdrawal constitutes a loss to voluntary sector activity in the relatively unpopular field of offender rehabilitation of certain specific personalities with expertise, experience and powerful contacts, we should perhaps more importantly concern ourselves with the wider significance of a process of professionalisation that takes place at the expense of volunteer sentiments. In particular, we should question whether the professional gains will be worth the disappearance of Lady Bountiful from the landscape of voluntary sector penal treatment.

The Griffins took a bold step towards closing the gap between sectors of society that rarely meet. Their regular presence in their projects symbolised and, more importantly, *enacted* the compassion of the privileged for the disenfranchised. As Payton (1988) observes, 'professionals replacing volunteers removed the necessity of direct contact between the rich and the poor, between the haves and the have nots, the comfortable and the distressed' (p.51-52). The crucial importance of human contact as a catalyst for the experience of the intrinsic pleasure of giving beyond the immediate reach of family, friends and class has already been considered. How long does such compassion survive the absence of contact between the benefactor and the beneficiary? As Wuthnow remarks, while there is clear merit in the institutionalisation of social programmes to ensure the equitable distribution of relief, there is an inherent paradox in taking this process so far that needs are bureaucratically met *irrespective* of the presence of human compassion: '[i]ndifference is now a possibility because much is done by institutions that depend on compliance and conformity rather than powerful or virtuous persons' (1995:32-3; also Wuthnow 1996). Yet, indifference to the plight of women offenders has impoverished their treatment in the penal system for decades (Rumgay 2000; 2004b).

> I've worked for lots of organisations. We talk a lot about tenants and quality and all that kind of thing. At the Griffins, I think we *talked* less but we *did* more. And we did more *before* other people. That stuff about social inclusion, not having that labelling, not having that barring of people, but also the importance of the relationship between staff and clients and management committees seeing their relationship with clients as being important and their relationship with staff as being important. That's something that some organisations are only *starting* to think about *now*—that you get what you deserve. [The Griffins] did that a long time ago. (Hostel manager)

It is not argued here that we should contemplate a wholesale return to days when female voluntary labour shored up fragmentary welfare provision. Yet it should not be impossible to integrate opportunities for

245

experiencing personal authenticity through the voluntary expression of compassion into the organisational requirements of professional bureaucracies. In return for that experience, the Griffins offered not only considerable savings in public expense and human concern of a different and complementary character to that of professional care (Handy and Srinivasan 2004), but also a unique philanthropic gift.

The practice of 'normal-smithing' flowed both from the pragmatic necessities of hostel life and from the non-professional status of Council members, whose common sense application of the standards and expectations of conventional life infused both the behaviour requested of residents and the respect with which those residents were treated. The hostel experience nurtured the process of natural desistance from crime and deviance by helping women not only to adapt to these norms but also to profit from them.

The Griffins, however, went further than this. A growing body of commentary now comments upon the importance of building social, as well as personal capital in order to encourage successful desistance from crime (for example, Bazemore and Erbe 2004; Farrall 2002; Sampson and Laub 1993). These arguments contend that acquisition of personal capital, in the form of skills tailored to the requirements of conventional life, is of limited value in social environments in which opportunities to practise them are scarce. It follows, then, that a thorough rehabilitation strategy will seek to develop, not only offenders' personal attributes, but also the range and quality of the social networks available to them (Clear and Karp 1999). This perspective has encouraged a strong critique of contemporary rehabilitative practices that confine attention exclusively to offenders' shortcomings (for example, Farrall 2002; Mair 2004).

Yet, the graduates of the Griffins Society's projects, however successful, would never access the social networks in which were invested considerable power over their destinies. The realities of their lives would always be circumscribed by structural limitations in their opportunities for personal development. Nevertheless, in a sense, through the Griffins, these socially excluded women 'borrowed' social capital that they would never personally achieve.

Altruists, philanthropists and volunteer helpers appear to share a characteristic self-efficacy: they have confidence in their capacity for effective action (Allen and Rushton 1983; Oliner 2003). We have seen that the Griffins were, indeed, supremely self-confident in this respect. Nor was their confidence misplaced: it derived from a clear and unsentimental recognition of their powerful influence as a social elite. Philanthropic activity on the part of such individuals is often suspected of serving the clandestine purpose of perpetuating class divisions by offering palliatives to the disenfranchised. It is true that the Griffins made no attempt to bring about revolutionary social change; indeed, their *modus operandi* for their enterprise relied largely on exploitation of their membership of the most powerful and privileged sector of society. Yet, since they were fundamental realists, perhaps they sensed all too clearly that class conditions were not readily amenable to change, *with or without* their philanthropic efforts. They knew, however, that they could manipulate that class structure to serve philanthropic ends. Ultimately, they were almost certainly the more effective for their willingness to struggle within, rather than against the class system. Thus, they lent their social capital to compensate for the irretrievable deficiency of that resource among severely socially excluded women.

The Griffins' unique philanthropic gift comprised their willingness to exploit their ability to take the fight to the centre. Because of their efforts, the voices of disadvantaged and disenfranchised women were heard, by proxy, in the very corridors of power from which issued many of their chances of successful integration into mainstream society. It is questionable whether the representations of professional bureaucracies could ever substitute for the sheer force of will of a small band of privileged, powerful and purposeful volunteer women.

Afterword

It was rare for anyone to have the last word in an encounter with the Griffins Society Council members. This project does not attempt to challenge that tradition. It leaves a final comment on the organisation's unique contribution to penal philanthropy to the organisation's chair, contemplating its future direction as a funder, rather than provider of community-based rehabilitative projects for women offenders.

I don't want to lose the human side to it. I don't want this to become a terribly scientific organisation and research projects all over the place. I want there to be, by what's left of the Council, a real under-standing of what we're there for…On the one hand, you have to move with the times, you have to accept change. I'm not frightened of change. But I do feel that there's still that thread and I don't want that thread broken. I think it would be very sad. I really do…There was tremendous *love* for this organisation. The Council members were so, not only were they committed, but they really *loved* it. People talk about it with tremendous warmth. That is unusual. That is really unusual. There are millions of voluntary organisations. They come, they go, some of them survive for longer than others. But I've *never* come across an organisation that has been talked about with such affection. They were a very brave group of women. You know, when you think about it, these were women who—okay, a couple of them were magistrates—[but they had] never seen that side of life before. But the confidence, the walking across [the street to the hostel], head up, absolutely no worries about anybody coming and trying to take the handbag. Do you know what I mean? I mean the total *confidence*. I just hope that we don't lose that. I don't think we will.

249

References

Adams, M. (1992). 'Hostel Staffing Crisis: NAPO Ballots for Industrial Action.' *NAPO News,* 37(February):1.

Adler, F. (1975). *Sisters in Crime: The Rise of the New Female Criminal.* New York: McGraw-Hill.

Advisory Council on the Treatment of Offenders. (1963). *The Organisation of After-care.* London: HMSO.

Allen, H. (1987). *Justice Unbalanced: Gender, Psychiatry and Judicial Decisions.* Milton Keynes: Open University Press.

Allen, N.J. and Rushton, J.P. (1983). 'Personality Characteristics of Community Mental Health Volunteers: a Review.' *Journal of Voluntary Action Research* 12(1)36-49.

American Correctional Association. (1990). *The Female Offender: What Does the Future Hold?* Laurel, MD: American Correctional Association.

Arkin, R.M. and Baumgardner, A.H. (1986). 'Self-presentation and Self-evaluation: Processes of Self-control and Social Control.' In R.F. Baumeister (ed). *Public Self and Private Self.* New York: Springer-Verlag, pp.75-97.

Baskin, D.R. and Sommers, I.B. (1998). *Casualties of Community Disorder: Women's Careers in Violent Crime.* Boulder, CO: Westview Press.

Bazemore, G. and Erbe, C. (2004). 'Reintegration and Restorative Justice: Towards a Theory and Practice of Informal Social Control and Support.' In S. Maruna and R. Immarigeon (eds). *After Crime and Punishment: Pathways to Offender Reintegration.* Cullompton: Willan, pp. 27-56.

Bloom, B. and Covington, S. (1998). *Gender-specific Programming for Female Offenders: What is it and Why is it Important?* Paper presented at the American Society of Criminology Annual Meeting, November 11-14, Washington, D.C.

Bottoms, A. and McWilliams, W. (1986) 'Social Enquiry Reports: Twenty-five Years after the Streatfeild Report'. In P. Bean and D. Whynes (eds) Barbara Wootton: Social Science and Public Policy. Essays in her Honour. London: Tavistock, pp. 245-276.

Brodsky, A.E. (1999). '"Making it": The Components and Process of Resilience among Urban, African-American Single Mothers.' *American Journal of Orthopsychiatry* 69(2):148-60.

Burnett, R. and Maruna, S. (2004). 'So "Prison Works" does it? The Criminal Careers of 130 Men Released Under Home Secretary, Michael Howard.' *Howard Journal of Criminal Justice* 43(4):390-404.

251

Cahill, M.A., Adinoff, B., Hosig, H., Muller, K. and Pulliam, C. (2003). 'Motivation for Treatment Preceding and Following a Substance Abuse Program.' *Addictive Behaviors* 28:67-79.

Camden Borough News: The Ham and High. (1969). 'Return to Freedom—The Homely Way.' Friday, May 16, p.9.

Clear, T.R. and Karp, D.R. (1999). *The Community Justice Ideal: Preventing Crime and Achieving Justice.* Boulder, CO: Westview Press.

Daniels, A. K. (1988). *Invisible Careers: Women Civic Leaders from the Volunteer World.* Chicago, IL: University of Chicago Press.

Department of Health. (1989). Caring for People: Community Care in the Next Decade and Beyond. Cm. 849. London: HMSO.

Department of Health and Social Security. (1988). Community Care: An Agenda for Action. London: HMSO.

Falkin, G.P. and Strauss, S.M. (2003). 'Social Supporters and Drug Use Enablers: A Dilemma for Women in Recovery.' *Addictive Behaviors* 28:141-155.

Farrall, S. (2002). *Rethinking What Works with Offenders: Probation, Social Context and Desistance from Crime.* Cullompton: Willan.

Fletcher, H. (1992). 'Dramatic Increase in Violence at Hostels.' *NAPO News*, 37(February): 2.

Forensic Psychiatry Team. (1989). Communication by letter. London: South West Thames Regional Health Authority.

Freedman, E.B. (1996). *Maternal Justice: Miriam Van Waters and the Female Reform Tradition.* Chicago, IL: University of Chicago Press.

Galston, W.A. (1993). 'Cosmopolitan Altruism.' *Social Philosophy and Policy* 10(1):118-134.

Giordano, P.C., Cernkovich, S.A. and Rudolph, J.L. (2002). 'Gender, Crime, and Desistance: Toward a Cognitive Theory of Transformation.' *American Journal of Sociology* 107:990-1064.

Giordano, P.C., Rossol, J. and Cernkovich, S.A. (2002). 'Emotion, Cognition and Desistance from Crime.' Paper presented at the Annual Meeting of the American Sociological Association, August 16-19, Chicago.

Gordon, L. (1995). 'Incest and Resistance: Patterns of Father-daughter Incest.' In B.R. Price and N.J. Sokoloff (eds). *The Criminal Justice System and Women: Offenders, Victims and Workers.* Second edition. New York: McGraw-Hill, pp. 280-296.

Graham, J. and Bowling, B. (1995). *Young People and Crime.* Home Office Research Study 145. London: Home Office.

Griffins Society. (undateda). Newsletter. London, The Griffins Society.

_____. (undatedb). The Griffins Society. London, The Griffins Society.

_____. (undatedc). Fundraising letter. London, The Griffins Society.

_____. (1975). Annual Report. London, The Griffins Society.

_____. (1976). Annual Report. London, The Griffins Society.

_____. (1977). Annual Report. London, The Griffins Society.

_____. (1978). Annual Report. London, The Griffins Society.

_____. (1979). Annual Report. London, The Griffins Society.

_____. (1981). Annual Report. London, The Griffins Society.

_____. (1982a). Annual Report. London, The Griffins Society.

_____. (1982b). Minutes of a Management Committee Meeting, 8 December.

_____. (1983a.) Annual Report. London, The Griffins Society.

_____. (1983b). Minutes of a Management Committee Meeting, 13 April.

_____. (1983c). Minutes of a Management Committee Meeting, 9 February.

_____. (1984a). Minutes of a Management Committee Meeting, 13 June.

_____. (1984b). Minutes of a Management Committee Meeting, 11 July.

_____. (1984c). Minutes of a Management Committee Meeting, 12 September.

_____. (1984d). Minutes of a Management Committee Meeting, 10 October.

_____. (1984e). Minutes of a Management Committee Meeting, 8 February.

_____. (1985). Annual Report. London, The Griffins Society.

_____. (1986a). Annual Report. London, The Griffins Society.

_____. (1986b). Minutes of a Management Committee Meeting, March 1986.

_____. (1988). Annual Report. London, The Griffins Society.

_____. (1989a). Annual Report. London, The Griffins Society.

_____. (1989b). Minutes of the Council Meeting, 11 May.

_____. (1990a). Annual Report. London, The Griffins Society.

_____. (1990b). Minutes of a Management Committee Meeting, 14 June.

_____. (1990c). Minutes of a Management Committee Meeting, 12 July.

_____. (1991a). Annual Report. London, The Griffins Society.

_____. (1991b). Minutes of the Council Meeting, 14 February.

_____. (1991c). Minutes of the Council Meeting, 9 May.

_____. (1991d). Memo concerning mother and baby project, 10 July.

_____. (1991e). Minutes of the Extra Council Meeting, 11 July.

_____. (1991f). Minutes of the Council Meeting, 12 September.

_____. (1991g). Minutes of a Management Committee Meeting, 9 May.

_____. (1991h). Minutes of a Management Committee Meeting, 14 February.

_____. (1992). Annual Report. London, The Griffins Society.

_____. (1994a). Annual Report. London, The Griffins Society.

_____. (1994b). Memo concerning future of Stockdale House, 1 December.

_____. (1994c). Minutes of the Council Meeting, 1 December.

_____. (1995a). Memo concerning closure of Stockdale House, 27 June.

_____. (1995b). Minutes of the Council Meeting, 13 February.

_____. (1995c). Minutes of the Council Meeting, 28 June.

_____. (1995d). Minutes of the Council Meeting, 16 November.

Handy, F. and Srinivasan, N. (2004). 'Valuing Volunteers: An Economic Evaluation of the Net Benefits of Hospital Volunteers.' *Nonprofit and Voluntary Sector Quarterly* 33(1):28-54.

Hedderman, C. (2004). 'Why are More Women Being Sentenced to Custody?' In G. McIvor (ed). *Women Who Offend*. Research Highlights in Social Work

44. London, Jessica Kingsley, pp. 82-96.

Heidensohn, F.M. (1968). 'The Deviance of Women: A Critique and Enquiry.' *British Journal of Sociology* 19(2):160-175.

Herman, J.L. (1992). *Trauma and Recovery*. Pandora: London.

HM Chief Inspector of Prisons. (1997). *Women in Prison: A Thematic Review*. London: Home Office, HM Inspectorate of Prison for England and Wales.

Home Office (1953) Report of the Committee on Discharged Prisoners' Aid Societies. Cmnd. 8879. London: HMSO.

_____. (1958) The After-care and Supervision of Discharged Prisoners. Report of the Advisory Council on the Treatment of Offenders. London: HMSO.

_____. (1961) Report of the Interdepartmental Committee on the Business of the Criminal Courts. Cmnd. 1289. London: HMSO.

_____. (1962) Report of the Departmental Committee on the Probation Service. Cmnd. 1650. London: HMSO.

_____. (1966). *Residential Provision for Homeless Discharged Offenders*. Report of the Working Party on the Place of Voluntary Service in After-care. London: HMSO.

_____. (1967). *The Place of Voluntary Service in After-care*. Second Report of the Working Party on the Place of Voluntary Service in After-care. London: HMSO.

_____. (2003). *Statistics on Women and the Criminal Justice System: A Home Office Publication under Section 95 of the Criminal Justice Act 1991*. London: Home Office.

Hough, M. (2000). 'Evaluation: A 'Realistic' Perspective.' In J. Fountain, R. Hartnoll, D. Olszewski and J. Vicente (eds). *Understanding and Responding to Drug Use: The Role of Qualitative Research*. EMCDDA Scientific Monograph Series No. 4. Luxembourg, Office for Official Publications of the European Communities, pp. 253-57.

Jackson, R., Wernicke, R. and Haaga, D.F. (2003). 'Hope as a Predictor of Entering Substance Abuse Treatment.' *Addictive Behaviors* 28:13-28.

Jones, E. H. (1966). *Margery Fry: The Essential Amateur*. London: Oxford University Press.

Kent, J. (1962). *Elizabeth Fry*. London: B.T. Batsford Ltd.

Koven, S. (1993) 'Borderlands: Women, Voluntary Action, and Child Welfare in Britain, 1840 to 1914.' In S. Koven and S. Michel (eds) Mothers of a New World: Maternalist Politics and the Origins of Welfare States. London: Routledge, pp. 94-135.

Koven, S. and Michel, S. (1993). 'Introduction: "Mother Worlds."' In S. Koven and S. Michel (eds). *Mothers of a New World: Maternalist Politics and the Origins of Welfare States*. London: Routledge, pp.1-42.

Kruttschnitt, C. (1993). 'Violence by and Against Women: A Comparative and Cross-national Analysis.' *Violence and Victims* 8(3):253-270.

Laub, J.H. and Sampson, R.J. (2003). *Shared Beginnings, Divergent Lives: Delinquent Boys to Age 70*. Cambridge, MA: Harvard University Press.

Leary, M. (2002). 'When Selves Collide: The Nature of the Self and the Dynamics of Interpersonal Relationships.' In A. Tesser, D.A. Stapel and J.V. Wood (eds). *Self and Motivation: Emerging Psychological Perspectives.* Washington, DC: American Psychological Association, pp. 119-145.

Lewis, J. and Glennerster, H. (1996). *Implementing the New Community Care.* Buckingham: Open University Press.

Lofland, J. (1969). *Deviance and Identity.* Englewood Cliffs: NJ, Prentice-Hall.

Loucks, N. (1997). *HMPI Cornton Vale: Research into Drugs and Alcohol, Violence and Bullying, Suicides and Self-injury, and Backgrounds of Abuse.* Scottish Prison Service Occasional Papers, Report No 1/98. Edinburgh: Scottish Prison Service.

Maher, L. and Curtis, R. (1992). 'Women on the Edge of Crime: Crack Cocaine and the Changing Contexts of Street-level Sex Work in New York City.' *Crime, Law and Social Change* 18(3):221-258.

Mair, G. (2004) (ed). *What Matters in Probation.* Cullompton: Willan.

Manton, J. (1976). *Mary Carpenter and the Children of the Streets.* London: Heinemann Educational Books.

Martin, M.W. (1994). *Virtuous Giving: Philanthropy, Voluntary Service, and Caring.* Bloomington and Indianapolis: Indiana University Press.

Maruna, S. (2001). *Making Good: How Ex-convicts Reform and Rebuild Their Lives.* Washington, D.C.: American Psychological Association.

_____. (2004). 'Desistance from Crime and Explanatory Style: A New Direction in the Psychology of Reform.' *Journal of Contemporary Criminal Justice* 20(2):184-200.

Maruna, S., LeBel, T.P., Mitchell, N. and Naples, M. (2004). 'Pygmalion in the Reintegration Process: Desistance from Crime through the Looking Glass.' *Psychology, Crime and Law* 10(3):271-281.

McCarthy, K.D. (1990). *Lady Bountiful Revisited: Women, Philanthropy, and Power.* New Brunswick, NJ: Rutgers University Press.

Mercier, C. and Alarie, S. (2002). 'Pathways Out of Deviance: Implications for Programme Evaluation.' In Brochu S., Da Agra, C. and Cousineau, M. (eds). *Drugs and Crime Deviant Pathways.* Aldershot: Ashgate, pp. 229-239.

North London Press. (1969). Untitled article. Friday, May 16, p.1.

Odendahl, T. (1990). *Charity Begins at Home: Generosity and Self-interest Among the Philanthropic Elite.* New York: Basic Books.

Oliner, S.P. (2003). *Do Unto Others: Extraordinary Acts of Ordinary People.* Boulder, CO: Westview Press.

Oliner, S.P. and Oliner, P.M. (1988). *The Altruistic Personality: Rescuers of Jews in Nazi Europe.* New York: The Free Press.

Ostrander, S.A. and Schervish, P.G. (1990). 'Giving and Getting: Philanthropy as a Social Relation.' In J. Van Til and Associates (eds). *Critical Issues in American Philanthropy: Strengthening Theory and Practice.* San Francisco: Jossey-Bass.

Ostrower, F. (1995). *Why the Wealthy Give: The Culture of Elite Philanthropy*. Princeton: Princeton University Press.

Page, R.M. (1996). *Altruism and the British Welfare State*. Aldershot: Avebury.

Payton, R.L. (1988). *Philanthropy: Voluntary Action for the Public Good*. New York: American Council on Education/Macmillan.

Prochaska, F.K. (1980). *Women and Philanthropy in Nineteenth-century England*. Oxford: Oxford University Press.

Ravenna, M., Hölzl, E., Kirchler, E., Palmonari, A. and Costarelli, S. (2002). 'Drug Addicts in Therapy–Changes in Life Space in the Course of One Year.' *Journal of Community and Applied Social Psychology* 12:353-368.

Rock, P. (1996). *Reconstructing a Women's Prison: The Holloway Redevelopment Project, 1968-88*. Oxford: Clarendon Press.

Rumgay, J. (1999). 'Violent Women: Building Knowledge-based Intervention Strategies.' In H. Kemshall and J. Pritchard (eds). *Good Practice in Working with Violence*. London: Jessica Kingsley, pp. 106-27.

_____. (2000). 'Policies of Neglect: Female Offenders and the Probation Service.' In H. Kemshall and R. Littlechild (eds). *User Involvement and Participation in Social Care*. London: Jessica Kingsley, pp. 193-213.

_____. (2004a) 'Scripts for Safer Survival: Pathways out of Female Crime.' *Howard Journal of Criminal Justice* 43(4):405-419.

_____. (2004b) 'Living with Paradox: Community Supervision of Women Offenders.' In G. McIvor (ed). *Women Who Offend*. Research Highlights in Social Work 44. London: Jessica Kingsley, pp. 99-125.

Sampson, R. and Laub, J. (1993). *Crime in the Making: Pathways and Turning Points Through Life*. Cambridge, MA: Harvard University Press.

Schlenker, B.R. (1986). 'Self-identification: Toward an Integration of the Private and Public Self.' In R.F. Baumeister (ed). *Public Self and Private Self*. New York: Springer-Verlag, pp.21-62.

Scott, A. F. (1990). 'Women's Voluntary Associations: From Charity to Reform.' In K. D. McCarthy (ed). *Lady Bountiful Revisited: Women, Philanthropy, and Power*. New Brunswick, NJ: Rutgers University Press, pp. 35-54.

Shover, N. (1996). *Aging Criminals*. Beverly Hills, CA: Sage.

Sinclair, I.A.C. (1975). 'The Influence of Wardens and Matrons on Probation Hostels: A Study of a Quasi-family Institution.' In J. Tizard, I.A.C. Sinclair and R.V.G. Clarke (eds). *Varieties of Residential Experience*. London: Routledge and Kegan Paul.

Simoneau, H. and Bergeron, J. (2003). 'Factors Affecting Motivation during the First Six Weeks of Treatment.' *Addictive Behaviors* 28:1219-1241.

Sommers, I., Baskin, D. R. and Fagan, J. (1994). 'Getting Out of the Life: Crime Desistance by Female Street Offenders.' *Deviant Behavior* 15:125-149.

Steffensmeier, D. and Streifel, C. (1993). 'Trends in Female Crime, 1960-1990.' In

C. C. Culliver (ed). *Female Criminality: The State of the Art*. New York: Garland.

Tangney, J.P. (2002). 'Self-conscious Emotions: The Self as a Moral Guide.' In A. Tesser, D.A. Stapel and J.V. Wood (eds). *Self and Motivation: Emerging Psychological Perspectives*. Washington, DC: American Psychological Association, pp. 97-117.

Tedeschi, J.T. (1986). 'Private and Public Experiences and the Self.' In R.F. Baumeister (ed). *Public Self and Private Self*. New York: Springer-Verlag, pp.1-20.

Thornberry, T.P., Krohn, M.D., Lizotte, A.J. and Smith, C.A. (2003). *Gangs and Delinquency in Developmental Perspective*. Cambridge: Cambridge University Press.

Wandersman, A. and Nation, M. (1998). 'Urban Neighborhoods and Mental Health: Psychological Contributions to Understanding Toxicity, Resilience, and Interventions.' *American Psychologist* 53(6):647-656.

Werner, E.E. and Smith, R.S. (1992). *Overcoming the Odds: High Risk Children from Birth to Adulthood*. Ithaca, NY: Cornell University Press.

Wilczynski, A. (1997). *Child Homicide*. London: Greenwich Medical Media.

Wright, R.T. and Decker, S.H. (1994). *Burglars on the Job: Street life and Residential Break-ins*. Boston, MA: Northeastern University Press.

_____. (1997). *Armed Robbers in Action: Stickups and Street Culture*. Boston, MA: Northeastern University Press.

Wuthnow, R. (1991). *Acts of Compassion: Caring for Others and Helping Ourselves*. Princeton, NJ: Princeton University Press.

_____. (1995). *Learning to Care: Elementary Kindness in an Age of Indifference*. New York: Oxford University Press.

_____. (1996). *Poor Richard's Principle: Recovering the American Dream through the Moral Dimension of Work, Business and Money*. Princeton, NJ: Princeton University Press.

Index

A service to remember Joanna Moriarty

Held at St Michael at the Northgate, Oxford

Oxford

2.30pm 17th October 2017

Remembering Joanna Moriarty

Let us pray:

Heavenly Father, you have not made us for darkness and death, but for life with you for ever. With you we have nothing to fear. Speak to us now your words of eternal life. Lift us from anxiety and guilt to the light and peace of your presence, and set the glory of your love before us; through Jesus Christ our Lord, **Amen**

Reading: Psalm 23

Music

Shared memories of Jo

Reflection: Revd Mary Gurr

Prayers:

Father in heaven, we thank you because you made us in your own image and gave us gifts in mind, body and spirit. We thank you now for Jo and what she meant to each of us. As we honour her memory, make us more aware that you are the one from whom comes every perfect gift, including the gift of eternal life, through Jesus Christ, **Amen**

God of mercy, as we mourn the death of Jo and thank you for her life, we also remember times when it was hard for us to understand, to forgive and to be forgiven. Heal our memories of hurt and failure and bring us to forgiveness and life in Jesus our Saviour, **Amen**

Our Father, who art in heaven, hallowed be thy name. Thy kingdom come, thy will be done, on earth as it is in heaven. Give us this day our daily bread. And forgive us our trespasses as we forgive those who trespass against us. Lead us not into temptation, but deliver us from evil. For thine is the kingdom, the power and the glory, for ever and ever, Amen

Commendation:

Joanna has fallen asleep in the peace of Christ. Her body has been returned to the earth. **We** entrust her with faith and hope in everlasting life, to the love and mercy of our Father. Surround her and all those who loved her with our love and our prayers. **Amen**